The Asian Financial Crisis

The Asian Financial Crisis:
Lessons for a Resilient Asia

edited by
Wing Thye Woo,
Jeffrey D. Sachs and
Klaus Schwab

The MIT Press
Cambridge, Massachusetts
London, England

Library of Congress Cataloging-in-Publication Data

The Asian financial crisis : lessons for a resilient Asia / edited by Wing Thye Woo, Jeffrey D. Sachs, and Klaus Schwab.
     p.   cm.
Includes bibliographical references and index.
ISBN 0-262-19452-X (hc. : alk. paper)—ISBN 0-262-69245-7 (pbk. : alk. paper)
    1. Financial crises—Asia—Case studies. 2. Asia—Economic policy—Case studies. I. Woo, Wing Thye. II. Sachs, Jeffrey. III. Schwab, Klaus, 1938– .
HB3808 .A859   2000
330.95—dc21   00-033255

Contents

Contributors

Frank Flatters (chapter 12)
Professor of Economics, Queen's
University, Canada

Donald Hanna (chapter 3)
Managing Director, Head of Asia
Pacific Economic and Market
Analysis, Salomon Smith Barney,
Hong Kong

Mumtaz Hussain (chapter 4)
Research Associate, Harvard
Institute for International
Development, Cambridge

Kiseok Hong (chapter 10)
Research Associate, Korea
Development Institute, Korea

Jong-Wha Lee (chapter 10)
Professor of Economics, Korea
Development Institute, Korea

Thomas G. Lewis (chapter 6)
Senior Vice-President and
Regional Chairman, Asia-Pacific,
The Boston Consulting Group,
Boston

Dwight Heald Perkins (chapter 11)
Harold Hitchings Burbank
Professor of Political Economy,
Harvard University, Cambridge

Richard P. Mattione (chapter 9)
Portfolio Manager and Member,
Grantham, Mayo, Van Otterloo &
Co. Inc., Boston

Steven C. Radelet (chapter 8)
Institute Fellow and Director of
the Macroeconomics Program at
the Harvard Institute for
International Development;
Lecturer on Public Policy, the
Kennedy School of Government,
Harvard University,
Cambridge

Jeffrey D. Sachs (chapters 1 and 2)
Galen L. Stone Professor of
International Trade, and Director,
Harvard Center for International
Development, Harvard
University, Cambridge

Klaus Schwab
President, World Economic
Forum, Switzerland

Sara Sievers (chapter 5)
Executive Director, Harvard
Center for International
Development, Harvard
University, Cambridge

Shang-Jin Wei (chapter 5)
Associate Professor, Kennedy
School of Government, Harvard
University, Cambridge

Wing Thye Woo (chapters 1, 2 and 7)
Professor of Economics,
University of California, Davis;
and Professorial Fellow, Institute
of Southeast Asian Studies,
Singapore

Preface

This book is the latest product of a longstanding cooperative research arrangement between the World Economic Forum and the Harvard Center for International Development to provide the latest thinking on economic growth and global competitiveness. Earlier versions of the papers in this book were published in *The Asia Competitiveness Report 1999*, which was released at the January 1999 meeting of the World Economic Forum in Davos, Switzerland. The Competitiveness Report received very favorable reviews, and many members of the Forum urged that its analyses be made available to a wider audience. We are therefore very happy to accept the kind offer of MIT Press to publish an updated selection of the papers. Quite a number of the papers, particularly the country studies, had to be rewritten to take recent developments into account.

This book examines the challenges facing East Asia at present Were the predictions that East Asia would become the strong third pillar of the world economy unrealistic and unfounded? Or, has East Asia only experienced a severe, but short-term, contraction? Although the Asian crisis countries have a clear need for reform, we believe that the outlook for a full recovery from the contraction is positive. The sharp region-wide economic rebound in 1999 certainly attests to the strong underlying strengths in the East Asian economies.

The papers in this book indicate that sound economic growth will be sustained provided that the right policies are adopted. The first chapter outlines a coherent agenda for restoring economic vitality and prosperity, and the second chapter provides an analytical overview of the Asian crisis in the last three years. We believe that the conclusions reached in this book can help accelerate economic recovery and will strengthen the process of globalization in a way that will benefit the people of East Asia and the rest of the world.

We would like to acknowledge the great contribution of Catherine Whitney Hoover, who worked very closely with us to ensure that the manuscript was clear in its exposition of the analytical issues. We also thank Mumtaz Hussain, who helped us put many of the data tables together.

Jeffrey D. Sachs
Klaus Schwab
Wing Thye Woo

February 14, 2000

The Asian Financial Crisis:
Lessons for a Resilient Asia

I

Lessons from the Asian
Financial Crisis

1   A Reform Agenda for a Resilient Asia

Jeffrey D. Sachs and
Wing Thye Woo

The Asian financial crisis is over. While this is a big relief, the fact that it occurred at all is a matter of great concern. What is of even greater concern was the unexpected[1] nature of the crisis, the large number of economies that were hit, and the depth of the output collapse in some countries. The troublesome question is whether there is a common element in the development strategies of Indonesia, Malaysia, South Korea and Thailand that rendered them vulnerable to sudden substantial falls in GDP. Before the crisis, these four economies had been grouped with Hong Kong, Japan, Singapore and Taiwan in a laudatory report by the World Bank entitled *The East Asian Miracle*.[2] Was the Asian miracle a myth, a Soviet-type mirage that imploded on the eve of what was expected to be the Pacific Century?

Malaysia, South Korea and Thailand have rebounded faster than anticipated by most analysts. In December 1998, the International Monetary Fund (IMF) had forecasted 1999 growth rates of −3.4 percent for Indonesia, −2 percent for Malaysia, −1 percent for South Korea and 1 percent for Thailand. The actual 1999 growth rates have turned out to be 0.2 percent for Indonesia, 5.4 percent for Malaysia, 9.4 percent for South Korea and 4.0 percent for Thailand. Is the recovery sustainable? A V-shaped recovery across the whole spectrum of crisis countries would vindicate the miracle view, whereas a W-shaped recovery would verify the mirage view.

The World Economic Forum (WEF) and the Harvard Institute for International Development (HIID) recognized from the very beginning that the Asian financial crisis was part of a more general financial phenomenon that went beyond the particular circumstances in the Pacific

---

1. Arguably Thailand could be an exception, but only in a limited sense. See footnote 3.
2. World Bank (1993).

Asia region. In mid-1998, WEF and HIID assembled an experienced international research team to analyze the causes and mechanisms of financial crises, and to formulate a reform agenda that could, first, help to reduce the likelihood of future international financial crises, and, second, help to restore and enhance the international competitiveness of Pacific Asia after the crisis is over. The assignment to the research team was not only to identify the policy changes that international organizations and governments in developed and developing countries could implement to improve global economic performance, but also to examine business opportunities in post-crisis Pacific Asia and recommend appropriate strategies to businesses operating in the region.

The initial working assumption of the WEF-HIID team that the Asian financial crisis was part of a larger problem of global finance was confirmed very quickly with the collapse of the Russian ruble in August 1998. The financial contagion then hit South America with the devaluation of the Brazilian real on January 13, 1999. Other currencies in Africa, Asia and Latin America soon came under attack.

It is important to be clear, however, that while the crisis in all cases was sparked off by the withdrawal of loans by panicked international banks, the depth of the crisis reflected more than the size of this reversal in capital flows. There were two other important reasons for why the crisis was so deep. First, these countries had some severe institutional weaknesses that made them unusually fragile financially. Second, some countries (at the advice of the IMF) responded with overly tight stabilization policies, and mishandled the restructuring of the financial sector.[3] The harshness of the Asian financial crisis was the joint product of external shock, internal weakness and policy mistakes.

After intensive analysis of the global financial crisis and the specific conditions in Pacific Asia, the WEF-HIID team has crystallized their results into thirty recommendations for global reform in the following seven areas:

- the financial and non-financial sectors of developing countries,
- the International Monetary Fund,
- the international monetary system,

---

3. Analysis of Thailand's financial collapse reveals that it can be seen as two crises. The first crisis was started by the unsustainable trade deficit caused by the overvalued baht. The second crisis, the more damaging of the two crises, was caused by the panicky flight of funds produced by the inappropriate stabilization-restructuring package implemented to counter the first crisis.

- the design of international "rescue" packages,
- the regulation of international capital markets,
- short-term Pacific Asian financial management, and
- long-term Pacific Asian institutional reform.

1.1   Financial Reforms Within Developing Countries

The institutional weaknesses of domestic corporations (both financial and non-financial) render them susceptible to creditor panic. Aiming to increase the resilience of the financial sector and the non-financial corporate sector when faced with external credit shocks, and to enable these sectors to recover rapidly after the occurrence of such shocks, the research team proposes eight reform measures in this area.

Proposal 1. Financial institutions should more quickly adopt internationally accepted accounting standards. Major international accounting firms should work together with the international agencies to increase the standardization of accounting practices in the emerging markets.

Proposal 2. The supervision of financial institutions must be enhanced, and BIS-style[4] prudential ratios must be enforced on the financial institutions. As part of this process of improved supervision, there should be:

- much wider membership of developing countries in the Bank for International Settlements (BIS);

- an intensive international effort to upgrade the technical capacity of banking supervisors; and

- new BIS standards that are appropriate for the volatile conditions of emerging markets. The capital adequacy ratio should take into account that the bank's capital may be denominated in the home currency, but a significant part of its loan portfolio may be denominated in another currency.

Proposal 3. The ownership structure of the banking sector in emerging economies should be diversified to include foreign ownership, in order to reduce the risks of systemic banking collapse, and to generate demonstration effects to the domestic banks regarding efficient operations and prudent risk management.

---

4. BIS = Bank of International Settlements.

Proposal 4. The development of the non-bank financial sector (e.g., the equity and bond markets) should be promoted because the over-reliance on bank credit in many developing countries has made them excessively vulnerable to financial panics.

Proposal 5. The legal underpinnings of corporate governance should be clarified, especially to protect minority shareholders. Part of the vulnerability to financial panic arises from the lack of clarity of property rights within the emerging market economies.

Proposal 6. Modern bankruptcy law should be introduced to forestall creditor panics (or "grab races") in the event of financial distress.

Proposal 7. Financial institutions should be required to file more frequent reports on their portfolios and their exposure to sectoral and currency risks, to allow better oversight by shareholders and the regulatory bodies.

Proposal 8. Short-term foreign borrowing by domestic banks should be tightly limited as a matter of prudential policy. Excessive short-term foreign debts of Asian, Russian, and Brazilian banks contributed to the onset of financial crises in all of these economies.

1.2   Reform of the International Monetary Fund

Grave flaws in the IMF's procedures and policy recommendations have become apparent in the course of the crisis. Each of the IMF's major packages in the past two years has failed to meet its targets, and many of the programs (for example, those for Korea, Russia and Brazil) have collapsed within weeks of their approval. To improve international management of future crises and to renew the legitimacy of the international financial system itself, the research team proposes four reform measures in this area.

Proposal 9. The international community should establish an IMF External Review Commission to review the functioning of the IMF in some of its major recent activities: its handling of the international financial crisis, its policy advice to developing countries, and the IMF's structural adjustment programs in the poorest countries.

Proposal 10. Archived IMF materials should be made public to allow outside surveillance of the institution.

Proposal 11. IMF voting powers should be reformed to give greater representation to developing countries, which, after all, constitute 85 percent of the world's population, and which bear the burden of failed IMF strategies.

Proposal 12. The functioning of the IMF Executive Board should be over-hauled: for instance, the Board should host public hearings, provide opportunities for outside parties to submit evidence to the Board, and solicit professional opinions from experts beyond the IMF staff.

1.3   Reforms of the International Monetary System

The third set of reform recommendations arises from the deep instabil-ities in the international financial system. The events in East Asia, Russia and Brazil demonstrate the instability of short-term capital flows, and their tendency to oscillate between waves of euphoria and waves of panic. These instabilities have been exacerbated by systems of pegged exchange rates, as were used in Thailand, Korea, Russia and Brazil, as is explained in our detailed essay in this volume. As a result, the research team recommends three main reform measures in this area.

Proposal 13. In general, countries should pursue flexible exchange rate arrangements (e.g., wide crawling bands and open floats). In every case of serious financial crisis—including Mexico in 1994, Argentina in 1995, Korea and Thailand in 1997, Russia in 1998, and Brazil in 1999—the country pursued a fixed exchange rate policy in the years leading up to the crisis, and the system of fixed rates clearly contributed to the onset of the crisis.

Proposal 14. Because the IMF is not (and cannot be) a true international lender of last resort, there is no justification for the monopoly position of the IMF as the sole international arbiter of monetary affairs. Regional monetary bodies, for example within Pacific Asia, or within other emer-ging market regions, could provide mutual support in the event of a financial crisis hitting a particular member country.

Proposal 15. An international bankruptcy system should be established to accelerate an orderly workout of international debts when a devel-oping country falls into an extreme indebtedness crisis. As an interim measure, the writing of contracts for Eurobonds should be amended to create "standing committees of creditors," and to introduce some of the standard bankruptcy procedures, e.g., the automatic-stay provision (to prevent grabbing of assets before resolution of bankruptcy in domestic court), and the debtor-in-possession provision (to enable the firm to continue to obtain working credit while the domestic bankruptcy process takes place).

1.4   Reforming International "Rescue" Packages

The IMF has launched five major "rescue" packages in the past two years: Thailand (August 1997), Indonesia (November 1997), Korea (December 1997), Russia (July 1998) and Brazil (December 1998). None of these packages succeeded in re-establishing market confidence or in reducing the adverse macroeconomic effects of international financial panic. Indeed, all of these packages quickly collapsed and required renegotiation. This suggests that there have been major flaws in the design and implementation of these policy packages. The research team has identified at least three areas of needed change.

Proposal 16. Debt relief often needs to be an integral component of "rescue" packages in order to encourage creditor-debtor bargains to stretch out loans, convert debts to equity, and occasionally achieve a permanent write-down of claims.

Proposal 17. IMF programs must not be designed to defend pegged exchange rates (as in the Brazil and Russia programs) because, at best, such IMF programs promote sharp recessions, and at worst (as in Russia and Brazil) the currency collapses anyway.

Proposal 18. Rescue packages should "bail in" (rather than "bail out") the international private investors by insisting that the private creditors bear the major burden for renegotiating the timing and repayment terms on existing debts when a financial crisis emerges. For example, the private creditors may be called upon to roll over existing claims, as occurred in the case of Korea in December 1997.

1.5   Regulatory Reforms of International Capital Markets

The fifth set of reform recommendations addresses the dangers of premature capital account liberalization in emerging markets before the necessary supervisory and regulatory standards are in place. Because short-term capital movements can destabilize an economy, and force a government into an expensive financial bailout of the banking system, the research team recommends the following four reform measures.

Proposal 19. Controls on short-term capital inflows into emerging markets can help to maintain macroeconomic and financial stability. But while controls on short-term capital inflows may be advisable in many countries, controls on capital outflows should almost always be avoided, since controls on outflows tend to undermine government credibility and provide an inducement towards irresponsible policies.

Proposal 20. While excessive short-term capital inflows should be discouraged, long-term capital inflows (especially foreign direct investment) should be promoted. There are still major strides to be taken in many developing countries (e.g., in areas of telecommunications, banking and other modern services) in allowing foreign investors to gain ownership of domestic enterprises.

Proposal 21. There should be informative and timely disclosure of hedge funds, cross-border lending, and derivatives transactions to enable policy makers in the developed and developing countries to know the external financial exposures of their national financial institutions.

Proposal 22. There should be greatly enhanced regulation of highly speculative activities such as highly leveraged hedge funds.

Proposal 23. The international community should immediately constitute a working group on international capital flows, including representatives of the developed countries, the developing countries, the major international institutions (IMF, BIS, WTO, UNDP, WB and others)[5], as well as private-sector observers, to report to the respective international institutions within one year on improvements in the oversight and regulation of cross-border capital flows.

1.6   Short-term Financial Measures to Restore Growth in Pacific Asia

The most serious immediate problem of the Asian crisis countries is the tremendous amount of bad debts in the banking and corporate sectors. The answer to the bad debt problems must be a series of negotiations between creditors and debtors to restructure the debts. At the same time, a large-scale infusion of public money to recapitalize the banking systems in Asia is unavoidable. The research team makes the following four recommendations for financial workouts in Asia.

---

5. WTO = World Trade Organization, UNDP = United Nations Development Program, and WB = World Bank.

Proposal 24. The recapitalization of banks in Pacific Asia should be accelerated, through a combination of public money, foreign investment and contributions by existing owners.

Proposal 25. The government should replace the non-performing loans (NPLs) of the banking system with government bonds, and in return the bank owners should agree to repay the government bonds over a set period, or to convert the government bonds into bank equity if the banks cannot service the bonds.

Proposal 26. Having acquired the banks' NPLs at a discount, the government should give debt relief to the firms based on their capacity to pay. Specific guidelines for debt relief would include the following:

- debt relief should be concentrated on small and medium-sized firms because they have been hit the hardest by the credit crunch; and

- debt write-downs for the larger corporations should be conditional on debt-equity swaps, in which the government gains some equity share in the corporations. This equity share would later be auctioned as a form of "re-privatization" of the government's stakes.

Proposal 27. The barriers to entry by foreign banks should be lowered to provide the competition that is needed to prevent domestic banks from imposing wide spreads between deposit and lending rates in order to earn their way out of the crisis (but with disastrous costs to domestic corporations).

1.7   Long-term Measures to Enhance Asian Competitiveness

In our opinion, the greatest long-term challenges to Pacific Asia lie not in financial regulation, macroeconomic stability or exchange rate management but in "social software," such as the improvement of the quality of education, the overhaul of public institutions, the enhancement of science and technology, and the promotion of democratic political structures.

The annual Global Competitiveness Report (GCR) gives some clear and quantifiable evidence of the shortcomings in these areas. While the Asian manufacturing countries (China, Indonesia, Japan, Korea, Taiwan, Malaysia, Thailand and the Philippines) achieved an average overall ranking of 21st out of 53 countries in the 1998 GCR rankings, and a particularly high ranking of 9th on fiscal management, these countries received a surprisingly low rank of 30th in technology, and 34th in quality of governmental institutions.

The research team makes three very general recommendations to address fundamental problems of harnessing technology and skilled manpower and establishing adequate social infrastructure for sustained economic development.

Proposal 28. The Southeast Asian countries should make a determined effort to raise the standards of science and technology within their societies. Among other steps, this will require much greater support for higher education, as well as encouragement of much closer links between universities and the private sector, such as the collaborative relationships found in the high-tech areas of the U.S. economy (such as information technology and biotechnology).

Proposal 29. In enhancing the quality of public institutions, appointments and promotions should be based primarily on merit and not on, say, ethnic identity or ideology.

Proposal 30. Pacific Asia must launch a concerted effort to upgrade its public institutions, particularly its civil service and its judiciary system. For example, according to the 1998 GCR, Indonesia was ranked 53rd out of 53 countries with respect to the independence of the judiciary, with Malaysia, Thailand, Korea, China, Taiwan and the Philippines all ranked worse than 30th.

2   Understanding the Asian Financial Crisis

Jeffrey D. Sachs and
Wing Thye Woo

2.1 Introduction

At the height of the Asian financial crisis in the middle of 1998, pundits often pronounced that it would take three to five years for Asia to recover. American triumphalists loudly proclaimed that Asian capitalism, just like Soviet socialism a decade ago, had come to the end of its economic logic. The Pacific Asian economies that had long been hailed by many analysts as models for the rest of the developing world were depicted by some of. the same analysts during the crisis as unsustainable nests of crony capitalism.

The Asian financial crisis is as puzzling as it has been far-reaching in its consequences. The sharp region-wide plunge in output after the devaluation of the Thai baht in July 1997 was unexpected,[1] and the strong region-wide recovery in 1999 was equally unexpected. The World Bank and the International Monetary Fund have long shared a common policy framework, but they are now divided on the causes of the crisis, and on what the policy advice should have been given. All across Pacific Asia, the crisis has brought about many fundamental changes: governments have changed, internationally well-known conglomerates have collapsed, the banking systems are paralyzed by large amounts of non-performing loans, and barriers to entry by foreign financial institutions have been lowered.

Broadly speaking, there were two initial explanations for the unexpected nature of the Asian financial crisis, the large number of economies that were hit, and the depth of the output collapse in some countries. The first explanation emphasized the common structural problems ("soft rot") in the crisis Asian countries as the primary cause

---

1. See the empirical investigation in Woo, Carleton and Rosario (forthcoming).

of their sudden output collapses, and viewed their crises as "inevitable disasters that finally happened." The second explanation emphasized the primary role of financial contagion in the crisis. Just as external creditors had been excessively optimistic about economic prospects earlier in 1994–96,[2] they became overly pessimistic at the end of 1997. If irrational exuberance exists, as warned by Alan Greenspan, then disconsolate melancholia must also occur occasionally.

Over time, various synthesis views have emerged. However, many so-called synthesis views that admitted to the existence of panics by external creditors were actually soft rot explanations, because they identified the "fallen" countries as the countries with the most severe cases of soft rot. A more balanced synthesis view would differentiate "fallen" countries into three categories: countries with advanced soft rot, countries that experienced the greatest bouts of financial panic,[3] and countries where inappropriate IMF advice led to overly tight macroeconomic policies and badly designed and badly handled restructuring programs.

The claim that the Pacific Asian economies had imperfect economic institutions (for example, inadequate banking supervision and collusive relations between big business and government officials) is surely correct, but to go on to claim that these flawed economic institutions reached breaking points simultaneously, and thereby ignited the region-wide economic crisis, is also surely incorrect. The second claim would be like focusing exclusively on deforestation in Central America when discussing the damage wrought by Hurricane Mitch, while ignoring the damage from the hurricane itself. Policy failures matter, but they are only part of the story of Asia's financial storm. As much attention should be paid to the financial "hurricane" itself, specifically, the tendency for international financial markets to overreact to both positive and negative news. It was financial panic among international investors that brought Pacific Asia to its knees in 1998. Fortunately, the underlying fundamental strengths of the region have brought about an economic recovery more quickly than was widely predicted.

In general terms, we can say there were few specifically "Asian" features of the Asian financial crisis. Official Washington, led by the IMF, proclaimed the crisis to be one of Asian capitalism, but the more

2. When net private capital inflow to Indonesia, Malaysia, the Philippines, South Korea and Thailand increased from US$40.5 billion in 1994 to US$102.3 billion in 1996, the spread on the Eurobonds issued by these countries fell.
3. For example, panic caused by domestic political problems.

generic character of the crisis became all too clear during 1998, as the crisis spread to Russia, South Africa and Latin America. Rather than an Asian crisis, the world is experiencing a type of global crisis that reflects the rapid arrival of global capitalism in a world economy not yet used to the integration of the advanced and developing countries. The 1994–95 foreign exchange crises in Mexico and Argentina and, less severely, in the rest of Latin America via the "tequila effect" of 1995, were the high-profile precursors to the financial market crisis that hit Pacific Asia in mid-1997. The Asian financial crisis is really another example of financial panic involving international creditors, though of course the onset of financial panic reflected some of the conditions specific to Asia in 1997. [4]

The extent of economic devastation in each Asian country differs according to specific national structural conditions and policy reactions: for example, the amount of international debt; the proportion of international debt that is short term; the adequacy of financial sector regulation; the amount of foreign reserves available to the monetary authorities; the tenacity with which the country defended its exchange rate; the degree to which IMF-style high interest rates and bank closures were implemented (with adherence to IMF programs often doing more, rather than less, short-term damage); and the ability of the political system to preserve social stability while coping with economic shocks. The solutions to the crisis require responses at both the international level, to address shortcomings in the nascent global capitalist system, and at the regional and national levels, to maintain and improve Asia's competitiveness in a globalized economy.

Naturally, professional opinion remains deeply divided about the sources of the crisis (national versus international), the reasons for Asia's extreme vulnerability (poor policies versus private-sector instabilities), the appropriate policy responses (IMF-style financial orthodoxy versus financial heterodoxy of various forms), and the best ways to guard against a recurrence of crisis in the future (national level reforms versus a new global architecture). We review the arguments here and stake out our own position on the basis of the evidence in this volume. In our view, the crisis was built on national weaknesses that were greatly magnified by a flawed international financial system. In addition, the initial policy recommendations from Washington, especially suggestions to

---

4. A less well-known, but also dramatic, precursor was the Turkish financial panic in 1994.

raise interest rates sharply and to close a large number of financial institutions, were deeply flawed and made matters worse, not better. Long-
term crisis prevention requires actions both at the national and international levels, including a basic change of strategy in exchange rate
management and recognition of the inherently destabilizing risks of
short-term capital flows.

The most general and important point is that global capitalism has to
be understood better by global policy makers, national political leaders,
and business people in all parts of the world. All of these participants in
the new global economy have to recognize the types of shocks that have
been magnified and rendered more common by the processes of deep
economic integration and of institutional harmonization that are key
forces of global capitalism. Only with a better comprehension of the
new realities will the world community be able to take true precautionary measures to head off a future crisis, and will Asia be able to make a
swift recovery from the deep crisis which engulfed the region. In short,
we need to rise to the challenge of developing new policies and new
business strategies that are appropriate for global capitalism.

Our analysis is organized as follows. Section 2.2 offers a conceptual
framework to understand the onset and evolution of the 1997–98
financial crisis. As explained below, the crisis resulted from the interaction of (1) problematic macroeconomic policies (especially exchange
rate policies) in the emerging markets, (2) shortcomings in the financial
sectors of the borrowing countries, and (3) intrinsic instabilities in the
global financial markets. These problems interacted with some deeper
weaknesses in Asian competitiveness to trigger the sharp financial
crisis. Section 2.3 outlines the different stages in the recovery process,
relates the 1997–98 crisis to earlier financial crises in developing countries, and presents our assessment about the sustainability of the ongoing recovery in the Asian crisis countries. Section 2.4 discusses a wide
range of policy options for the reform of international financial architecture, including macroeconomic policy design in developing countries;
the regulation of international capital flows; the revision of the roles of
the IMF, the United Nations agencies and other institutions; and the
redesign of international financial assistance itself, including accelerated
debt reduction.

2.2 Understanding the Asian Financial Crisis

A Theoretical Framework

Before we delve into the specifics of the Asian crisis, we need a general theoretical understanding of how international capital markets work—and fail to work—in the new global capitalist system. Thus, we start with some general theoretical ideas, and afterward focus on the Asian experience.

Emerging market financial crises, such as in Asia in 1997–98, are characterized by an abrupt and significant shift from net capital inflow to net capital outflow from one year to the next. These crises typically reflect a three-stage process that hits a developed country engaged in large-scale international borrowing. In the first stage, the exchange rate becomes overvalued as a result of internal or external macroeconomic events. In the second stage, the exchange rate is defended, but at the cost of a substantial drain of foreign exchange reserves held by the central bank. In the third stage, the depletion of reserves, usually in combination with a devaluation, triggers a panicked outflow by foreign creditors holding short-term claims. The trigger in most cases is the devaluation itself, resulting from the exhaustion of reserves. The panicked outflow of short-term capital leads to macroeconomic collapse, characterized by a sharp economic downturn, soaring interest rates, depressed equity prices and a plummeting currency.

Some observers have attributed such crises to currency devaluation, because the panics have almost always followed a movement in the currency. This was certainly the case in Asia: the Asian crisis followed soon on the heels of the unexpected devaluation of the Thai baht on July 2, 1997. Similarly, Korea's extreme crisis came in December 1997, following the devaluation of the Korean won. Generalizing from these instances, and from the earlier case of Mexico's devaluation in December 1994, these observers have concluded that currencies should be fixed in value and never allowed to weaken. We disagree. In our view, it is not the devaluation, but rather the defense of the exchange rate preceding the crisis that opens the door to financial panic. A gradual weakening of the currency by itself is not harmful—as exemplified by the successes of many countries with flexible exchange rate arrangements, including Chile, Canada, Australia and New Zealand.

The real damage comes from the depletion of foreign exchange reserves while trying to defend an overvalued currency. A devaluation that follows the depletion of reserves can indeed trigger a panic, but the lesson is to allow the currency to weaken *before* the reserves are depleted. When foreign reserves are depleted, short-term inter-bank credits in particular become subject to an abrupt, self-fulfilling loss of confidence. In summary, the devaluation signals the depletion of reserves; the depletion of reserves signals the inability of the central bank to act as a lender of last resort vis-à-vis foreign creditors; the short-term foreign creditors flee in panic; and the macroeconomy collapses as a result of the creditor flight.

Creditor Panic

The ubiquitous feature of recent emerging market crises is that the exchange rate defense, typically ending in a devaluation, has often been followed by a rapid and ferocious withdrawal of credits by foreign investors. It is the panic, not the devaluation itself, which leads to the acute damage to the emerging market and to the creditors.

Typically, some key segments (e.g., banks, non-financial enterprises and government) of the fast-growing Asian economies are heavily in debt to foreign investors, including international banks, hedge funds and other investment funds. Much of this debt is short-term, i.e., with maturity under one year. Additionally, much of the debt has trigger clauses, such that repayment is immediately accelerated in the event of a contractual default by the debtor to other creditors. The borrowing, in general, is converted into long-term, relatively illiquid investments. As a result, total short-term debt is often significantly greater than the available short-term assets that might be mobilized to repay creditors in the event of a withdrawal of new lending.

The level of central bank foreign exchange (forex) reserves is crucial because the central bank is widely, and rightly, understood to be the lender of last resort not only to the banks, but to the government and corporate sector as well, in the event of an external creditor panic. Suppose that foreign banks begin to withdraw credit lines from domestic banks, demanding repayment of outstanding loans. This immediately leads to financial distress in the banking system, since the banks have transformed the foreign loans into long-term investments. The bank may, to some extent, use liquid domestic assets to purchase dollars in the foreign exchange market, but even so, the bank is unlikely to have sufficient liquid assets on hand to meet a large-scale withdrawal of funds. Thus, the central bank will almost surely have to extend credit, either directly as foreign exchange loans, or as domestic credit which is then sold in the forex market. In the latter case, of course, the exchange rate will depreciate in the absence of official intervention.

Once forex reserves have been depleted, the central bank's lender-of-last-resort functions are deeply compromised, and international creditors understand this fact very well. In these circumstances (depletion of forex reserves, and a high level of short-term debt), the economy becomes vulnerable to a self-fulfilling run. Even if economic fundamentals are adequate to ensure long-term debt servicing without default, they are not adequate to guarantee short-run debt servicing in the event of a panic. Thus, a panic can unfold simply from the self-fulfilling belief of creditors that it will indeed occur. This explains the finding by Radelet and Sachs (1998) that when the ratio of short-term debt to forex reserves is greater than 1, the country is prone to a creditor panic.

In the past five years, financial panics have been triggered mainly by three types of events:

1. the sudden discovery that reserves are less than previously believed;

2. unexpected devaluation (often in part for its role in signaling the depletion of reserves); and

3. contagion from neighboring countries, in a situation of perceived vulnerability (low reserves, high short-term debt and overvalued currency).

It is important to stress that currency devaluation, following a long defense of the exchange rate, has typically been the most important trigger of panic. This seems to be the result of several factors. First, many investors have been caught off guard by the devaluation, even when it has been widely discussed previously. These investors seem, incredibly enough, to have taken at face value the solemn commitments of governments not to devalue. Second, the devaluations are often the signal that forex reserves are at a lower level than publicly announced up to that point. In Mexico, the late-December 1994 devaluation "revealed" the steep loss of reserves in early December 1994. In Thailand, the July 2, 1997 devaluation was followed by public announcements that the Thai Central Bank had a large book of forward dollar sales. These dollar sales were not previously announced, and came as a large jolt to the market. In Korea, the December 1997 devaluation was the occasion for revealing that much of the central bank's announced forex reserves were actually illiquid claims on Korean banks, the result of preceding unannounced deposits of the reserves in offshore Korean banks experiencing a run on inter-bank loans (in effect, the central bank had been making unannounced extensions of credit to offshore Korean banks). Speaking in the most general terms, the collapse of pegged exchange rate regimes appeared to have been regarded as "serious breaches of faith" by foreign investors, causing them to recall their loans even though the devaluation has already occurred.

When the panic gains full force, the effects are devastating. The rational behavior of each short-term creditor is to demand repayment as rapidly as contractually possible, and to suspend routine inter-bank lines that support letters of credit and other standard trade financing operations. Long-term fundamentals cease to play any role in investor thinking, since the logic of *sauve qui peut* dominates in a creditor scramble in which creditors are serviced on a first-come, first-serve basis. The macroeconomic results are a huge overshooting: (1) debt is drawn down even when domestic investments (e.g., in working capital and letters of credit) have a rate of return vastly greater than the world cost of capital; (2) the real exchange rate depreciates sharply, far overshooting any real correction that needs to be made; (3) the current account swings wildly from deficit to outright surplus; (4) the banking system suffers illiquidity, and perhaps an ancillary panic by domestic savers; (5) market real interest rates soar to astronomical levels, as each borrower scrambles to mobilize funds to avoid default; and (6) partial default on forex obligations becomes almost assured. The key effects on macroeconomic contraction are (1) the collapse of bank lending, leading to a collapse of trade and production; and (2) the conversion of illiquidity into insolvency over the course of a few months, as loans become nonperforming under the weight of reduced production and sales, and the crushingly high interest rates on working capital.

Economic Policies During a Financial Panic

In order to minimize the output collapse, it is imperative that the central bank takes the following two steps to keep the payments mechanism of the economy intact. The first step is to prevent the generalized panic sparked off by the failure of the bad banks from rendering the good banks illiquid and causing the good banks to fail too. This means that the central bank must extend sufficient reserves to the good banks to meet the withdrawal of deposits but not sufficient for them to extend new loans to finance speculation against the currency.

The second step to protect the payments mechanism is for the central bank to ensure that the good customers (especially if they are exporters) of the failed banks continue to receive working credit to keep production going. This means that the central bank must keep the operations of failed banks going while restructuring their balance sheets for eventual sale. Again, the emphasis is on maintaining the volume of working credit to existing clients. The crucial point to keep in mind is that the creation of new reserves is to accommodate the private sector's shift out of bank deposits into currency and not to fuel the run from domestic assets to foreign assets.

During a financial panic, the central bank has to choose maintenance of the domestic payments system and output level over maintenance of the existing exchange rate. The central bank should float the currency and allow currency depreciation to discourage capital outflow. Some banks may fail because of the exchange-rate-induced increase in the value of their foreign liabilities, and the central bank must keep the operations of these banks going in order to keep production credit going to the good firms. With the amount of working credit in the economy unchanged by the financial panic, domestic firms can increase exports to take advantage of the currency depreciation.

The resulting growth in exports, coupled with the stability of output, will help to restore confidence in the economy, prompting domestic agents to repatriate their capital from abroad and foreign creditors to resume lending. The final outcome will be an appreciation of the currency from its over-depreciated value (although possibly not up to its pre-crisis value). The important implication is that banks that had been bankrupted by the exchange-rate-induced increase in the value of their foreign liabilities are now likely to be solvent again.

In light of the analysis above, we see the error of the first IMF packages that were implemented in Thailand, South Korea and Indonesia. The tightening of monetary policy in order to raise interest rates to prevent further currency depreciation, the abrupt closure of bad financial institutions, and the raising of prudential ratios, all created a tremendous credit crunch that dramatically deepened the output decline and inflamed the panic. The closure of the bad financial institutions, particularly in Indonesia, where there was no depositor insurance, spread the financial panic to the good banks. The fact that fiscal policy was also tightened ensured the crashing of these economies.

Our objection to the first IMF packages that were implemented in the crisis countries should not be interpreted as a general objection to closing bad banks or adopting higher prudential ratios similar to those used by the Bank for International Settlements. We only object to the implementation of these two actions in the middle of a financial crisis. The timing of the implementation of these two policies was wrong.

Applying the Framework to Asia

Our interpretation of financial crises is a general one, not specific to Asia. But the analysis fits the Asian experience very well. All of the countries that got into trouble in Asia (especially Indonesia, Korea, Malaysia and Thailand) shared three main characteristics. First, they were very successful economies, so they were able to attract significant inflows of capital during the 1990s. Second, all of the countries maintained exchange rates that were practically fixed to, or depreciating at predetermined rates against, the U.S. dollar during the 1990s. Third, the combination of capital inflows and fixed exchange rates pushed these economies into positions of vulnerability, characterized by an overvalued currency, falling foreign exchange reserves, and a high level of foreign debt, especially short-term debt. As discussed earlier, once the overvaluation of the currency became apparent to investors (by the end of 1996 in the case of Thailand, and by mid-1997 in the case of the other economies), currency speculation led to the worst of all worlds. To honor their exchange rate commitments, these countries simply depleted their foreign exchange reserves to defend their overvalued currencies. When reserves fell to low levels, the foreign creditors panicked and demanded immediate repayments of loans, rather than rolling the loans over, which would have been mutually beneficial for both creditors and debtors.

In fact, in the case of Asia, we can definitely view the crisis as a "crisis of success" rather than a "crisis of failure." Only successful economies would have been able to attract so much capital inflow as did the Asian economies. Ironically, these economies did not really need so much foreign capital. During their high growth phase of the 1980s, the Asian countries tended to save around 25–30 percent of GDP and to invest a similar amount, so that they relied little on foreign borrowing. In the early 1990s, these countries liberalized their financial markets, with the effect that domestic banks and corporations could suddenly borrow from abroad, thereby raising the investment rates even higher than the already high levels of domestic saving. There was certainly no shortage of willing foreign lenders. As a result, the ratio of investment to GDP rose to around 35 percent or more, with 5 percent of GDP or more being financed by foreign loans.

There is plenty of evidence that neither the foreign nor domestic financial markets were able to allocate the increased investments very efficiently. Both microeconomic and macroeconomic data support the view that the incremental investments in the 1990s were only moderately profitable. Too much money was poured into speculative real estate projects, e.g., in downtown Bangkok. There was also a fairly clear over-investment in sectors such as memory chips, especially among the copy-cat Korean conglomerates (chaebols). Still other investments were thoroughly wasted in crony projects such as the abortive "national car" program linked to former President Soeharto's family. Yet, even though the incremental investments added little to economic growth, they were hardly a disaster on average, and certainly not a sufficient explanation for an abrupt economic collapse.

The collapse came mainly because of the macroeconomic problems outlined earlier, not the microeconomic inefficiencies of the investment boom, though such inefficiencies certainly added to the trouble. More important was the fact that the investments were financed by short-term loans, under conditions of pegged exchange rates (or, in the case of Indonesia, a crawling peg). As the capital inflows proceeded in the 1990s, domestic prices and wages were bid higher. As a result, the wage level expressed in dollars began to creep up to unsustainable levels. The steady devaluation of the Chinese yuan in 1991–94 (through the swap market mechanism) further decreased the competitiveness of these countries. When the U.S. dollar appreciated sharply relative to the Japanese yen and the European currencies in 1995 and 1996, these currencies then appreciated alongside the dollar, further eroding their international competitiveness. Export growth faltered severely in 1996 as a result. By the end of 1996, market participants began to suspect the need for a currency depreciation in several Asian countries, most notably Thailand.

The rest, as they say, is history. Thailand depleted its foreign reserves in an ill-fated attempt to stabilize its currency. After using most of its reserves, it announced defeat on July 2, 1997, allowing the baht to depreciate. The IMF insisted on several draconian measures for the Thai economy, most notably a sharp increase of interest rates, a significant cut in budget outlays, and a dramatic closure of 58 finance companies.

The combination of depleted foreign reserves, high levels of foreign short-term debt, and market anxieties surrounding the tough IMF measures, all conspired to produce a full-fledged financial panic. The panic spread to the rest of Pacific Asia, engulfing Indonesia and Malaysia in the fall of 1997, and Korea in December 1997.

When the crisis hit, many observers began to point out some of the weaknesses of the Asian economies: poor banking supervision, excessive lending in the 1990s, cronyism in the allocation of loans, and so forth. These weaknesses were, and are, real, but they hardly explain Asia's collapse. The Asian economies were not "miracle" economies to be sure, but they were also not disasters waiting to happen, except as victims of global panic. Overall, these economies were somewhere in the middle of the world's major economies in terms of institutional quality; they were good enough to achieve rapid growth, given that they were starting at fairly low levels of income (and therefore with plenty of room to import technologies to catch up with the leaders). For example, the World Economic Forum's *Global Competitiveness Report* consistently ranked the Asian economies just a bit above average in overall competitiveness. For example, of the 53 countries evaluated for competitiveness in 1997, Indonesia ranked 15th, Thailand ranked 18th and South Korea ranked 21st. Investors knew about the weaknesses, at least in broad terms, but they also knew about Asia's great strengths: high rates of domestic saving, export promotion policies, a skilled and disciplined labor force, and private-market orientation. What nobody counted on was a sudden withdrawal of foreign credits that would bring these economies to their knees.

2.3 Setting the Stage for Asian Recovery

Three Stages of Asian Recovery

When a financial panic hits, all macroeconomic systems go awry. Lenders demand immediate repayments on short-term loans, and credit dries up entirely. Most firms are completely cut off from further borrowing, while market interest rates soar to the stratosphere. Cash-strapped enterprises, pressed to repay foreign debts that are being called, try to buy up dollars at any price. The exchange rate therefore eventually collapses, reaching absurdly depreciated levels. The banking system becomes illiquid. Not only are domestic banks unable to open letters of credit on behalf of exporters (since foreign banks no longer trust the liquidity or solvency of the domestic banks), they are unable to borrow from each other. If the central bank is playing by IMF orthodox rules, it too will not provide emergency credits to cash-strapped commercial banks. Even the fear of central bank orthodoxy can trigger a banking panic, as the bank's creditors try to escape before the onset of illiquidity, thereby triggering the illiquidity that they fear.

The overall result is economic collapse. Production ceases because of the lack of working capital. Illiquid firms become insolvent as production and sales collapse, while bad debts pile up. The banking sector itself is destroyed as a result of creditor panic, a loss of depositor confidence, and a explosion of bad loans.

Economic recovery, as a result, displays three fairly distinct phases. The first phase is the end of panic, which comes faster than expected by most observers. The idea is simple. The huge panicked outflow of capital comes to an end after a few months, for a combination of three reasons: some of the short-term debts are repaid, some are rescheduled, and some are simply defaulted upon. In any event, the panicked outflow ceases. When this occurs, several healthy developments ensue. The exchange rate strengthens from its absurdly depreciated levels. Interest rates come down from the heavens. Working capital begins to flow again, at least moderately, to cash-strapped firms. This first stage began in summer 1998, when interest rates returned to more normal levels and exchange rates strengthened, even in countries such as Indonesia and Malaysia, where political risks were still very high. Panic had pushed the exchange rates and interest rates to such absurd levels that a rebound to more normal financial market prices was inevitable.

The second stage of recovery is much trickier. The financial panic leaves a legacy of bad debts throughout the economy, which must be cleared up. The banking sector is usually in deep trouble. Bank capital is wiped out by non-performing loans, and perhaps by exchange rate depreciation. (If the banks have borrowed in dollars and lent in domestic currency, they are caught in a whipsaw of currency depreciation.) Domestic non-bank enterprises also tend to be in trouble. Months of high interest rates, shortages of working capital, and depressed domestic markets lead to a buildup of unpayable debts. Foreign creditors are often left with a large stock of non-performing loans, so debt workouts require agreements not only with domestic creditors but also with foreign creditors, thereby adding to the administrative and political complexities of the needed adjustments.

All of these problems need to be addressed through a series of debt write-offs or stretch-outs. The banks must be recapitalized, usually through an infusion of public funds (e.g., a takeover of bank capital), followed by a privatization of the public sector's new stakes in the banks. The corporations must renegotiate with their creditors. Debts can be rescheduled, or partially reduced, or swapped for equity (in which case the creditors become part or full owners of the enterprises). These renegotiations can happen informally or in the context of formal bankruptcy procedures. Unfortunately, most of the Asian countries lack adequate bankruptcy legislation and procedures to ensure that the process can run smoothly and efficiently. Until these debts are written down, one way or another, economic performance will continue to be deeply impaired. Companies with a large stock of debt will be unable to get adequate working capital, much less capital for needed long-term restructuring. The banking sector will remain in a shriveled state, unable to serve as an effective financial intermediary because of inadequate bank capital and a loss of confidence on the part of the banks' depositors and creditors.

The third stage of the crisis—after the end of panic and the cleanup of debt—is to raise long-term competitiveness. Part of the solution to long-term competitiveness is a turn to flexible exchange rates (thus ending a period of currency overvaluation), but this is rarely enough. Governments must take steps to improve the effectiveness of basic political and economic institutions: for example, they must control corruption, improve financial market oversight, and reduce the chances of a future bank panic through improved risk management (for example, through a better-capitalized banking sector). Even more fundamentally, they must work to improve the quality of the human and physical capital in the economy. Is the education system adequate to keep pace with global technological innovations? Are the country's scientific and technological institutes of sufficient caliber? Is the country stuck in a unproductive export niche (and thereby subject to growing international competition from low-wage economies) or is it able to establish competitiveness in new sectors? As we have noted, the Asian economies were only marginally above average in overall competitiveness, even before the onset of the financial crisis. They clearly had lots of work to do in institutional improvements.

Prognosis for Selected Pacific Asian Countries

Before assessing the economic prospects of selected Pacific Asian countries, it is important to note that there have been at least four financial panics in the first half of the 1990s: Argentina in 1995, Mexico in 1995, Turkey in 1994 and Venezuela in 1994. Part A of table 2.1 shows the GDP growth rates of these economies for the period two years before the panic and two years after the crisis (except for Venezuela, for which data is also shown for three years after the crisis). In three of the four cases (Argentina, Mexico and Turkey) the financial panic caused a sharp drop in output for one year, followed by a sharp rebound. The result was a V-shaped movement in GNP.

Despite these previous experiences with V-shaped recoveries, throughout 1998 the IMF predicted a U-shaped recovery for East Asia. The IMF forecasted at the end of 1998 that Indonesia, Malaysia and South Korea would experience continued output decline in 1999, and that Thailand would have a lethargic recovery (see part B of table 2.1). The IMF's gloomy predictions followed from its diagnosis that the Asian financial crisis reflected deep-seated structural flaws (advanced soft rot) within these economies, and that growth would return only after a complete makeover.

Part B of table 2.1 shows a V-shaped recovery in East Asia, just as in the crises reported in Part A. There was a similarly sharp output decline for Indonesia, Malaysia and South Korea in 1998, followed by a strong rebound in output growth in 1999. The widely held expectation of continued strong recovery in 2000 is certainly more in line with the financial panic explanation than the soft rot explanation for the Asian financial crisis. The soft rot explanation could be salvaged only if the recoveries across East Asia turn out to be W-shaped, i.e., if there is a sudden prolonged collapse in 2000 or 2001.

To anticipate the detailed discussion, we are, on the whole, optimistic about the return of economic growth to the Pacific Asian countries in 2000. However, while the region has moved beyond the panic stage into economic recovery, the return to sustained high rates of growth is still open to question, because of remaining uncertainties about the clean-up of debt and of long-term institutional reforms. It should also be noted that our optimism is conditional upon the United States and Western Europe continuing to ensure sufficient liquidity in world financial markets by cutting interest rates as necessary, and keeping their domestic markets open to imports, despite the left-of-center character of their governments.

Table 2.1
Financial panics and real GDP change (in percent)

A. The precedents

Country and year of panic (= T)	T–2	T–1	T	T+1	T+2	T+3
Argentina, 1995	5.7	8.0	–4.0	4.8	8.6	—
Mexico, 1995	2.0	4.5	–6.2	5.2	7.0	—
Turkey, 1994	6.4	8.4	–5.0	6.7	7.3	—
Venezuela, 1994	7.3	0.3	–2.9	3.4	–1.6	5.1

B. The Pacific Asian cases

	1995	1996	1997	1998	1999	2000[a]	IMF's prediction of 1999 growth rate (issued Dec. 1998)
Indonesia	8.2	8.0	4.6	–13.6	0.2	4.0	–3.4
Malaysia	9.5	8.6	7.7	–7.5	5.4	5.5	–2.0
South Korea	8.7	7.3	5.5	–5.8	9.4	6.3	–1.0
Thailand	8.8	5.5	–0.4	–10.0	3.9	5.3	1.0

a. The 1999 estimates and 2000 projections are from HSBC Asian Economies Weekly, March 6, 2000.

In the discussion that follows, we begin with the two largest countries of the region, China and Japan. Even though these countries did *not* experience panic, each faces a very tricky situation in 2000. We then proceed to the panic cases of Korea and Southeast Asia.

China

China's GDP growth has been slowing every year since 1992, and declined to the still-enviable rate of 7.1 percent in 1999. Inflation has been wiped out, and retail prices have actually been falling since October 1997. The slowdown in the 1993–97 period was part of a deliberate policy action to deny loss-making state-owned enterprises (SOEs) their accustomed allotments of credit, in order to force them to improve their efficiency and to change their ownership forms if necessary. The safety valve of this strategy of restructuring the inefficient SOE sector through tight credit policy was the export market.

That safety valve strategy was briefly under threat in 1998 and 1999, when the negative growth in many Pacific Asian countries in 1998 rendered China's export growth in 1998 to be almost zero.[5] In response to the unexpected sharp drop in external demand in mid-1998, China greatly increased the scale of the reflation measures that began in early 1998. The big expansion in bank credit and state investments kept GDP growth above 7 in 1998 and 1999.

Has China managed to avoid, or merely postponed, being part of the Asian financial crisis that has been marked by a severely devalued currency, a collapsed banking sector, and a large output decline? A large speculative run on the renminbi (RMB) is clearly not possible because of capital controls. Furthermore, China's external short-term debt is less than US$30 billion, while its non-gold reserves stand above US$150 billion; most of the foreign funds in China are tied up in physical investments; and foreign participation in China's stock market has been limited to trade in B-shares, which are denominated in U.S. dollars and can be owned only by foreigners.

Some China watchers have claimed that bank depositors are, or will soon be, worried by the large amount of non-performing loans (NPLs) in the state banks, and that a bank run is inevitable. The result would be a bank crash followed by an output collapse. We find such a scenario implausible despite the high NPL ratio (possibly one-third of all loans), because we think that the depositors regard the NPL problem to be one that the government is financially and technically capable of solving. The fact is, if the government were to assume all of the NPLs of the state banks, this would raise China's public debt-GNP ratio to about 50 percent, which is still far below the U.S. federal debt-GNP ratio of 70 percent (which in turn is among the lowest of the G7 countries). Nonetheless, the fiscal costs of future bank restructuring will be very large, and tricky to carry out.

China's capital controls have made the current account balance the primary determinant of the equilibrium exchange rate. Although China's trade account balance was US$43 billion in 1998 and about US$30 billion in 1999, devaluation pressures would be hard to resist in 2000 if there is a significant drop in exports due to displacement in North American, European, and Japanese markets by Korean and Southeast Asian products.

---

5. Omitting Hong Kong because of its entrepot character, 33 percent of China's exports in 1996 went to Indonesia, Japan (which alone took 20 percent), Malaysia, the Philippines, Singapore, South Korea, Thailand and Taiwan.

We see China's biggest challenge to lie not in warding off a dramatic financial crisis but in choosing the correct tradeoff between maintaining low urban unemployment and continuing to move decisively on systemic reforms. The choice is between short-term political comfort but future crisis versus short-term political conflicts but future stability. The latest example of this policy dilemma was the fast expansion of credits in the last half of 1998 to the banks' traditional client base, the state-owned enterprises, in order to boost production. Because of the enormous pressures on the bank managers since 1994 to prevent a worsening of their NPL ratios, the only way that the central bank could induce the banks to lend more to the SOEs was to implicitly guarantee that the bank managers would not be punished if these new loans were to become non-performing.

Many of China's structural problems, such as the stagnation of agricultural productivity, the slowdown in the growth of rural enterprises, the continued inefficiency of the SOEs, and the large NPLs at the state banks, can only be solved by promoting normal forms of private ownership, e.g., partnerships, cooperatives and shareholding corporations. Until land truly belongs to the peasants, the local cadres in many areas will continue to appropriate agricultural land at will for other uses and to redistribute land every four or five years, despite the mandated tenure of 30 years. Until the peasants have constitutionally secured tenure rights on the land, they will not make the investments in the land that are necessary to raise agricultural productivity.

Until the rural enterprises that are registered as collectively owned are reorganized to become normal corporations whose shares are freely traded, they will find it hard to raise funds to expand their operations, and to be free from the interference of the local cadres. Similarly, until the state banks and SOEs are converted into shareholding enterprises, losses will continue to grow. The clarification and protection of property rights over land, rural enterprises, banks and SOEs require the following actions for their success:

• the development of a modern legal framework to lower the cost of economic transactions; and

• the transparent distribution of these property rights to the local communities, to prevent social outrage over embezzlements that occur under the guise of reforms.

China's forthcoming entry into the World Trade Organization (WTO) marks an important transition on many fronts for China. First and foremost, China's admission into the WTO will improve the economic security of China. The requirement for annual renewal by the U.S. Congress of China's normal trading relationship with the United States made China's economic growth vulnerable to the vagaries of American domestic politics. Through WTO membership, this engine of growth will no longer be unilaterally shut off by the United States without the action being a major violation of international law.

Second, China's willingness to join such an institution reflects more than a desire to protect itself from potential blackmail by the United States; it also reflects China's realization that the active ingredient in Deng Xiaoping's recipe for growth was the convergence of China's economic institutions to the economic institutions of modern capitalist economies, particularly of East Asian capitalist economies. The important point is that China's decision to join WTO reflects the political leadership's willingness to bear the considerable costs that compliance with WTO rules will create. China is a natural food-importer and a natural factory-oriented society, given its low land-man ratio. The agricultural sector employs over 320 million people, which is over two-thirds of the rural labor force. The bulk of China's state-owned sector survives only because of various forms of subsidies and import barriers, but such instruments contravene WTO regulations. Because the SOEs employ over 40 percent of the urban labor force, job shifts in the labor force are inevitable. Conservatively, a fifth of China's workers may have to change jobs, and this could be a politically destabilizing process if not handled adeptly, and if external shocks were to slow down economic growth.

Japan

Japan's economic recovery still hangs in the balance. After being in recession throughout 1998, Japan grew 1.5 percent[6] in 1999:1Q and 1 percent in 1999:2Q. That was the end of the good news, however. Japan slipped back into recession with growth of −1 percent in 1999:3Q and −1.4 percent in 1999:4Q, to produce a 0.3-percent growth rate for 1999, which was much lower than the 1-percent growth predicted by the IMF in October 1999.[7] Part of the weakening in growth could no

---

6. On a quarter to quarter basis.
7. "Japan is back in recession," *New York Times*, March 14, 2000; and IMF (1999).

doubt be attributed to the strengthening of the yen in the second half of 1999. The exchange rate went from an average of 120.9 yen per US$ in 1999:2Q to 104.5 yen per US$ in 1999:4Q.

As Richard Mattione makes clear in this volume, the traditional instruments of macroeconomic policy—interest rate cuts and fiscal expansion—are not available to undergird the Japanese economy. Interest rates are already nearly zero, while fiscal deficits are approaching a remarkable 10 percent of GDP! Neither instrument offers much room for maneuver. Not is all lost, however, because other more novel forms of policy change could be effective in stimulating Japanese growth. They are, at least partly, being implemented.

Japan's aggregate demand is weak on several fronts. Business investment and consumer spending have both been hit hard by a loss of confidence in the economy. Exports have been hit hard by the fall in incomes in the rest of Asia. Small and medium-sized businesses in Japan are suffering from a squeeze on lending, as Japan's sick banks have cut back on loans as part of their attempts to reconstruct their capital bases. Unfortunately, the increasingly aggressive supervision of banks (including the closure of major Japanese financial institutions) has had the short-run effect of intensifying the credit squeeze.

So where, then, can Japanese growth come from in the near term? The first step, without question, would be the implementation of a major reorganization of the banking system, built around a huge infusion of public funds to reestablish capital, to finance orderly bank closures and mergers, and to prepare the sick banks for eventual purchase by other domestic and (especially) foreign investors. The Diet has voted for several initiatives to use public funds to support the rehabilitation of the banking sector. This step is almost surely the *sine qua non* for effective growth in the medium term.

A second source for growth would be a recovery in exports to parts of Asia, based on two factors. First, the continued recovery of the East Asian crisis countries will provide some lift to Japan. Second, and perhaps more important, Japan could provide additional credits to the hard-hit countries of Asia to finance purchases of Japanese output. This idea is embodied in the Miyazawa Plan, which provides US$30 billion in aid to the region. To be really effective for both Asia and Japan, the program should be even larger, around $60 billion. These funds could come in the form of grants (for example, in the case of Indonesia, the hardest-hit country in the region) and in the form of loans. It is estimated that the loss of East Asian markets cost Japan perhaps 1.5 to

2.0 percentage points of GDP in 1998. A combination of Asian recovery plus an aggressive assistance program could reverse those losses in 2000.

A third source of growth should be monetary expansion. This may seem odd, since there is so much talk about "liquidity traps" in the air, a theory which holds that Japan has done all that it could with monetary expansion. It is true that Japan's nominal interest rates cannot be much lower, but Japan could still accomplish several important things by a further aggressive increase of the money supply. First, with a dose of money-induced inflation (e.g., around 3 to 5 percent per year in the next few years), land and other asset prices in Japan would stop falling and perhaps begin to rise, thereby easing the problems of bad debts in the banking system. Second, real interest rates (that is, nominal interest rates minus inflation) would be reduced, even if nominal interest rates did not fall more. The upshot would be easier borrowing terms for business and households, which would stimulate investment and consumption demand.

The next effect of monetary expansion would be a further deprecia-tion of the yen. This is perhaps the reason that the Bank of Japan does not carry out a more aggressive monetary expansion, but the reasoning is wrong. The U.S. is, inappropriately, against a further yen depreciation, even though the chances of a vigorous Japanese recovery at 105–120 yen to the dollar are very low. Japan needs a further depreciation of the yen.

The U.S. fears a more aggressive monetary expansion because it believes that a significant yen depreciation (e.g., to 150 yen per dollar) would trigger protectionism in the U.S. and adverse consequences in the rest of Asia. Both fears are misplaced. First, monetary expansion would increase Japan's imports as well as its exports. While the yen would depreciate, thereby boosting exports, the concomitant boost in consumer and investment spending would draw in imports. The effect on net exports would be very small, and not enough to trigger a serious protectionist backlash. Second, the effects on Asia could be undone, in most cases, by a slight further depreciation of other currencies in Asia (such as the won and baht) vis-à-vis the U.S. dollar.

It is notable that the U.S. has pushed repeatedly for Japan to expand fiscal policy rather than monetary policy. Unfortunately, these pressures have greatly exacerbated Japan's long-term fiscal problems (especially the heavy burden of future social security expenditures with a rapidly aging population), without providing real stimulus in the short term. It seems that as the government has reduced its own saving (in fact, increased its dis-saving), households have increased their own saving.

Without wanting to claim that all fiscal instruments are exhausted—
since a reduction in marginal income tax rates, and an investment tax
credit for investment could both help to stimulate aggregate demand—
the fact is that the deficit is now so large as a percentage of GDP that
any more talk of outright Keynesian fiscal stimulus should simply be
dismissed.[8]

In short, Japan has the makings of a gradual recovery in 2000, if large-
scale banking rehabilitation, significant foreign assistance to Asia, and
aggressive monetary expansion are combined. These measures would
reestablish working capital flows; boost domestic prices, thereby easing
the bad debt problems; and invigorate exports. Japan could begin a
recovery by the second quarter of 2000, but with a yen value closer to
140–150 yen per dollar than its current value of 105–115 yen per dollar.
With the depreciated yen, it could be possible to see GDP growth of up
to 1.5 percent in 2000.

Note, finally, that in any circumstances—even with the most brilliant
and determined reforms—Japan will not be able to recreate the high-
growth era. Because Japan is now a mature economy, per capita growth
rates of 1.5 to 2.0 percent per year are the highest that could be expected
on a long-term basis. So, with a population growth rate of around 0.2
percent per year, Japan will experience medium-term growth of perhaps
2.0 percent per year.[9]

South Korea

The recovery of South Korea in 1999 was spectacular. GDP grew 4.5
percent in the first quarter, 9.9 percent in the second, and 12.3 percent in
the third. The growth for the year is expected to be 9.4 percent. The
won-dollar exchange rate has dropped from its historical high of 1,962
won/US$ on December 23, 1997 to 1,120 won/US$ on March 13, 2000,
and the stock market index increased over 220 percent in the same
period. Interest rates, which once topped 35 percent, now stand below
10 percent. Korea has further increased its ability to withstand speculative attacks: its non-gold foreign exchange reserves stood at US$65
billion in 1999:3Q compared to short-term foreign debt of about US$38

8. Ironically, if the U.S. had not unwisely pushed Japan towards fiscal stimulus in earlier
years, there would be more fiscal room to maneuver today.
9. Note that with the U.S. population growing at around 0.9 percent per year, the U.S. will
have 0.7 percentage points higher overall GDP growth than Japan, even when per capita
growth rates are the same.

billion. Moreover, the proportion of short-term debt in total debt has dropped to 20 percent from more than 40 percent in 1997.

The large amount of non-performing loans (NPLs) in financial institutions is one of the most serious obstacles to these institutions' ability and willingness to extend credit. The fact that the increase in bank credit has been slower than the increase in bank deposits suggests that banks prefer to purchase government securities rather than make loans. To speed up the recapitalization of the banking sector, the government passed legislation in 1998 that allowed foreigners to buy Korean banks. Korea First Bank, which was taken over by the government in late 1997, has been sold to the U.S. group Newberg-GE Capital.

Many critics of Korean industrial organization have attributed the depth of the Korean collapse to the excess capacity and the over-stretched management in the over-diversified chaebols. Under government pressure, the biggest five chaebols promised to reduce their activities to about five industries by the middle of 1999. The government has taken an active monitoring and enforcing role in consolidating products under fewer chaebols. For example, Arthur Andersen was commissioned to study how the electronics industry should be restructured, and the firm recommended that the electronics branch of the LG chaebol be merged with the electronics branch of Hyundai. When LG resisted handing over its electronics branch to Hyundai, the government called upon Korean banks to limit loans to the LG chaebol, which soon capitulated to the government's wishes.

The extent of restructuring that has occurred in industrial organization seems quite insignificant so far. The 30 largest chaebols produced 12 percent of GDP in 1998, down from the peak value of 16.5 percent in 1995. The extent of restructuring within the chaebols may also have been insignificant, although they have met the state-stipulated target of reducing their debt-equity ratios below 200 percent by the end of 1999.

In the paper on South Korea in this volume, Kiseok Hong and Jong-Wha Lee warn that caution about the Korean economy is still warranted despite the remarkable growth performance in 1999. They point out that since the expansionary macroeconomic policies were an important cause of strong growth in 1999, it is likely that the resumption of a less expansionary policy stance and the speeding up of financial and corporate restructuring would slow GDP growth in 2000 to about 6 percent. However, if structural reform efforts are diluted and the current stance of expansionary macroeconomic policy extends to 2000, Hong and Lee think that Korea may experience another episode of financial instability and recession in the medium term.

There is also concern about fiscal soundness. In restructuring the financial sector and extending the social safety net, the government has rapidly increased its borrowing. The central government debt increased from 13.6 percent of GDP in 1997 to 31 percent in 1998. Even these figures may underestimate the true government liabilities, since the consolidated budget does not include many quasi-fiscal and extra-budgetary activities. The inclusion of these extra items will raise government liability to over 70 percent of GDP in 1999.

The crisis left many social problems in its wake. The unemployment rate remains high (5.4 percent in August 1999), and it is unlikely to recover its pre-crisis average of 2 to 3 percent in the near future. Furthermore, the recovery has not been even in every sector of the economy. The recent rapid recovery has concentrated on several manufacturing industries, especially the semiconductor and automobile industries. The service sector, by contrast, remains relatively sluggish. As many unemployed workers shifted to the services sector, nominal wages in the personal services sector decreased by 3 percent in the first half of 1999, in contrast to the 8-percent increase of the total industry wages. If these social problems result in political instability, then full recovery will be delayed.

The Southeast Asian Crisis Trio

Thailand not only precociously fell victim to the Asian financial crisis in mid-1997, but also suffered a larger GDP decline in 1998 than Malaysia and South Korea, and registered lower growth in 1999 than these two countries. Nevertheless, most signs of future growth prospects are positive. Short-term trade-related capital has returned, and as a result, exports have increased. Longer term foreign capital has also returned. For example, foreign investors bought most of the assets of the 56 closed finance companies, and the Electrical Generating Authority of Thailand borrowed, with guarantees on debt-servicing given by the World Bank, US$300 million from the international markets. These positive developments on the current account and the capital account have helped to strengthen the currency to 37 baht/US$ in March 2000, from 47.0 baht/US$ two years ago. Interest rates have dropped sharply as well. The short-term interest rate has fallen to 3.91 percent on March 1, 2000 from 25 percent on September 24, 1997. The only significant indicator that appears gloomy about Thailand's economic prospects is the stock market index, which was 371.6 on March 1, 2000, compared with 372.7 on December 31, 1997 and 547.0 on September 24, 1997.

Thailand is now well into the second stage of the recovery process; namely, the stage of working out the NPLs of the banks and the debt overhang of the corporations. However, the process of debt workout has been slow because the government is unwilling to use large amounts of public funds to effect a speedy removal of bad debts from the banks. Frank Flatters, in his chapter on Thailand in this volume, reports that it is "the government's view that leaving the bad loans with the banks would ensure more effective management of these portfolios." The government is determined to minimize the "strategic NPL" phenomenon, in which good firms refrain from servicing their bank debts in anticipation of their "defaulted" loans being written off by the banks because of government pressure to do so.

There is, however, another way whereby the government could handle this "strategic NPL" behavior without prolonging the debt workout process. The alternative strategy is for the government to finance a massive removal of NPLs from the banks and then implement rigorous auditing of the bad corporate debts that it takes over from the banks.

Once beyond the financial crisis, Thailand's competitiveness will depend crucially on the removal of several well-known obstacles to its long-term growth: inadequate physical infrastructure, a low level of human capital, and a corrupt administrative structure. Unless these long-term development challenges are met, Thailand will find it difficult to maintain its previous growth rate of approximately 7 percent.

Beginning in 1998:3Q, Malaysia sought to fix its collapsing economy with reflation carried out behind temporary capital controls. Banks were assigned an 8-percent credit growth target, bank prudential standards were relaxed, and government spending was increased. The ringgit was pegged at 3.8 ringgit per US$ while the regional currencies appreciated against the US$. Since the decline in output was caused by a fall in aggregate demand and not by a destruction of productive capacity, these policies helped GDP to grow 5.4 percent in 1999.

Unlike Thailand, Malaysia moved quickly to solve the NPL problems of the banks and the heavy debt burdens of the corporate sector through massive bailouts with public money. While the bailouts certainly helped to boost aggregate demand in 1999, this pervasive use of bailouts definitely strengthens the moral hazard problems that already exist. For example, the bailout of Bank Bumiputra was the third bailout in the 32-year history of the bank.

The chief reason that the government moved decisively ahead with the bailouts is because Malaysia's race-based policy of increasing the Malay community's share of corporate assets was carried out to a large extent through bank loans to Malays to buy corporate shares, which would then be used as collateral for the loans. As a consequence, the fluctuations of the stock market have come to exert disproportionate influence on the politics within the ruling Malay party (especially when there is an internal power struggle, such as now). The collapse of the stock market after 1996 created margin calls on many influential Malays, who at the same time found that the lower profits generated by the economic slowdown were not sufficient to service their debts. The good news is that the speedy debt workouts restored the credit mechanism, but the bad news is that they are likely to create more debt workouts in the future through the moral hazard mechanism.

The Industrial Coordination Act (ICA) of 1975 requires that all enterprises with equity above a certain amount sell 30 percent of their shares to Malays. These designated Malay shares are usually sold at a significant discount to Malay individuals or Malay organizations selected by the government. The evidence shows that the most internationally competitive manufacturing sectors in Malaysia are the sectors that have been exempted from the ownership requirements and are dominated by foreign direct investors. The bulk of the import-substituting light industrial firms are owned by Chinese-Malaysians, and the evidence is that few of them ever grow large enough to start exporting. The dilemma faced by such firms is that if they grow larger, they become subject to the rules of the ICA, but if they do not become larger, they are not likely to be able to export. As a result, it appears that the incentive structure rooted in the ownership legislation has inhibited the development of an export capacity among import-substituting light manufacturers.

For Malaysia to address the long-run problems of maintaining high growth and increasing international competitiveness, it must take the following actions:

• relax the ownership restrictions of ICA to enable the needed recapitalization of the banks and large firms; and

• institute a weeding-out process within its infant industry program to prevent high-cost inputs from undermining international competitiveness by including expiration dates for state subsidies and import protection.

Malaysia is now at a crucial point in its history, and extraordinary political leadership is required. This leadership must have the political courage to assess objectively whether the continuation of the race-based programs and the industrial policies has more to do with political patronage than with providing "infant industry protection" to Malay professionals and businesses. If political patronage is behind these policies, then the economic costs from a rigid ICA are not serving the social justice motivation behind the race-based policies. A fast-growing and internationally competitive economy will do more to enrich the Malay community than state-generated rents can ever hope to do.

Indonesia came close to a complete meltdown in 1998, when GDP fell 13.6 percent and riots broke out across the country. Only agricultural output did not experience a decline (it grew by 0.15 percent). Industrial output fell 19 percent and service output fell 17 percent. The real wage dropped about 50 percent, and the greatest job loss appears to have occurred among rural professionals and urban professionals,[10] two politically vocal groups. The crisis has certainly wiped out a part of the progress against absolute poverty achieved in the last 30 years, raising the official poverty rate from 11 percent in 1996 to 40 percent in 1998. Riots in the first half of 1998 ended the 32-year reign of President Soeharto, and resulted in the burning of Jakarta's Chinatown. Since then, inter-religious and inter-island conflicts have surfaced occasionally, and there are continuing breakdowns in basic law and order on personal safety and protection of property rights. The erratic downward course of the exchange rate reflected, and contributed to, the instabilities and fragilities of the Indonesian situation. The end-of-year rupiah-US$ exchange rate went from about 2,400 in 1996 to 4,650 in 1997, to 8,050 in 1998, and then to 7,085 in 1999—but not before collapsing to 16,000 in May 1998, around the time of Soeharto's resignation.

Economic policy-making was paralyzed for most of the time since then because of political uncertainty. Bacharuddin Habibie, who succeeded Soeharto, was replaced by Abdurrahman Wahid in October 1999. The financial panic has ended, but it still casts a long shadow because of continued uncertainty about social instability, and because Indonesia's short-term foreign debt is probably still greater than its non-gold foreign reserves. Nevertheless, interest rates have almost returned to their pre-crisis level; for example, the end-of-year lending rate was 19

---

10. See Azis (1998).

percent in 1996, 25 percent in 1997, 35 percent in 1998, and 21 percent in 1999. There is even the strong possibility that GDP actually grew in 1999.

The two most important economic problems faced by Indonesia are the bankrupt banking system and the huge debt burden on private corporations. The Indonesian Bank Restructuring Agency (IBRA) was established in January 1998 with wide powers to restructure the banking sector. IBRA has proceeded with increasing assertiveness in addressing the banks' problems, but progress has been slow because of the inadequacy of the legal system, and interference from political figures.

The Indonesian Debt Restructuring Agency (INDRA) was set up in June 1998 to help the non-bank corporations to deal with their foreign debts. After creditors and debtors have reached agreement on the restructuring of the loans, INDRA acts as the intermediary to receive rupiah payments from the debtor and to make dollar payments to the creditor. INDRA protects the debtor from future depreciation of the rupiah by guaranteeing an exchange rate value that is close to the existing value. However, few private corporations have used INDRA's facilities for the following reasons:

• many creditors have resisted writing down their loans; and

• in the absence of exceedingly generous debt relief, many debtors are still insolvent at the current exchange rate, so a guarantee against future rupiah depreciation is irrelevant.

Political stability, not economic restructuring, is the over-arching factor in restoring economic growth and determining future international competitiveness. Without resolution of the big political questions, economic reforms not only cannot proceed rapidly, they also cannot produce benefits that are close to their potential levels.

2.4   The Seven Pillars of Reform

Our analysis of the Asian financial crisis indicates the clear need for important reforms in many areas, including domestic markets, domestic institutions, international organizations, and international financial architecture. In the first chapter, "A Reform Agenda for a Resilient Asia," we drew upon the analysis here and the analyses in other chapters to propose 30 specific policy actions that cover seven issues.

First and foremost, the financial markets in developing countries require root-and-branch reform in many cases. To enhance the resilience of the financial system to creditor panic, prudential regulation and supervision must be strengthened; accounting practices must be brought up to international standards; balance sheets of financial institutions must be reported more fully, more frequently, and more timely; and regulations for the entry of foreign banks must be relaxed.

Second, the performance of the International Monetary Fund (IMF) left much to be desired. The IMF actually contributed to the financial panic that helped to bring down the Asian economies. External supervision of the IMF must be increased and improved, and this requires that the IMF's decision-making process must become more transparent and include the input of a larger number of developing countries.

Third, the IMF cannot, and should not, be either the international lender of last resort or the international deposit insurance agency. In such circumstances, generalized floating of exchange rates should be the norm for the international monetary system. The new monetary system should establish regional monetary bodies, and an international bankruptcy court to speed up international debt restructuring.

Fourth, the failure of the first IMF programs for Thailand, Indonesia and South Korea, as well as subsequent programs for Russia and Brazil, makes it clear that international rescue packages must be re-designed. Among other things, there should be ways to "bail in," rather than bail out, the foreign creditors. Debt relief, standstills for existing debt, priority payment for new loans, and other standard features of domestic bankruptcy procedures should be part of international rescue packages. IMF funds should certainly not be used to defend overvalued exchange rates, as was done (unsuccessfully) in Russia and Brazil.

Fifth, the regulation and monitoring of international capital markets should be stricter and internationally coordinated. The chief regulatory reforms are prudential restrictions on short-term capital inflows, and the further liberalization of long-term foreign direct investments. The United Nations should take the lead in convening a meeting of international organizations on this important question. Such a meeting would help to bridge the differences and misunderstandings between the developed and developing countries.

Sixth, the bad debts of the financial and corporate sectors in Pacific Asia must be decisively and quickly resolved because they are paralyzing the credit system and inhibiting investment. The key steps to re-capitalizing the banking sector are the infusion of public money, and the takeover of some large domestic banks by foreign banks. The key steps to reviving the corporate sector are debt write-downs and debt-equity swaps.

Seventh, there is a serious mismatch in Pacific Asia, particularly in most of Southeast Asia, between investment in physical hardware (factories and machinery) and investment in the social software (scientific research centers, administrative and judiciary systems, and growth of civil society). While it is now increasingly recognized that the enrichment of the domestic scientific base is crucial for sustaining high economic growth, it is less recognized that Asia's flawed social infrastructure and inadequate political institutions—which have allowed for too much corruption and mismanagement—are a cause for serious concern. In a world of growing international competitiveness, when foreign direct investors are courted not just by Asia but Central Europe and Latin America, the concerns over governance are bound to grow, and to weigh increasingly heavily on the unreformed countries of Asia. In short, the long-term competitiveness of Asia rests as much on "getting the institutions right" as on "getting the prices right."

References

Azis, Iwan. 1998. "Outlook of the Indonesian economy and strategic issues," manuscript, Cornell University, December.

International Monetary Fund. 1999. *World Economic Outlook*, October.

Radelet, Steven, and Jeffrey Sachs. 1998. "The East Asian financial crisis: Diagnosis, remedies, prospects," *Brookings Papers on Economic Activity*, 1: 1–90.

Woo, Wing Thye, Patrick Carleton, and Brian Rosario. (forthcoming). "The unorthodox origins of the Asian financial crisis," *ASEAN Economic Bulletin*.

3

Restructuring Asia's Financial System

Donald Hanna

3.1 The Sorry State of Asian Finance

Although more than two years have passed since Asia's economic crisis began, much of the region's financial system remains in tatters. Non-performing loans (NPLs) are staggeringly high, and real credit growth is dismal (table 3.1).

In Japan, the region's largest economy, the government injected ¥25 trillion (or 5 percent of GDP) in new public funds for bank recapitalization. Domestic credit growth has since hovered around 0–1 percent since mid-1997, despite the lowest nominal interest rates in the world. Last year, in a desperate effort to prompt more lending and growth, the Bank of Japan resorted to leapfrogging commercial banks and buying commercial paper directly from the country's leading firms.

In China, the region's most populous economy, estimates of NPLs run to 35–40 percent of loans outstanding, or 30 percent of GDP. In the region's other highly populated country, India, NPLs are about 16 percent of total loans. Only massive holdings of government bonds, the counterpart of India's outsized fiscal deficit, buttress the capital base of its banking system.

In the Asian crisis countries, i.e., Indonesia, Korea, Malaysia and Thailand (ACC-4), conditions remain fragile. In Thailand, 56 finance companies and 8 commercial banks, representing over 13.5 percent of the financial system's assets, have been closed or merged. NPLs constitute nearly 38 percent of outstanding loans over two years into the crisis. Standard & Poors estimates that as of October 1999, Thailand still needs US$23 billion in additional equity, which amounts to roughly 65 percent of the banking system's existing capital, for banks that remain open.

The author is grateful to Wilbur Maxino for his assistance in preparing this chapter.

In Indonesia, of the 240 banks operating before the financial crisis, 64 have been closed, 13 have been nationalized and are undergoing shareholder negotiations, and 8 have received capital injections from the government. Seventy-three private banks remain operating, under the recent government-imposed condition that they maintain a capital adequacy ratio (CAR) of at least 4 percent. Bank Indonesia recently mentioned it may hand over two of these banks to the restructuring agency for failing to maintain the required 4-percent CAR. The government has issued around Rp500 trillion (US$70.4 billion) in bonds for the capitalization of troubled banks and to compensate Bank Indonesia for its liquidity support in the past and the settlement of inter-bank claims. It envisages issuing another Rp140 trillion (US$19.7 billion) to complete the recapitalization of state banks. Indonesia's recapitalization effort, including estimated interest payments, has cost the government some 58 percent of GDP.

Korea's Financial Supervisory Commission, the entity that oversees bank restructuring, has nationalized Korea's six largest and oldest banks, and has budgeted about W64 trillion to boost capital in troubled banks (though so far, only around 86 percent of the total budget has actually been spent). Another W3 trillion has been put into two investment trust companies (ITCs) as equity, and a bond stabilization fund of W30 trillion has been set up to support the assets of other ITCs.

In the wake of the financial panic that swept through the ACC-4, credit growth in real terms took a dramatic dive to the negative (see figures 3.1–3.4).[1] The contraction was most severe and abrupt in Indonesia, although the story was much the same throughout the crisis region. Even in countries less heavily affected, such as Singapore or Hong Kong, credit growth slowed dramatically as banks remained cautious about credit quality. This collapse of domestic credit was closely associated with collapsing GDP (figures 3.1–3.4).

---

1. Real credit is calculated using a constant exchange rate for foreign currency denominated credit to avoid counting the increase in the local currency value of that credit as a new flow. As usual, local currency denominated credit is deflated by the local CPI. Some of the continued decline in credit is due to more aggressive write-offs of bad loans as recapitalization has moved forward.

Table 3.1
State of the banking sector

	NPL ratio	Reached peak NPL ratio	Loan to deposits		
			Nov. 1999	1998	1996
Korea	20.5	26.0	56	58	75
Malaysia	12.0	18.5	90	96	93
Philippines	14.6	17.0	83	88	100
Thailand	38.0	48.5	112	146	151

Source: CEIC, Salomon Smith Barney estimates.

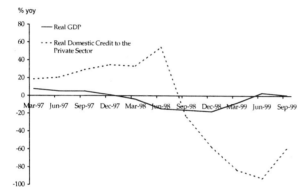

Figure 3.1
Indonesia: Real domestic credit and GDP.

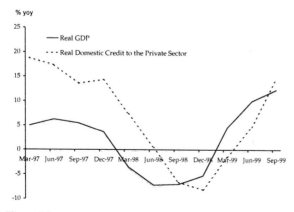

Figure 3.2
Korea: Real domestic credit and GDP.

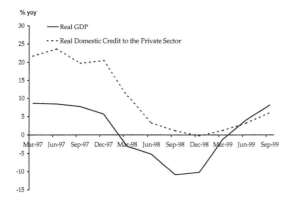

Figure 3.3
Malaysia: Real domestic credit and GDP.

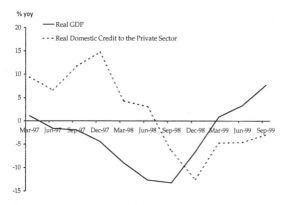

Figure 3.4
Thailand: Real domestic credit and GDP.

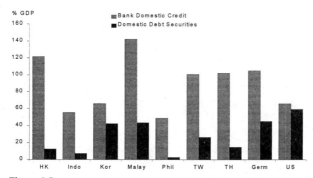

Figure 3.5
Sources of formal finance. Source: CEIC, BIS and GS estimates.

The discussion so far has focused on the banking system, mainly because banks dominate Asia's financial system. Other sources of formal finance such as pension funds, insurance companies, or the bond market are generally small (figure 3.5). Therefore, problems in the banking system largely correspond to problems for the financial system overall.

3.2   How Did Asia Get Into This State?

The most plausible explanation of the crisis points to the massive outflow of capital after June 1997 that reversed an equally massive capital inflow in the preceding three years.[2] Understanding these flows is crucial to understanding the state of Asia's financial system and what can be done about it.

After the fall in world real interest rates in 1989, capital flows to Asia began to increase, pulled in by attractively high GDP growth rates (and expected high returns) and pushed by lower returns in the rest of the world. Net capital inflows averaged 1.8 percent of GDP in the ACC-4 between 1989 and 1992, and 6.4 percent of GDP after 1992. In Thailand, capital inflows in 1995 hit 13 percent of GDP. This compares with a net capital inflow of 0.6 percent of GDP in the same period in the developed economies of the G-7.

Not only were capital flows extremely large, they were increasingly short term. This move toward greater amounts of short-term capital increased the risks of collapse should flows reverse, as they did in the second half of 1997. Data on commercial bank loans from the Bank for International Settlements (BIS) illustrate the extent of inflows and their reversal. Over 1989–94, banks that reported to the BIS saw their external claims on Asia rise to US$372 billion from US$141 billion. Between 1995 and mid-1997, reporting banks pumped US$203.2 billion into Asia. In the last six months of 1997 and the first quarter of 1998, US$63.2 billion flooded out. Over the remainder of 1998 and the first half of 1999, another US$270.5 billion left the region.

The flip-side of capital inflows into the region was a sharp buildup in the leverage of the region's economies (figure 3.6). Thailand, Korea and Malaysia had total debt to GDP ratios of about 200 percent of GDP. Japan's was nearly 300 percent. These levels of indebtedness far exceeded comparable numbers for other emerging market countries. Total debt shown in figure 3.6 combines external and domestic debt. To avoid double

---

2. A financial boom and bust is also the chief explanation of the weakening of Japan's banking system, although the timing is far earlier.

counting, the foreign debt of the banking system is netted out on the assumption that funds raised overseas were on-lent domestically.

Not only were debt stocks high, so too was debt service; for example, debt service amounted to almost 41 percent of GDP in Thailand in 1997 (figure 3.7). These high and rising ratios of debt and debt service made Asian economies especially sensitive to interest rate shocks or the withdrawal of finance.

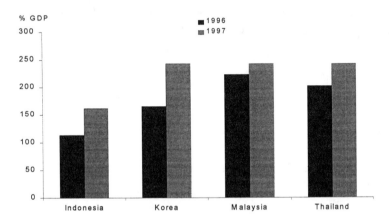

Figure 3.6
Total debt in the ACC-4. Source: GS estimates.

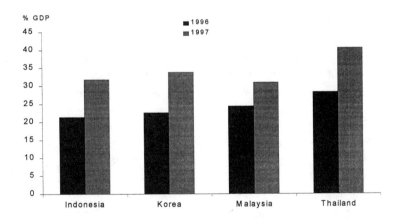

Figure 3.7
Debt service ratios in the ACC-4. Source: GS estimates.

Table 3.2
Total loan disbursements as percentage of net capital inflows

	1994	1995	1996
China	69	105	86
India	62	148	70
Indonesia	351	170	172
Malaysia	(178)	122	146
Philippines	81	98	57
Thailand	74	82	56

Source: CEIC, World Bank and GS estimates.

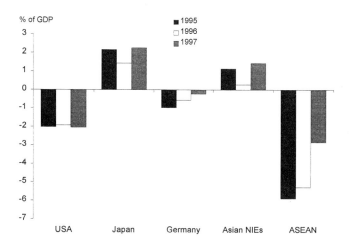

Figure 3.8
Current account. Source: CEIC, GS estimates.

Foreign capital inflows came largely in the form of debt, chiefly via the region's banks (table 3.2). While some countries, notably China, received most of the inflows as foreign direct investment, this was the exception rather than the rule.

The inflows found their way chiefly into investment in Asia rather than into consumption. Despite the world's highest savings rates, the pace of investment, chiefly private, absorbed the lion's share of the inflows. This savings/investment gap was reflected in the large current account deficits that East Asia, outside Japan, ran in the mid-1990s (figure 3.8). Unlike earlier episodes of yawning current account deficits,

52   Don Hanna

such as those Latin America in the 1980s, the imbalance and the debt
occurred largely in the private sector. Most East Asian countries (except
Japan) increased their fiscal surpluses over the years of strong inflows in
an attempt to offset the boost to domestic demand generated by the
capital inflows.

Unfortunately, attempts to moderate the effect of the inflows on
demand were not successful. Real exchange rates appreciated, though
generally only modestly (table 3.3). This real appreciation affected the
allocation of capital in East Asia (as it had in Japan in the late 1980s).
Non-traded sectors such as real estate and services got an increasing
share of credit in most ACC-4 countries, with the exception of Korea
(figure 3.9). This sectoral allocation became especially problematic in the
aftermath of the 1997 devaluations. The sharp shift in the real exchange
rate soured the loans of the non-traded sector that had been built up in
the heyday of capital inflows.

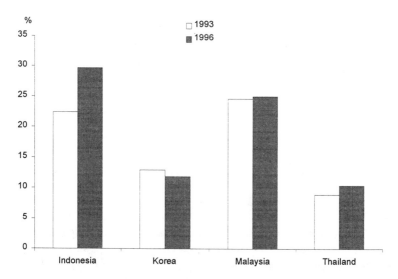

Notes: Indonesia – proxied by loans to the services industry as percentage of total commercial
banks credits. Korea – proxied by housing loans as percentage of total of deposit money
banks. Malaysia – proxied by merchant banks' property loans as percentage of total, less the
portion that went to the Cagamas (the state-owned mortgage refinancing agency) and to
stockbrokers. Thailand – proxied by the mortgage receivables portion of gross total loans and
business receivables in finance companies.

Figure 3.9
Share of non-traded sectors in total credit. Source: CEIC, GS estimates.

Table 3.3
Spot and GSDEEMER exchange rate values

	End of period: 1995		
	Spot	GSDEEMER	% Overvaluation
China	8.3	8.1	**(2.2)**
Hong Kong	7.7	8.0	3.3
India	35.2	35.8	1.5
Indonesia	2,293.6	2,376.9	3.6
Korea	774.0	804.5	3.9
Malaysia	2.5	2.6	1.5
Philippines	26.2	28.1	7.2
Singapore	1.4	1.5	4.9
Taiwan	27.3	27.1	**(0.8)**
Thailand	25.2	25.9	2.8
	End of period: 1996		
	Spot	GSDEEMER	% Overvaluation
China	8.3	8.6	3.8
Hong Kong	7.7	8.1	4.2
India	35.9	39.8	10.9
Indonesia	2,362.3	2,610.6	10.5
Korea	844.6	863.6	2.3
Malaysia	2.5	2.7	7.7
Philippines	26.3	28.7	9.1
Singapore	1.4	1.5	7.0
Taiwan	27.5	28.2	2.4
Thailand	25.7	26.8	4.4
	End of period: June 1997		
	Spot	GSDEEMER	% Overvaluation
China	8.3	8.6	3.0
Hong Kong	7.7	8.5	10.1
India	35.8	41.6	16.1
Indonesia	2,432.0	2,898.5	19.2
Korea	887.9	926.6	4.4
Malaysia	2.5	2.9	13.7
Philippines	26.4	30.2	14.5
Singapore	1.4	1.6	9.7
Taiwan	27.8	28.8	3.7
Thailand	24.7	28.3	14.7

Note: GSDEEMER (Goldman Sachs Dynamic Equilibrium Emerging Market Exchange Rate) is a proprietary model for estimating the long-run nominal exchange rate that will balance a country's current account. It relies on observed econometric links between a country's real and trade-weighted exchange rates, and its terms of trade, openness, international real interest rates and relative productivity. Other, more standard measures of real effective exchange rates also show real appreciation, although such measures do not capture whether the appreciation was consistent with underlying changes in the equilibrium real exchange rate. Numbers in bold are undervaluations. Source: Bloomberg, GS estimates.

3.3   Why the High Inflow of Money? Why Was It Not Better Allocated

Questions about the allocation and magnitude of capital inflows received by Asia are tightly interwoven. Integral to the story are the pegged
or quasi-pegged exchange rates (i.e., those managed within a tight band)
that East Asian countries, excluding Japan, used as part of their strategy
of export-led development.

A feature of tightly managed exchange rates is that daily variations
are small. However, there is still a slight probability of exchange rates
changing dramatically, as they did in 1997. Markets often underestimate
the risk of unlikely but drastic events. Tightly managed exchange rates
make foreign borrowing appear less risky and cheaper than it actually
is; and such borrowing increases as long as there seems to be little
chance of a radical change, and prices continue to reflect the inaccur-
ately estimated risk.

Figure 3.10 shows that foreign capital inflows for the ACC-4, as
proxied by the increase in foreign liabilities of the commercial banking
system, increasingly took a bigger share of the strong growth of domestic credit that characterized the ACC-4 prior to 1998. Indonesia, which
was operating with a band, exemplifies the problem. Until 1993, the
rupiah's intervention band was only 1 percent. As capital flows
increased, the band was gradually widened to 10 percent by mid-1997,
with the currency generally trading on the strong side of the band.
Despite the widening, foreign currency borrowing gathered pace prior
to mid-1997, reaching over US$65 billion, up from US$42 billion in
1994.[3] After the baht devaluation, Bank Indonesia accelerated the
widening of the band, but the rupiah quickly reached the new weaker
level. In September 1997 Bank Indonesia eliminated the band rather
than spend massive amounts of reserves or push interest rates to
exorbitant real levels. A panic among foreign borrowers ensued, contributing to the subsequent sharp depreciation in the rupiah.[4]

---

3. Bank for International Settlements.
4. By the end of December the rupiah was trading near Rp5,000 per US$1.00—roughly
double its September value. By that time, external private debt repayments had largely
ceased. The further deterioration of the rupiah to nearly Rp17,000 was caused by the
increase in political uncertainty and the collapse of the banking system.

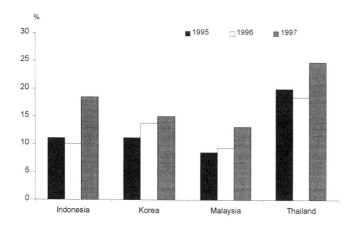

Figure 3.10
Commercial banks' foreign borrowing as share of domestic credit. Source: CEIS, GS
estimates.

Some have argued that mispricing through inaccurate risk assessment
is not the only problem.[5] There is also the deliberate increase in risk that
lending institutions take on if they feel that, in the event of devaluation,
they will not suffer the full losses stemming from their lending decisions.
This moral-hazard problem is especially applicable for large commercial
banks because of the support generally given to such banks, and their
depositors, in the event of a currency or banking crisis. In practice,
liquidity support to the banks in Asia has been huge. In Thailand, the
Financial Institution Development Fund extended loans worth over 25
percent of 1998 GDP in an effort to shore up weak banks. In Indonesia,
liquidity support amounted to more than 20 percent of 1998 GDP.

One has to be careful with *post hoc ergo propter hoc* arguments. In
Thailand, large depositors were not bailed out during the banking crisis
in the mid-1980s. While principal was returned to depositors of failed
institutions, this was drawn out over ten years at below-market interest
rates. In Indonesia, the large depositors of one of the top-ten private
banks suffered losses when the bank was liquidated in 1991. These
measures would, in principle, have put depositors on notice that they
stood to lose money if they invested in risky banks. The massive shift of
deposits to foreign or state-owned banks as fears rose about the banking
systems in ASEAN, despite the announcement of government guarantees

---

5. Krugman (1998) emphasized moral hazard as the key factor behind the financial crisis.

of all deposits, demonstrates that the public did not view all institutions as equally safe. The riskiest banks in Korea were merchant banks, not commercial banks, though the latter are larger. The disparate behavior of banks, even large banks, seems to reflect more the expectations and risk appetite of managers and owners rather than a pervasive sense of moral hazard, i.e., a sense of invulnerability resulting from the high probability of government support. Managers have also been punished for corruption and poor lending in the past, which should have disciplined their behavior and reduced moral hazard. For example, managers of one of the seven Indonesian state-owned commercial banks were jailed for their dubious lending that bankrupted the bank. In sum, to claim that depositors viewed their accounts as safe without regard to a bank's lending, or that bank managers or owners thought themselves immune to the consequences of poor lending, is an inaccurate assessment of the situation.

What is clear is that prudential regulation and supervision of the ACC-4 banking systems was weak. This is documented, for example, in the work on regional banks done by Goldman Sachs.[6] It is also apparent from the concerted effort to bring prudential regulations and supervision to international standards that has been a part of the adjustment of the region to the crisis. Less-regulated entities were also those that took on greater risks. For example, the Korean government estimates that the NPL ratio of non-bank financial institutions (NBFIs) was 15 percent as of June 1998, compared with 10 percent in commercial banks. NBFIs also showed higher levels of NPLs in Malaysia and Thailand, which was more a reflection of a breakdown in supervision in an environment of misguided mania than a result of increased risk due to firms operating as if they were "too big to fail."

Another important element of the problem of financial excess and consequent distress was the region's accelerated efforts at financial liberalization in the 1990s. In Thailand, the authorities created the Bangkok International Bank Facility (BIBF), which was effectively an offshore banking system. This greatly increased Thai corporations' access to foreign-denominated lending. BIBF debt of Thai companies jumped to US$31 billion by the end of 1996, of which more than US$20 billion was short-term debt. The increase in BIBF lending accounted for roughly two-thirds of the increase in external debt between 1992 and 1996, and

6. See Roy Ramos (1997). A pull-out section compares prudential norms across Asia and in the U.S. The most widespread shortcoming was inadequate standards for the recognition of NPLs.

almost all of the increase in short-term debt. This increase in borrowing was partly stimulated by government regulations. Foreign banks operating under the BIBF were told that the granting of full banking licenses would be a function of the volume of BIBF lending.

While BIBF lending was ostensibly to go to companies with foreign exchange earnings, poor oversight and a lack of compliance by the banks meant that, in practice, many loans funded projects in the non-traded sector. Access to these large borrowings in foreign currencies made it very difficult for the Thai authorities to slow aggregate demand (given their quasi-fixed exchange rate), despite efforts to increase the fiscal surplus as the economy overheated in 1995–96. These same loans were a crushing blow when the baht devalued in mid-July.

In Indonesia, liberalization of the types of services and the number of institutions that were given licenses was a more important factor than easier access to foreign exchange in explaining the financial boom and bust. Entry and service provision was liberalized in 1989, leading to a mushrooming of banks and assets. The number of banks rose threefold in three years, far outstripping the government's ability to supervise them adequately. Credit growth leapt to more than 70 percent at one point in early 1990, fueling a housing and stock market boom. Bank Indonesia subsequently clamped down, but NPLs created during that time weakened the banks, thereby helping to create the loss of confidence in 1997.

Korea also began financial liberalization during the 1990s as part of its effort to join the OECD. Concerned about capital inflows, the Koreans focused on allowing capital outflows, especially as the nominal cost of credit was high in Korea—a large attraction to offshore lenders. Despite Korea's efforts, portfolio net inflows between 1990 and mid-1997 totaled US$59 billion. In the previous seven years, net inflows had totaled roughly zero.

It was not liberalization alone that was the problem, so much as liberalization outstripping the regulatory structure of the country. For example, the Philippines also liberalized its capital account in 1993, sparking an increase in foreign currency denominated lending. But a better-developed regulatory structure (and a higher perceived risk premium on lending to the Philippines, given its history of default in the 1980s) sheltered the country from the excesses that plagued other ASEAN nations.

The other perverse interaction was between liberalization and corporate governance or transparency. The greater access to funding created by liberalization increased the importance of transparency and arm's-length transactions to ensure the efficient allocation of resources. The traditional control that a main lending institution could exert over a borrower in the relatively oligopolistic markets of Asia disappeared with the liberalization. However, it was not replaced by a transparent source of accounting information that would allow the new competitive lenders to assess risks accurately. Leverage increased dramatically with liberalization, but transparency did not.

3.4   What Has Been Done?

Efforts at overcoming the financial collapse in Asia have focused on two broad areas:

• restoring the balance sheets of financial intermediaries, partly through the use of public money (fixing the stock problem); and

• alleviating the credit crunch through restoring intermediation, but within a framework that ensures better future credit decisions (fixing the flow problem).

There are two main attitudes in dealing with the stock and flow problems. Call them the Old Testament Attitude (OTA) and the New Testament Attitude (NTA). The OTA advocates bankrupting banks or firms for past poor lending/borrowing decisions (sins). This view holds that not to force losses on decision makers is to risk future poor lending decisions (to encourage sin) or to prompt moral hazard. However, in practice this approach is problematic because of the sheer size of the bankruptcies required; the inadequacy of the legal framework for bankruptcy and liquidation, even after improved statutes in the last two years; and the shortage of professionals skilled in bankruptcy procedures.

The OTA in Indonesia is responsible for the closure of 14 financial institutions in November 1997 without deposit insurance in place or clarity about the soundness of other banks. This prompted a run toward foreign- and state-owned banks.

The NTA is summed up by Alexander Pope's phrase "To err is human, to forgive divine." The NTA was behind the moves throughout the region to provide near-blanket deposit guarantees, and in the cases of Korea, Thailand and Indonesia, to comfort external bank creditors by providing a government guarantee to repayments of loans to intervened banks (i.e., banks that the government has helped, bailed out or taken over).

In general, the ACC-4 were guided by both the NTA and the OTA. The OTA mainly dominated in the early days of the crisis, or in countries that were less affected. As the crisis deepened, sometimes due to the very measures that resulted from the OTA, the NTA became more common. For example, most countries tightened capital adequacy and NPL standards in the early days of the crisis (Malaysia, Thailand, Indonesia, the Philippines and Korea); however, as the situation worsened, either lower capital adequacy or looser NPL ratios became more common (Malaysia and Indonesia).

As the effects of the crisis wane, countries are likely to move back toward the OTA. Indonesia and the Philippines already have plans for future increases in capital adequacy ratios, and restrictive deposit guarantee programs are planned in Korea and Indonesia. This reflects the sensible view that the move toward the NTA was a reflection of the social costs of financial panic and not an indication of the preferred policy for normal times.

The basic strategy for restoring bank balance sheets has two components:

• Transfer NPLs to another specialized institution, generally state-owned (all ACC-4 countries).

• Seek new capital, either from the private sector at home or abroad, or from the state.

Governments have also used the recovery period to consolidate, for instance by forcing mergers or closing down institutions viewed as completely unviable. In the ACC-4, all depositors have been fully protected. However, governments have generally only used this strategy for a portion of the banks in their system. In the worst affected country, Indonesia, some private bank owners have been allowed to maintain a position in technically bankrupt banks, although this was not generally the case across the region. The decision, while smacking of favoritism, reflected a desire by the government to avoid the wholesale nationalization of the banking system and the subsequent risks of future poor lending decisions.

The strategy for restoring credit intermediation, besides the recapitalization of the banks, has focused on revamping prudential and supervisory norms to meet international standards. Besides the changes in NPL standards mentioned above, several countries have revamped their supervisory agencies (Korea, Thailand, Japan and Indonesia). Legal changes that promote stricter bankruptcy laws, and eliminate tax disin-centives to loan-loss provisioning, to merging, and to debt restructur-ings, are also part of the financial sector reforms in most countries. Greater transparency is being pushed by efforts to create more arm's-length relationships between banks and firms, or between firms, to avoid the problems caused by related lending, as in Indonesia, or the complex cross-guarantees of the chaebols in Korea. The aim is to ensure that future credit will be better allocated and, in the event of default, that claims can be settled more quickly and cheaply.

The entry of new firms in the financial sector, generally of foreign banks or institutions, has also been a part of the effort to improve financial intermediation. The hope is that foreign banks will bring higher credit standards and better screening processes, improving credit quality for the system overall.

3.5   What Problems Remain?

The chief remaining issue is the slow progress of financial restructuring at banks, and, to a greater extent, at corporations. Indonesia typifies this situation. In the banking sector, there has been significant progress in transferring assets to the Indonesian Bank Restructuring Agency (IBRA). As of August 1999, it holds Rp220 billion in bad loans received from state banks, nationalized or closed banks, and private banks that have received government equity. That is just under one-third of all domestic credit in the banking system.

The process of restructuring these assets has been slow. First, the country's strategy focused on avoiding fire sales. This necessarily meant a period of delay in sales. Second, the process has been set back severely by a corruption scandal involving IBRA, a nationalized bank, Bank Bali, and the political party of former President Habibie.

The fallout from the Bank Bali scandal is also slowing state bank restructuring. These banks were due to receive an injection of new equity from the government in July 1999, but as of December they were still waiting. In the meantime, their capital base continues to erode due to a negative interest margin.

The wider corporate sector is also suffering from the lack of progress on debt restructuring. Indonesian private external debt stands at roughly US$63 billion, including short-term trade credit. While this was a relatively modest 30 percent of GDP in mid-1997, it is now roughly three times that due to depreciation of the rupiah, even though the rupiah is now twice as strong as it was in at its weakest point in mid-1998. Given that, as in Thailand, much of the lending went into non-traded sectors, the ability of Indonesian firms to service their debt has shrunk dramatically. To handle this problem, the government, a committee of external creditors, and a committee of major debtors ironed out an agreement on debt restructuring in July 1998. Overseen by the Indonesian Debt Restructuring Agency (INDRA), the deal is modeled after the FICORCA plan used in Mexico in the mid-1980s. Assuming certain repayment terms (a minimum repayment period and maximum spread) are met, the banks/creditors would then have access to exchange rate cover under the program. However, the first year lapsed with only one firm, a state enterprise, entering the program. The window for access has since been extended and the minimum terms made more favorable. Still, to date, not one additional firm has entered the program. By contrast, the Mexican FICORCA plan led to the restructuring of 56 percent of total registered private-sector debt during its first year of operation (1983).

Thailand's difficulties now center more on the banks than on the corporate sector. A program announced in August 1998 that earmarked Bt300 billion in government funds for bank recapitalization has remained largely unused by the 7 banks and 15 finance companies eligible to draw on them. So far, only about 17 percent of the Bt300 billion has been drawn. Plans for setting up asset management companies at individual commercial banks are also proceeding slowly. As of January 2000, overall NPLs for the banking system are estimated at 38 percent of total loans (from a peak of 48 percent reached in May 1999).

This tepid response stems from banks worrying that drawing on public money will weaken the control of the families/managers in charge of most Thai banks. So far, the government has been unable to write down the equity of the existing owners because of their political clout, but at the same time it has been unwilling to bail them out. This quandary was behind the earlier government decision to leave NPLs on the books of respective banks rather than consolidate them, as was done in the United States and Sweden.

Banks have gone to the private capital markets for equity, raising about Bt396 billion in common equity. However, recent efforts to continue the capital-raising exercise have failed as international investors worry about the continuing high level of NPLs and wonder whether restructured loans will stay current. One of the best-managed local banks disclosed in November that over 10 percent of loans restructured since the start of the crisis had not met the new, easier terms.

The procedures for corporate restructuring have been improved, but resorting to corporate restructuring is still infrequent. A streamlined Chapter 11 law was introduced in 1998, with a law on foreclosure finally passed last summer.[7] The Financial Restructuring Advisory Committee, a private-sector panel set up to prompt out-of-court settlements, has been largely ineffectual. By September 1999, only 13 percent of outstanding loans had been restructured.

Korea has seen perhaps the most progress in corporate restructuring. Many of the major chaebols are complying with the agreements reached with the government that mandate lower leverage and less product diversification. However, these firms have fared better than their smaller counterparts, which have been largely cut off from credit and had to close down. An important portion of the reduction in leverage resulted from a rally in Korean equity prices.

Inadequate bank restructuring poses a risk to Asia's nascent recovery. Although GDP growth has rebounded so far without a restoration of credit growth, this is not sustainable. The beneficial effects of lower domestic interest rates, an absence of investment demand, and, for traded sector firms, better cash flows following the currency devaluations will not persist. As Asia's output gaps disappear over the next year or two, both inflation and investment demand will rise. Banks will need to be ready to supply credit.

3.6 What Can Be Done?

While there has been progress in financial restructuring in Asia, there is still a long way to go to put the banking system and its borrowers back on a sound footing. What can be done to accelerate this process?

Accelerate recapitalization by extending the NPL carve out. With real activity rebounding, but real credit growth shrinking, the key element of financial restructuring is restarting credit growth so that the recovery is not strangled. To do this, a crucial task is to restore sound balance sheets. This entails the two steps outlined earlier: (1) carving out NPLs from the balance sheets of the banks; and (2) filling the holes created by the bad loans with new capital. It is important to extend this process beyond the group of intervened banks where action is currently

---

7. Chapter 11 refers to the section of U.S. bankruptcy law covering corporate reorganization. Foreclosure is covered in a separate section. However, without the threat of foreclosure, the outcome of a corporate reorganization is stacked in favor of the existing owners.

being taken, because banking systems as a whole cannot earn their way out of NPLs at reasonable interest spreads.

Regulatory, legal and accounting improvements are fine for dealing with the flow of new credit, but for them to make a difference there must be a flow of new credit. Flaws in corporate governance, information, and transparency have contributed to Asia's difficulties, but the key factor behind the crisis has been financial panic and the sudden halt in credit. Improving transparency and governance can contribute to growth in the future. However, such institutional changes will take years—and the ACC-4 cannot wait that long.

The stock problem is not being dealt with effectively, but this is not chiefly a result of the lack of institutions. The ACC-4 already has the necessary institutions to purchase non-performing assets and recapitalize the banks. Public money has already been pledged in Thailand. The real lack is not money or institutions, but political consensus on the process—particularly about how to settle losses between internal and external creditors, depositors, debtors and taxpayers.

At present, efforts to recapitalize the banking system are viewed largely as a zero-sum game—everyone is focused on their short-term losses and not on long-term economic health. Governments fear that letting bank owners off the hook for making bad loans will incur a loss for taxpayers. It is unlikely to be a loss to depositors since governments have generally made guarantees for them.[8] Meanwhile, bank owners fear that letting corporations off the hook by writing down loans will cost them their banks, and corporations do not want to repay their loans because they do not expect new financing any time soon and fear losing control of their companies.

However, there is something to be gained by moving forward: avoidance of the serious cost to economic growth being borne by everyone due to the malfunctioning financial system. One relatively crude way of measuring this cost is to look at the amount of excess liquidity in the banking system. With a properly functioning banking system, these funds would be expanding credit and thereby economic growth, creating jobs and reducing poverty. In Indonesia and Korea, the elasticity of real credit growth to real GDP growth, all things being equal, is at 0.48.

---

8. There are efforts under way to limit deposit insurance in both Korea and Indonesia, but for the moment, imposing significant losses on depositors would only trigger bank runs—hardly a palatable outcome.

Use the case of Indonesia as an example. As of September 1999, excess reserves were about Rp5 trillion more than their five-year average. Multiplying by the money multiplier of 8 means that credit was some Rp40 trillion or 3 percent of GDP less than it could have been.[9] A government looking to reduce unemployment and poverty should then be willing to pay out public money in order to avoid this cost.[10]

In practice, some governments have already pledged far more than this due to their decisions to guarantee depositors and external creditors. However, having given that guarantee, it is clearly time to move forward with restructuring that will allow economic activity to pick up. In Indonesia, for example, the government expects to spend Rp50 trillion in interest payments on bonds issued to recapitalize banks. Yet trillions in assets held by the Indonesian Bank Restructuring Agency remain largely unsold.

Moving forward means largely relinquishing the desire to bankrupt either bank or company shareholders. After all, given the extent of financial distress in ACC-4, it is not feasible to replace bank and company owners wholesale. On the margin, new foreign owners and consolidations are useful, but the fact is that there is little practical alternative but to have existing managers continuing in many of the banks and firms.

In Korea and Indonesia, the government is focusing on co-payments by existing owners as a means of sparking recapitalization. The idea is to avoid moral hazard by forcing bank owners to reveal their interest in continuing to operate the bank. But capital is not really the issue today in running banks in Asia, rather it is expertise. What is needed is management with a stake in the future soundness of the banks. Only when the banking system has normalized and government retreats, will private capital be needed.

One way to interest the owners in quick restructuring would be for the government to agree to swap the NPLs at a discount for government

---

9. There are many ways to criticize this estimate. In particular, why take the recent rate of money growth as optimal? It is not. Given that most of the crisis countries have an IMF program structured around relatively tight money, this analysis probably understates the loss to growth from the dysfunctional financial system. It also implicitly assumes that credit, rather than money, is more important for GDP growth. There is extensive literature on the subject. See Bernanke and Gertler (1995) for an overview of the links between credit and GDP growth. GS estimates using October 1998 official figures.

10. Interestingly, the Indonesian government expects to pay about Rp34 trillion in interest costs on bonds issued to cover the losses in the banking system, a number very close to the estimated amount of credit not issued.

bonds.[11] The government would contribute any capital shortfall created by the discount sale. In return, the existing owners would agree to pay down the government bonds and/or replace government capital with common equity over a set number of years. Those owners who judge that their banks are incapable of generating profits and attracting common equity in the future would not agree to the NPL carve out/recapitalization today. Those with a more sanguine outlook would opt for the program. Having already guaranteed the deposits, the government would then have the option of closing or merging any bank that did not raise its own capital or accept capital from the government.

This is roughly the program that Indonesia is implementing, with an important exception. Indonesia is giving away the potential capital gains in its recapitalization of private banks by allowing old shareholders to buy back their shares, not at their market price, but rather at a rate of interest the represents the government's cost of providing the original funding. Given that it is management expertise, not capital, that is needed in restoring banking systems in the near term, there is no need for adding this subsidy to that already provided to depositors.

Where would the governments source the capital for the bank recapitalization? Given the expected size of the losses in the banking system, which run, in some cases, to 20–30 percent of GDP, this looks like a daunting problem. In practice, it is far less so. Recapitalization using government funds does not require that the governments provide the full amount of the loss immediately in either domestic or international bond markets. All that needs to occur is that government bonds be issued directly to the distressed banks. New funds would be needed to service the interest on the government bonds so as to ensure a cash flow to the banks holding the bonds. Repayment of principal can be made after the economies have recovered. However, assuming there are no runs on the restructured banks, and that real interest rates are manageable (say 5–10 percent), this would cost, at best, 3 percent of GDP, even in countries where the net loss is 30 percent of GDP.

What would the governments do with the purchased NPLs? They would be transferred to an asset management company set up in each of the ACC-4 countries. (This entity would have NPLs as its assets and bonds outstanding to the banks as its liability.) These entities already

---

11. Swapping at a discount allows for greater transparency in the accounts of the bank and simplifies the process of liquidation of the loans by the entity purchasing them. However, if the loans are swapped at book value, the process can proceed more rapidly.

exist in each ACC-4 nation. However, at present the institutions are generally only dealing with a select group of assets—usually those of the financial institutions that have already been intervened, or those sold under voluntary programs. By purchasing the rest of the distressed assets, the expertise built up in the institutions could be levered, potentially helping to resolve the problem more quickly.

Reduce Leverage at the Corporate Level.[12] The establishment of an asset management company dealing with most of the system's NPLs would alleviate most of the debt problems for the banks. However, the borrowers still have their obligations. To restore economic activity, the debt and debt service of borrowers needs to be linked to their capacity to pay.

Realistic assessment of investment and growth prospects will reveal losses for both debtors and creditors relative to their original expectations. Hence, there is reticence to move forward, given the impaired capital of the banking system. Fortunately, with the rapid rebound in Asia's growth, the size of the losses is shrinking.

Settling claims is the realm of a bankruptcy court or some informal bankruptcy proceeding (such as the advisory committees set up in Thailand, Indonesia and Malaysia). All the ACC-4 nations are moving ahead with revamped bankruptcy laws, hoping to accelerate the restructuring process and lower the social cost of inoperative firms. However, waiting for these to become fully operational is likely to take too long. The existence of an asset management company can further accelerate the process by consolidating much of the bad debt with one creditor, easing the collective action problem of debt settlement.

The risk here is that by consolidating assets with a public AMC, borrowers will choose to default despite having the resources to pay, on the expectation that the public AMC will not be able to enforce a settlement. The solution to this problem is not to avoid consolidating the assets, but rather to enhance the collection powers of the public AMC, something that Malaysia and Indonesia have done.

---

12. This section concentrates on adjustment to either the stock of debt or to its servicing. Leverage can also be reduced through faster growth. However, as the 1980s in Latin America showed, growing out from under debt burdens can be excruciating. Besides, Asia today is a capital exporter, having largely generated current account surpluses on the back of collapsing imports. If excessive capital inflows and unwise investment were the root of the problem, then writing down or restructuring debt would be less costly to near-term growth than sticking to the original terms.

An AMC dealing with most bad loans purchased at a discount is also in a position to pass on debt relief to the enterprises. However, to date this has been politically difficult, especially in Korea, where there is opposition to the power of the chaebols and the sense that their aggressive expansion plans contributed to the crisis. There are two possible alternatives that would resolve this issue.

1. Concentrating debt restructuring and relief exercises on small and medium-sized business. This has the advantage of being much more politically palatable and addressing institutions that have been hardest hit by the credit crunch.

2. Pushing for debt-for-equity swaps in the larger corporations in exchange for debt write-downs. Having received a stake in the upside, the political opposition to debt restructuring would diminish. How could this be elicited given the strategic nature of some of the current corporate non-payments? In larger companies, transferring the debt to a government body can allow for more leverage to be used to effect restructuring. This is especially true in Korea, where the banks are less influential than the main chaebol.

So far, governments have attempted to use the threat of bankruptcy to prompt settlements. However, there are a wide variety of other avenues that governments can use to induce corporations to come to the bargaining table: licenses, taxes, regulations, and criminal or civil law for fraud and malfeasance. To the extent that it is more realistic for an AMC to write-down debt than an undercapitalized bank, so is the chance that a government will succeed in encouraging settlements.

In the end, internal debt restructuring in Asia may not prove as difficult as in Latin America in the 1980s. Because of the initial solvency of the public sector in countries such as Thailand and Korea, increases in public debt that leave depositors largely whole, and managers in place, can work.. The level of public debt is low in the ACC-4, with the exception of Indonesia. Therefore, adding more debt to recapitalize banks will not raise debt to dangerous or unsustainable levels. The politics of the burden-sharing are still messy and likely to be protracted, even with efforts to accelerate the process listed above. However, the fiscal cushion substantially reduces fears that pressures will end in desperate monetization, as they did in Argentina in 1989.

Table 3.4
Share in total external debt

	Public	Private	
		Financial sector	Non-financial sector
Latin America (1981)			
Argentina	29.6	34.1	n.a.
Bolivia	84.6	2.5	n.a.
Brazil	56.9	24.3	n.a.
Mexico	55.0	13.0	n.a.
Peru	70.4	7.4	n.a.
Venezuela	35.9	11.2	n.a.
ACC-4 (1997)			
Indonesia	42.5	11.1	46.4
Korea	11.7	60.9	27.3
Malaysia	39.2	52.7	8.0
Thailand	27.2	42.6	30.2

Source: World Bank, GS estimates.

3.7   Risks

One risk to the strategy of using public funds more aggressively to recapitalize banks is that the restructured banks would still refuse to lend, out of a concern about excessive risks. Alternatively, they might prefer to lend only to a handful of borrowers, but at high spreads, thus rebuilding their profits to facilitate the eventual repurchase of the government's share of the equity.

However, to date this has not been a hindrance to GDP growth. While aggregate lending in the ACC-4 is still down, GDP growth through the first three quarters of 1999 is up spectacularly. Korea and Malaysia are growing at double-digit seasonally adjusted rates. Improved cash flows due to lower nominal interest rates, weaker exchange rates (for traded sector firms) and tax breaks have helped. So, too, has an absence of investment demand and a surge in local bond finance. Going forward, though, bank lending will need to contribute to GDP growth, albeit in a less dominating fashion.

One solution to ensuring a flow of credit is to introduce more competition into the respective systems. The entrance of foreign banks, unencumbered by the need for the future repurchase of shares, would put downward pressure on margins, helping to avoid the chance that lending gets held back by exorbitant interest rates.

Another concern is that the introduction of government ownership, without the full write-down of existing bank shareholders, will perpetuate moral hazard. As we argued earlier, this is really an issue of trade-offs—growth today against the risk of future problems. The most reasonable means of going forward is to accelerate the regulatory and supervisory changes, corporate governance, and legal changes needed to provide the information to make less risky loans in the future. These same changes need to not only provide the information to banks but also to put in place a framework that ensures banks use the information, either due to fear of regulatory reprisal or out of lust for profit. Thus, while long-term structural reforms have a relatively small role to play in accelerating Asia's recovery, they have a huge role to play in avoiding a future debacle.

References

Bernanke, B.S., and M. Gertler. 1995. Inside the black box: The credit channel of monetary policy transmission. *The Journal of Economic Perspectives* 9(4): 27–48 (Fall 1995).

Krugman, P. 1998. *What Happened to Asia?* http://web.mit.edu/krugman/www/disinter. html (January 1998).

Ramos, Roy. 1997. Prudential norms and CAMELOT: How real are reported earnings and book values? *Asia Banking Survey Part II.* Goldman Sachs.

4

Export Competitiveness in Asia

Mumtaz Hussain and Steven Radelet

Manufactured exports were at the heart of Asia's rapid economic growth and development between 1965 and 1997. Asia's push into labor-intensive manufactured exports provided many benefits to the region. It accelerated technological progress by fostering closer connections with international firms that were using leading-edge technologies, encouraged economic specialization, promoted high rates of investment into profitable economic activities, and provided foreign exchange to finance imports of capital goods which could not be produced locally. It also provided a large number of jobs for low-skilled workers, thereby helping to alleviate poverty across the region. In the wake of the financial crisis, many Asians are pinning their hopes for an Asian recovery on renewed export expansion.

How realistic is this hope? After all, export growth dropped dramatically across the region just before the crisis in 1996 and 1997, partially contributing to the onset of the crisis itself. Moreover, exports have grown only slowly, at least in value terms, following the large currency depreciations that were the hallmark of the crisis. Has Asia reached the end of line for export-led growth? Are the problems in the region now so deep and the competition from other emerging markets so intense, that exports cannot be the engine of growth that they once were?

Asia's future is particularly murky at the present juncture, and depends not only on decisions made in Asia, but also on events in the rest of the world, such as the rise of protectionist sentiments in the West. However, even in the aftermath of the crisis, the balance of the evidence indicates that Asian firms are likely to be quite competitive on world markets in the future. Barring a worldwide inward turn towards protectionism, manufactured exports are likely to be an integral part of Asia's long-term recovery.

4.1   The Changing Patterns of Trade in the Early 1990s

In thinking about the future of Asian exports, it is useful to start by recognizing the dramatic ways in which trade changed in Asia during the last two decades. Both the composition of Asia's exports and its major markets have shifted remarkably since the early 1980s. In 1980, primary products dominated the exports of the four large ASEAN countries (Indonesia, Malaysia, the Philippines and Thailand), accounting for 86 percent of all exports. In China and India, primary products made up more than half of all exports. By 1996, the year before the onset of the crisis, the share of primary products in total exports had fallen sharply in these countries, displaced by rapid growth of an array of labor-intensive manufactured exports, especially textiles, garments, and basic electronics (figure 4.1). In Hong Kong, Korea, Singapore and Taiwan (the Newly Industrialized Countries, or NICs), which had seen the initial shift to labor-intensive exports a decade earlier, the 1980s and 1990s brought a decline in the share of labor-intensive and primary product exports in favor of rapid expansions in exports of electronic equipment, machinery and scale-intensive products (such as automobiles and steel). Thus, two distinct stages of export development seem to be evident from Asia's recent economic history: the first from primary products to labor-intensive manufactured exports, and the second from labor-intensive to more highly skilled manufactured exports.

These shifts in the composition of Asia's exports were accompanied by changes in the destination of exports (figure 4.2). For the large ASEAN countries, Japan became a much less important market, while the shares of exports to the United States and Europe changed little. The most dramatic change was the rise of the Asian countries themselves (other than Japan) as a market. The share of exports from the four large ASEAN countries sent to each other, the four NICS, and China rose from 18 percent to 33 percent between 1980 and 1996, with the lion's share of the exports going to the NICs. The pattern of exports from the NICs was a bit different: the share sent to Japan changed little, while share of exports to the U.S. and Europe fell sharply. China became a major export destination, accounting for 16 percent of exports from the NICs in 1996. The four NICs also traded more intensively with each other, as the intra-regional trade share grew from 9 percent to 14 percent. To some extent these changes in destination are simply reflections of the shift in composition: Japan is the major market for primary products in the region, so the shift away from primary products entailed a shift away from Japan as a market. But the change in composition is also indicative of the increasing complexity of manufactured production chains in the region, as firms in different countries in the region now handle different stages of the production process, giving rise to the rapid increase in intra-regional trade. As we discuss later, the growing importance of countries in the region as export destinations for each other is a major reason why export growth has been weak in the aftermath of the crisis.

4.2 Export Slowdown Before the Crisis

Exports, and particularly manufactured exports, grew rapidly across Asia during the 1980s and early 1990s. Throughout the region (excluding Japan), exports grew on average by 16 percent between 1990 and 1995, with manufactured exports growing 19 percent per year (table 4.1).

Table 4.1
Asian export growth (% per year)

Country	Total exports (US$)				Manufactured exports (US$)	
	1990–95	1996	1997	1998	1990–95	1996
China	19.1	1.6	21.0	0.4	21.2	5.6
Hong Kong	16.2	4.0	4.0	−7.5	15.9	4.6
India	11.3	7.4	3.6	−3.9	13.2	−4.2
Indonesia	12.1	9.7	7.3	−8.6	21.1	15.0
Japan	9.0	−7.3	2.4	−7.8	8.9	−7.6
Korea	14.0	3.7	5.0	−2.8	13.4	4.7
Malaysia	20.3	5.8	0.7	−6.9	27.7	9.3
Philippines	16.8	16.7	22.9	10.7	19.7	26.1
Singapore	17.5	5.7	0.0	−12.1	21.5	7.7
Taiwan	10.7	3.8	5.4	−9.5	11.8	−0.7
Thailand	19.6	−1.3	3.3	−5.1	23.4	−7.5
Average (excl. Japan)	15.8	5.7	7.3	−4.5	18.9	6.0
Average (incl. Japan)	15.1	4.5	6.9	−4.8	18.0	4.8

Sources: Total exports data are from International Financial Statistics, IMF. Manufactured exports data are from the United Nations Trade Database.

Four Large ASEAN Countries: 1980 and 1996

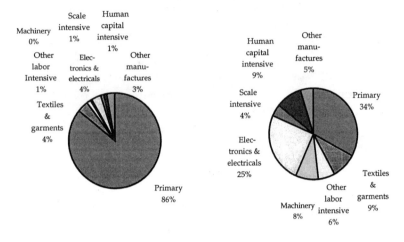

Four Asian NICs: 1980 and 1996

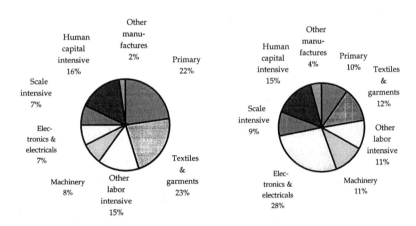

Source: United Nations Trade Database

Figure 4.1a

Composition of Asian exports

China: 1980 and 1996

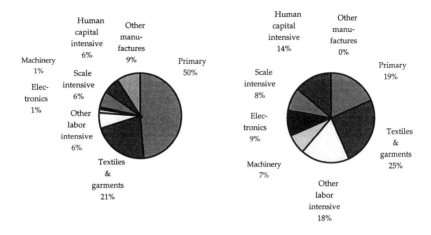

India: 1980 and 1996

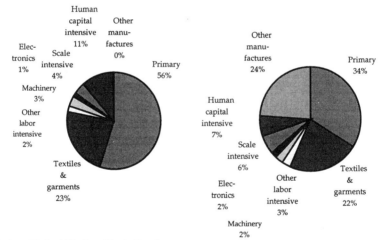

Source: United Nations Trade Database

Figure 4.1b

Composition of Asian exports

Four Large ASEAN Countries: 1980 and 1996

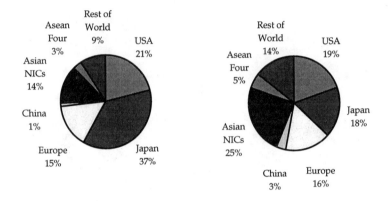

Four Asian NICs: 1980 and 1996

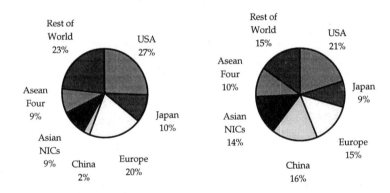

Source: United Nations Trade Database

Figure 4.2a
Asian exports by destination

China: 1980 and 1996

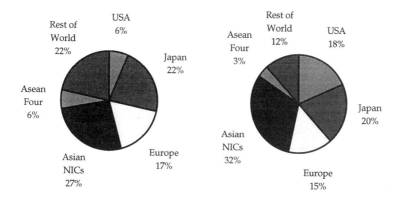

India: 1980 and 1996

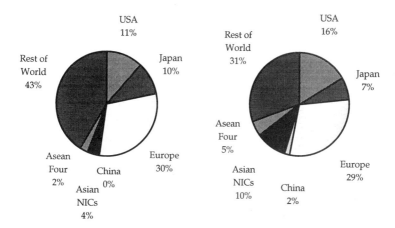

Source: United Nations Trade Database

Figure 4.2b
Asian exports by destination

But in 1996, export growth abruptly slowed in several countries, and export growth rates generally remained low in 1997. Thailand and Japan experienced export *contractions* of 1 percent and 7 percent, respectively, in 1996. Korea's exports grew by just 4 percent and Malaysia's by just less than 6 percent. Taiwan, Singapore and Hong Kong also saw an export slowdown. Even in China, where exports had boomed in the early 1990s, they grew less than 2 percent in 1996, before rebounding in 1997. Indonesia followed a slightly different pattern, with export growth slowing earlier, but not as sharply. After growing at an annual average of 23 percent between 1987 and 1992, growth in Indonesia's exports (excluding oil and gas) slowed in 1993, and averaged just 12 percent between 1993 and 1996. The Philippines was the only country in which export growth remained robust, reaching 17 percent in 1996 and 23 percent in 1997, driven by a surge in electronics exports.

One reason that export growth slowed so suddenly was an erosion of cost competitiveness in many countries in the region. Domestic production prices climbed more quickly than did world export prices, and since most countries kept their exchange rate fixed (or nearly fixed) against the U.S. dollar, profit margins were squeezed. Ironically, the massive inflows of foreign capital into the region in the early 1990s was partly to blame for the loss in competitiveness, as they drove up the prices of non-traded goods and services, such as property. The sharp appreciation of the U.S. dollar vis-à-vis the Japanese yen and European currencies after 1994 exacerbated the trend. As the dollar/yen exchange rate moved from 85 in June 1995 to 127 in April 1997, each of the pegged Asian currencies appreciated sharply against the yen. For example, each 100 yen of Thai exports to Japan brought in 29 baht in early 1995, but only 20 baht by early 1997. There were some benefits to Asia of the appreciation of their currencies against the yen: imports from Japan became cheaper, as did the cost of servicing yen-denominated debt. Nevertheless, exporters were squeezed by the fixed rates against the dollar, and the appreciations against other currencies.

This erosion of competitiveness can be illustrated in a very simple way by an index of the "real exchange rate" (RER). This index is calculated as the ratio of a weighted average of the wholesale prices prevailing in each country's trading partners (converted to domestic currency by the exchange rate) to domestic production costs (approximated by the domestic consumer price index). An increase in this ratio (referred to as a depreciation of the RER) means that foreign prices, when converted by the exchange rate, are rising faster than domestic prices, providing a very rough indication of improved price competitiveness. Conversely, a decline in the ratio (an appreciation of the RER) suggests a loss of competitiveness, usually brought about by relatively rapid increases in domestic prices that are not compensated by currency depreciation or increases in world prices.

Between 1990 and early 1997, the RER in most East and Southeast Asian countries fell, or appreciated, by between 12 and 47 percent, as shown in table 4.2b. In each of the four Southeast Asian countries, the RER fell by more than 22 percent. In Korea, the real appreciation was about 12 percent. These changes indicate a moderate erosion of competitiveness in these countries during the early 1990s.

Another indication of deteriorating competitiveness was the rapid growth of wages in some countries of the region during the early 1990s. While complete and comparable data on wages are not available, table 4.3 shows developments in wages in the apparel sector between 1990 and 1995 for most countries in the region. Wage rates in Malaysia, Indonesia and Thailand all grew by 12 percent per year or more, with Malaysia recording the fastest growth of all at 23 percent per year. Whereas Malaysia's apparel wages were only about 60 percent of Mexico's in 1990, wages in the two countries were almost equal by 1995. By contrast, apparel wages in China and India actually fell slightly during the period.

Of course, rising wages are an important and in many ways desirable sign of economic development, and these wage increases indicate a substantial boost to worker welfare. If these wage hikes were matched by gains in labor productivity, they could be sustained over time. But if productivity gains lag behind wage hikes, firms will begin to lose their competitive position, and neither export growth nor job growth can be sustained. Unfortunately, data on labor productivity are not available on a consistent basis for these countries, so a full analysis of the productivity-wages nexus is not possible. The broad macroeconomic evidence, however, is more consistent with a fall in competitiveness than a rise in productivity. We have already noted the fall in export growth. At the same time, current account deficits rose across the region, to as much as 8 percent of GDP in Thailand and Malaysia, and close to 4 percent of GDP in Indonesia and Korea.

Table 4.2
Exchange rates

a) Nominal exchange rate

	Change (%) against US$			Change (%) against Yen		
Country	12/90–6/97	6/97–12/97	6/97–6/99	12/90–6/97	6/97–12/97	6/97–6/99
China	37.0	−0.1	−0.1	46.5	−13.9	−6.2
Hong Kong	−0.7	0.0	0.2	14.4	−13.7	−5.8
India	49.5	8.8	17.4	57.1	−3.7	12.4
Indonesia	22.3	47.4	63.6	34.0	40.1	61.4
Korea	19.5	47.5	23.2	31.6	40.3	18.5
Malaysia	−7.3	35.3	33.8	8.8	26.4	29.8
Philippines	−6.2	34.0	30.6	9.8	24.9	26.4
Singapore	−22.2	14.8	16.1	−3.9	3.1	11.0
Thailand	1.9	45.4	30.1	16.6	37.9	25.9
Taiwan	2.6	14.8	13.9	17.2	3.0	8.7

b) Real exchange rate index (December 1990=100)

				Change (%)		
Country	June 1997	Dec. 1997	June 1999	12/90–6/97	6/97–12/97	6/97–6/99
China	80.8	75.7	76.0	−19.2	−6.4	−5.9
Hong Kong	57.8	54.2	54.5	−42.2	−6.2	−5.8
India	100.8	101.9	96.9	0.8	1.1	−3.9
Indonesia	77.3	125.4	99.2	−22.7	62.3	28.3
Korea	87.6	152.9	98.0	−12.4	74.6	12.0
Malaysia	73.4	105.3	94.1	−26.6	43.5	28.3
Philippines	52.5	74.0	60.2	−47.5	41.0	14.8
Singapore	71.8	79.6	79.3	−28.2	10.8	10.4
Thailand	74.9	122.8	90.1	−25.1	63.9	20.3
Taiwan	84.2	95.2	93.4	−15.8	13.1	10.9

Notes: An increase (positive change) in the nominal exchange rate indicates a nominal depreciation. The real exchange rate is calculated as the ratio of the trade-weighted average of the major trading partners' wholesale price indices to the local consumer price index. An increase in the real exchange rate index indicates a depreciation.

Table 4.3
Hourly labor costs in apparel manufacturing (US$)

Country	1990	1993	1995	Annual growth 1990–95
Taiwan	3.41	4.61	5.18	8.70
Hong Kong	3.05	3.85	4.32	7.20
Singapore	2.43	3.06	4.01	10.50
Korea	2.46	2.71	3.29	6.00
Mexico	0.92	1.08	1.61	11.80
Malaysia	0.56	0.77	1.59	23.20
Thailand	0.63	0.71	1.11	12.00
Philippines	0.46	0.53	0.72	9.40
Sri Lanka	0.24	0.35	0.41	11.30
Indonesia	0.16	0.28	0.33	15.60
India	0.33	0.27	0.29	−2.60
Pakistan	0.24	0.27	0.29	3.90
Vietnam[a]	n.a.	0.26	0.29	5.61
China	0.26	0.25	0.25	−0.80
Bangladesh[a]	n.a.	0.16	0.20	11.80

Source: *Apparel Hourly Labor Cost*, Werner International, Inc., New York, 1996.
a. Growth rates for 1993–95.

Although the erosion in competitiveness in the mid-1990s is an important part of the story, we need to keep its magnitude in appropriate perspective. The real appreciations in Asia during the 1990s were relatively modest compared with other developing countries. Brazil and Argentina, for example, have seen real appreciations of more than 40 percent since 1990. Thus, while the loss in price competitiveness probably contributed to the export slowdown and perhaps to the financial crisis as well, the magnitude of the effect appears to have been relatively modest.

A second possible explanation for the export slowdown in 1996 is that it was a result of a glut in world markets for some of Asia's export products, with the glut itself driven by Asia's rapid export growth during the previous decade. Too many countries were all trying to export the same products, so this argument goes, thus flooding the markets for manufactured goods. World prices for manufactured products rose slightly in the early 1990s, but then fell 3 percent in 1996 and 8 percent in 1997. Prices were especially weak in some markets, such as for semiconductors. World prices for semiconductors rose by about 50 percent between 1992 and 1995, but then quickly plummeted 20 percent between 1995 and 1997.

To some extent, these weak prices were at least partially a result of over-expansion and the creation of excess capacity in some key sectors in certain countries. Perhaps the clearest example is the rapid expansion of semiconductor production capacity by Korean conglomerates (or *chaebols*), that contributed to the sharp decline in prices. In addition, to some degree the weak prices reflected the entrance of new competitors, such as China, Mexico and India into world markets. China's manufactured exports grew more than twelve-fold from a mere $10 billion in 1980 to $127 billion in 1996. Mexico's more recent opening led to a jump in manufactured exports from $1.9 billion in 1980 to $71.2 billion in 1996, with a large increase in its share in the U.S. market. Manufactured exports from India grew by more than 13 percent between 1990 and 1995. Were the newcomers pushing out Asia's "original" exporters? The evidence suggests that this might have been the case with some specific products, but probably not for manufactured exports on the whole. Generally speaking, the rapid growth in exports by the newcomers was basically matched by the export growth rates in the "original" exporters. We can see this by examining the performance of the original exporters at two levels: first, against the three main newcomers, China, India and Mexico; and second, against manufactured exports from the rest of the world.

Manufactured exports from the ASEAN-4 (Indonesia, Malaysia, the Philippines and Thailand), together with Korea, Singapore, Hong Kong and Taiwan, grew from $70 billion in 1980 to $650 billion in 1996. Consider these eight countries, plus the two most important (in quantitative terms) "new" competitors, China and Mexico, as a group. The share of the total value of manufactured exports from this group originating in China and Mexico grew steadily from 1980 to 1992, suggesting that these countries, especially Mexico, did take some market share from the older exporters, as shown in table 4.4b. Between 1992 and 1996, both countries' share continued to increase, but not substantially. In some markets, such as textiles and apparel, China gained substantial market share, but other sectors lost some ground. From a global perspective, despite the increased competition from China and Mexico, the ASEAN and NICs shares of world manufactured exports were *rising* rather than falling. This evidence suggests that the entrance of new competitors into world markets put some pressure on Asian exporters, especially in certain markets.

Table 4.4
Manufactured exports

a) Annual average growth rate: 1981–96

Country	1981–92	1993–95	1996
China	17.5	20.9	5.6
Hong Kong	15.9	12.8	4.6
Indonesia	24.9	12.2	15.0
Korea	13.4	17.0	4.7
Malaysia	21.9	27.2	9.3
Philippines	11.2	24.0	26.1
Singapore	14.7	26.8	7.7
Taiwan	13.3	12.2	−0.7
Thailand	23.2	23.3	−7.5
Mexico	27.4	23.5	9.8
Asian-9 average	17.3	19.6	7.2
World	8.3	11.3	3.3

b) Share within the group of ten countries listed

Country	1980	1992	1996
China	12.3	14.1	15.1
Hong Kong	23.2	22.8	19.7
Indonesia	1.2	2.9	2.7
Korea Rp	19.6	14.9	14.3
Malaysia	3.0	5.4	7.0
Philippines	2.5	1.5	2.1
Singapore	11.8	10.3	12.9
Taiwan	21.9	16.5	13.2
Thailand	2.2	4.4	4.4
Mexico	2.4	7.2	8.5
Total	100.0	100.0	100

c) Share of world manufactured exports

Country	1980	1992	1996
China	0.9	2.4	3.1
Hong Kong	1.7	3.8	4.0
Indonesia	0.1	0.5	0.6
Korea Rp	1.4	2.5	2.9
Malaysia	0.2	0.9	1.4
Philippines	0.2	0.3	0.4
Singapore	0.9	1.7	2.7
Taiwan	1.6	2.8	2.7
Thailand	0.2	0.7	0.9
Mexico	0.2	1.2	1.8
Total	7.3	16.8	20.6

Source: United Nations Trade Database.

To some extent, these new entrants probably pushed the original exporters into higher value export products, rather than just displacing them from world markets completely. In any event, this pressure probably contributed to the export slowdown in some countries, but the effect does not appear to have been large enough to fatally undermine long-run export growth.

A final contributor to the slow export performance in 1996 and 1997 was the weakness of the Japanese economy, which grew by just 2 percent between 1995 and 1997. The value of Korea's exports to Japan fell by more than 12 percent in 1996 alone, partly due to the fall in semiconductor prices, but also because of weak demand. As we pointed out earlier, Japan is a much smaller export destination for Asian firms than it once was, but it still accounts for nearly one-fifth of exports from the large ASEAN countries and China, and about one-tenth of exports from the NICs.

We can conclude that the slowdown in Asia's exports in 1996 and 1997 was due to a number of factors, including some loss in price competitiveness, over-capacity in certain markets, slow economic growth in Japan, and increased competition from new entrants in world markets. The slowdown probably contributed somewhat to the onset of the financial crisis by raising concerns among creditors about the ability of Asian firms to service their debts, but seems to have been too small to have been a major cause of the crisis in and of itself. Some of the factors behind the export slowdown are indicative of longer-term trends in world markets, and some are due to cyclical changes or correctable weaknesses in domestic policies. Although Asian export growth is unlikely to return to the heady days of the late 1980s when production costs were relatively low and there was little competition from other emerging markets, there is little in the evidence to suggest that export-led growth has hit a dead end in Asia.

4.3   Exchange Rates and Exports in the Aftermath of the Crisis

Exchange rates in the crisis countries depreciated massively in late 1997 before rebounding in early 1998 (late 1998 in the case of Indonesia). Although the depreciations wrecked havoc on the balance sheets of many banks and corporations that had borrowed abroad, they should be a boon to exporters. Table 4.2 shows the depreciations in both nominal and real terms. Comparing June 1999 to June 1997, currencies depreciated against the dollar on a net basis by between 23 and 33 percent in Korea, Thailand, Malaysia and the Philippines. The Indonesian rupiah lost about 64 percent of its value, an enormous shift, although substantially less than the 80 percent or more it had lost at the height of the crisis. As a result of these depreciations, export prices in domestic currency terms have increased substantially. Some of this extra incentive for exporters has been offset by domestic inflation, which has raised production costs. This is especially true in Indonesia, where inflation in 1998 topped 80 percent before dropping off late in 1998 and falling to near zero during most of 1999. In Thailand and Korea, however, inflation remained below 10 percent throughout the crisis, so there was less erosion of the effects of the exchange rate depreciations.

The net effects of the nominal exchange rate changes and inflation are captured by the real exchange rate index examined earlier in table 4.2. According to this broad index, in mid-1999 Asian exporters were more competitive than they had been prior to the crisis, but in general had not quite returned to the price competitiveness that they enjoyed in 1990. Following the crisis, the RERs depreciated by between 12 percent (Korea) and 28 percent (Indonesia and Malaysia) between mid-1997 and mid-1999. However, even with these real depreciations, the RER had returned to approximately its 1990 level (set equal to 100 in each country) in only Korea and Indonesia. (Recall that a decline in this index represents a loss in competitiveness.) In Malaysia the RER was about 6 percent below its 1990 level, and in Thailand it was about 10 percent below the 1990 benchmark. These figures suggest that firms in these countries are in general more competitive on world markets than they had been in the years just prior to the crisis. But the changes in the RER are not large enough to expect a huge expansion in exports.

Export performance has been very weak across the region since the onset of the crisis, at least as measured by export values. In value terms, export growth in 1998 contracted in every country in the region except the Philippines and China, as shown previously in table 4.1. Korea's export growth of –2.8 percent was the third best in the region! China registered essentially no change in exports in 1998. Only in the Philippines, where exports are heavily concentrated in basic electronics, have exports continued to expand, with growth of 23 percent in 1997 and 11 percent in 1998. By contrast, Malaysia, Hong Kong, Indonesia, Taiwan, Japan and Singapore all saw exports contract by 7 percent or more in 1998.

Table 4.5
Export growth after the Asian crisis (percent change from four quarters earlier unless otherwise noted)

a) Export value growth rates (US$, %)

Country	1997 Q3	Q4	1998 Q1	Q2	Q3	Q4	1999 Q1	Q2
China	20.5	14.0	12.6	2.5	−2.0	−7.3	−6.9	−1.6
Hong Kong	2.5	7.4	−0.9	−3.2	−10.4	−13.7	−9.0	−5.9
Indonesia[b]	14.0	8.0	12.0	−1.0	−4.0	−12.0	−19.0	−6.0
Korea	16.1	4.4	8.4	−1.9	−10.8	−5.5	−5.9	3.4
Malaysia	2.6	−5.4	−10.8	−9.1	−10.0	5.3	—	—
Philippines	24.3	19.6	23.5	14.4	39.9	−28.6	16.3	24.1
Singapore	3.2	−3.9	−6.6	−13.9	−14.8	−12.4	−10.8	1.1
Taiwan	17.1	7.1	−0.3	−7.5	−9.6	−12.9	3.3	7.7
Thailand	5.4	4.3	−1.8	−6.9	−6.2	−6.5	−8.4	6.9

b) Export volume growth rates (%)

Country	1997 Q3	Q4	1998 Q1	Q2	Q3	Q4
China	—	—	—	—	22.1[a]	—
Hong Kong	4.4	9.6	1.4	−0.5	−7.1	−9.6
Indonesia	19.0	17.0	29.0	18.0	13.0	3.0
Korea	35.3	23.2	32.6	20.6	11.4	8.6
Malaysia	—	—	—	—	—	—
Philippines	—	—	—	—	—	—
Singapore	10.5	7.8	7.6	−0.2	−0.7	−3.7
Taiwan	9.7	11.4	3.8	0.8	—	−7.8
Thailand	11.7	16.3	14.1	12.8	5.7	1.0

a. Percent change during the first 10 months over the same period in 1997.
b. Indonesian data exclude oil exports. We thank Peter Rosner for supplying these data.
Sources: Data for export volumes are from World Economic Outlook (WEO) and International Financial Statistics (IFS), except for China and Indonesia. Volume data for China are from news media reports. Export data are from IFS except for data on Indonesia and Taiwan. Indonesia's data are based on information from the Indonesia Bureau of Statistics. Taiwan's data are from WEO.

Table 4.6
Growth rate of exports (US$ value)

	Export destination (1998)						
Exporter	U.S.A.	Japan	Rest of industrialized world	China	NICs	ASEAN	World
Indonesia	19.1	−20.9	15.7	−1.0	5.4	−0.9	3.2
Korea	4.5	−21.2	0.0	0.4	−38.1	−13.8	−7.4
Malaysia	10.9	−21.4	7.8	17.3	−20.9	−14.9	−4.5
Philippines	11.4	−7.5	9.4	57.0	13.0	29.8	7.3
Thailand	12.9	−12.6	10.5	21.4	−24.9	−14.5	−1.8

Source: Directions of Trade Statistics, IMF.

These figures on export *values* are somewhat misleading, however, since they disguise different trends in export *volumes* and *prices*. Export volumes grew very strongly through the first half of 1998 in both Korea and Indonesia, as shown in table 4.5. In the four quarters between mid-1997 and mid-1998 export volumes grew by about 20 percent in both countries. Thailand's response was more muted, with export volumes growing around 13 percent, but still well above the 1 percent growth in volumes recorded during the first half of 1997, and certainly much better than the value figures indicate. Volumes grew by much less in the economies that had smaller currency depreciations, such as Hong Kong, Singapore and Taiwan. However, export volume growth began to slow again in late 1998. Export volumes in the fourth quarter of 1998 in Korea were just 8.6 percent higher than in the fourth quarter of 1997. In Indonesia and Thailand, the increases were just 3 percent and 1 percent, respectively. For the year as a whole, however, export volume growth was very strong. Indonesia's export volume for all of 1998 (excluding oil) was 18 percent larger than in 1997, and the volume of manufactured exports was up 22 percent.

The main factor behind the decline in export *values* in 1998 was a sharp decline in export *prices* around the region. The fall in export prices is in large part due to the crisis itself, both because regional demand has fallen sharply, and because the currency depreciations have made Asian exports much cheaper in dollar terms. Price falls have been especially large for commodities. The World Bank estimates that during

1998, world energy prices plunged 32 percent, agricultural raw materials prices dropped 17 percent, and metals prices also fell 17 percent.
The world price of manufactured products has also been weak, falling
by about 8 percent in 1997 and 1.5 percent in 1998. Asian export prices
probably fell by even more than average world prices because of the
massive currency depreciations. For example, the price of Malaysian
logs exported to Japan dropped by half, and world prices for rubber
and copper dropped by over 40 percent. These price declines have been
very costly to the Asian economies, which desperately need foreign
exchange earnings in the midst of the crisis. The World Bank estimates
that unfavorable trade prices cost Thailand, Indonesia, Malaysia, the
Philippines and Korea the equivalent of about 3 percent of GDP. Indonesia lost about $4 billion dollars in revenues from weak oil prices in
1998, and an additional $3 billion from price declines for other commo-
dities.[1] This loss of $7 billion in export earnings from these price declines
was the equivalent of about one-third of Indonesia's foreign exchange
reserves at the end of 1998, and was larger than Indonesia's total
borrowings from the IMF in 1998 ($5.7 billion). Unfortunately, with the
exception of oil prices (which rose sharply in 1999) the outlook for
world tradables prices remains rather bleak.

   Low world prices are partly due to the crisis itself, of course, since
demand in the region has fallen sharply. Weak regional demand has
also hurt export volumes, since, as we saw earlier, the region has
become an important market for its own products. Indeed, the performance of Asia's exports in 1998 varies widely by different destinations,
as seen in table 4.6. The value of exports from Thailand, Indonesia,
Malaysia, the Philippines and Korea to the United States and other
industrialized countries (excluding Japan) grew very rapidly in 1998,
despite the weak world prices (Korea's exports to the U.S. grew
modestly, and its exports to other industrialized countries registered no
change). By contrast, the value of exports from these five countries to
Japan, the large ASEAN countries, and the NICs plummeted. Exports to
Japan fell by an average of 17 percent. Unlike Mexico after the Tequila
crisis in 1994–95, which was able to send the bulk of its exports to the
robust U.S. market next door, recovery in Asia is being hampered by
the collapse in demand in some of its most important markets. For the
immediate future, Asian export receipts are unlikely to rebound
because of continuing low world prices and weak regional demand,

---

1. We thank Peter Rosner for supplying this estimate.

despite the increased international competitiveness of export firms in the region.

4.4 Looking Ahead

Perhaps the biggest threat to exporters in the near future is the possibility of renewed protectionism around the globe in the wake of the crisis. As Asian exporters have become more competitive, competing firms in industrialized countries have come under growing pressure. Some industries, such as the U.S. steel industry, are pushing for the U.S. government to impose anti-dumping measures against low-cost competitors. Some firms are calling for tariff and other import barriers to protect their home industries. Past financial crises, such as the global crash in 1929, have led to prolonged periods of protectionism and a worldwide turn away from trade, and a similar outcome is possible in the aftermath of this crisis. If this were to happen, the prospects for the global economy and for a rapid return to growth in Asia would deteriorate markedly.

Currencies across the region appreciated dramatically during 1998. These appreciations provided a welcome respite for firms struggling to service foreign debts, and have largely corrected for the initial overshooting of the exchange rates that took place in late 1997 and early 1998. However, further appreciation could undermine export growth and slow the region's rebound from the crisis. For competitiveness reasons, additional strengthening of these currencies is unwarranted. This will be especially true for these countries if, as many analysts believe, China eventually devalues the yuan to ensure the competitiveness of its industries.

Of course, depreciation and lower dollar costs alone will not ensure Asia's competitiveness over the longer term. Asian governments face several challenges to ensure that firms remain competitive over a sustained period of time. Perhaps the most important is the need to improve the skills of the workforce, especially in Indonesia and Thailand, where educational efforts have lagged in recent years. Firms across the region are likely to be continually challenged by new countries shifting to an export-promotion strategy, creating pressures to upgrade into higher-end products. Continued pressure on Asia's "original" exporters can be expected in the future from several countries within Asia, especially China, but also India, Vietnam and Bangladesh, as well as countries outside of Asia. In addition, in some countries, infrastructure must be expanded and upgraded to relieve bottlenecks that had added to exporter's costs before the crisis. Finally, a return to sustained export growth in the near future will depend on the pace of overall economic recovery in Japan and the crisis economies themselves. As pointed out earlier, markets in the four large ASEAN countries, the four NICs, and Japan account for almost half of the exports from the four large ASEAN countries, and about one-third of the exports from the NICs.

Even with these challenges in mind, in the absence of a return to protectionism in the industrialized countries, prospects over the longer term for Asian exporters seem relatively bright. Asian firms have partially restored their competitiveness in world markets. Some dislocation and uncertainty from the crisis will remain, especially in Indonesia. But Asian firms continue to have many advantages over the rest of the world: they generally have access to a well-trained workforce, have many years of experience in competing on world markets, and most firms enjoy a favorable location near the major markets of Japan and China. Investors recognize Asia's advantages, and are beginning to come back to Korea and Thailand. In the Philippines, exporters have hardly missed a beat, and rapid growth continues there almost unabated. Although the extraordinarily rapid export growth of the past is unlikely to be repeated, most indications point towards strong export growth from Asia in the future.

5   The Cost of Crony Capitalism

Shang-Jin Wei and
Sara E. Sievers

5.1 Introduction

A common explanation of the financial crisis in East Asia points to "fast-moving white envelopes" filled with won, or baht, or rupiah or perhaps dollars, and claims that financial resources in many of the Asian economies were fatally misallocated due to corruption, whether of the white-envelope sort or something more subtle. Now is the time to pay the piper, the story goes, for as was believed all along, financial systems that base their distribution of investment capital on stuffed envelopes or personal relationships, rather than sound financial statements, are bound to collapse eventually. After a few years of wondering whether Asian growth would prove to be an exception, it turns out that the rule holds.

The story of Asia's turbulence is significantly more complicated than mere corruption. Overvalued currencies, short-term debt, and panic in the international capital markets are all important factors in the timing and extent of the 1997 crash. This does not let corruption off the hook, however. There is an increasing body of literature that estimates the costs to national economies of non-transparency in business and government, and an increasing number of indices that attempt to measure levels of corruption or perceived corruption in individual countries. Corruption levels in the Asian crisis economies, and in Russia and Brazil (which have experienced heavy Asian contagion), are higher than the world average, are generally higher than non-crisis Asian Tiger economies, and are largely worsening over time. Non-transparent lending practices certainly did help to create the environment in which domestic banking crises became widespread. While corruption is not the sole culprit in the financial woes of 1997–1998, it is most certainly an enabler to the crisis, and costly in a wide variety of other ways as well.

Table 5.1
Corruption ratings for selected countries

	BI (1–10 scale)	TI97 (1–10 scale)	GCR98 (1–10 scale)
Asian countries			
Singapore	1	2.34	1.84
Hong Kong SAR	3	3.72	2.31
Japan	2.25	4.43	2.50
Taiwan	4.25	5.98	3.43
Malaysia	5	5.99	5.01
Korea	5.25	6.71	5.50
Thailand	9.5	7.94	6.13
China	n.a.	8.12	6.73
India	5.75	8.25	7.32
Philippines	6.5	7.95	7.98
Indonesia	9.5	8.28	8.40
Pakistan	7	8.47	n.a.
Bangladesh	7	9.2	n.a.
Non-Asian countries			
Canada	1	1.90	1.84
United Kingdom	1.75	2.72	1.71
Germany	1.5	2.77	1.92
United States	1	3.39	2.11
France	1	4.34	2.77
Mexico	7.75	8.34	5.83
Kenya	6.5	8.70	7.08
Colombia	6.5	8.77	6.81
Russia	n.a.	8.73	7.08
Nigeria	8	9.24	7.83

Notes:
1. See section 5.2 for sources of the BI, TI and GCR indices.
2. All the indices in the table have been re-scaled so that large numbers imply more corruption.

5.2 Measuring Corruption

How to define corruption and measure it accurately is difficult and hotly debated. To be sure, these measurements and terms need refinement, something that continued work on the subject will likely provide over time. In the meanwhile, we define corruption as bribes from private sector parties to government officials; the latter abuses their power to extract payments from the former for personal benefit. This is to be distinguished from political corruption such as vote buying in an election, or legal or illegal campaign contributions by the wealthy and other special interest groups to influence laws and regulations. Such forms of corruption are without doubt costly, but are not the specific focus of this analysis.

The very nature of corruption—its secrecy, illegality and variations across different economic activities—makes it impossible to obtain precise information on its extent in a given country. This difficulty also precludes a precise grading of countries according to their relative degree of corruption. Like pornography, corruption is difficult to quantify, but you know it when you see it. That said, useful information on the seriousness of corruption in a country is available. Several survey-based measures of "corruption perception" are becoming increasingly widespread, and credibly reflect the general level of transparency in the countries for which such data exist. Four of these indices are described below. Table 5.1 displays corruption ratings for Asian and non-Asian countries, as determined by three of these indices.

The Business International (BI) index is based on surveys of experts and consultants (typically one consultant per country) conducted during 1980–1983.[1] It ranks countries from one to ten, according to "the degree to which business transactions involve corruption or questionable payments."

The International Country Risk Guide (ICRG) corruption index has been produced annually since 1982 by Political Risk Services, a private international investment risk service. The index is based on the opinion of experts, and intends to capture the extent to which "high government officials are likely to demand special payments" and "illegal payments are generally expected throughout lower levels of government" in the form of "bribes connected with import and export licenses, exchange controls, tax assessments, police protection, or loan applications."

Unlike the BI and ICRG indices, the Global Competitiveness Report (GCR) index is based on annual surveys of firm managers rather than experts or consultants. Sponsored by the World Economic Forum (WEF), and designed by the Harvard Institute for International Development, this survey asks business executives in the responding firms about various aspects of national competitiveness. Approximately 3,000 firms in 53 countries answered the question on corruption that asked the respondent to rate the level of corruption on a one-to-seven scale according to the extent of "irregular, additional payments connected with import and export

---

1. Business International is now a subsidiary of the Economist Intelligence Unit.

permits, business licenses, exchange controls, tax assessments, police protection or loan applications." The GCR corruption index for a particular country is the average of all respondents' ratings for that country.

The Transparency International (TI) index has been produced annually since 1995 by TI, an international non-governmental organization dedicated to fight corruption worldwide. The index is based on a weighted average of approximately ten surveys of varying coverage. It ranks countries on a one-to-ten scale.

It is worthwhile to emphasize that these indices are people's perceptions, as opposed to objective measures of corruption. Perception can be different from reality. That said, for many questions, such as how corruption affects foreign investment, perception is what actually matters; thus, perhaps our measure usefully reflects reality. In addition, despite the very different sources of the surveys, the pair-wise correlations between the indices are very high. For example, we know from previous work that the correlation between the BI and TI indices and that between the BI and GCR indices are 0.88 and 0.77, respectively. These high correlations bolster the reliability and credibility of all four indices.

5.3   Economic Consequences

We now assess the costs of corruption with respect to a variety of factors crucial to sustained economic achievement. First, we look at the connection between corruption and domestic investment, and then turn to the effects of corruption on foreign direct investment. We examine the impact of non-transparency on the financial sectors and on government expenditure, in particular social sector and poverty-reduction spending. We also consider the overall correlation between corruption and economic growth. It is worth noting that Asia's traditionally superior economic performance may tempt one to call into question the correlations we explain below. In nearly all cases, however, Asian performance would have been even better had levels of corruption been lower. In this sense, corruption in parts of Asia caused the affected regions to under-perform when compared to potential accomplishment.

Domestic Investment

A recent story in *China Youth Daily* offers anecdotal evidence of the costs of petty corruption on domestic investment.[2] Huang Shengxin started a private restaurant in Guangxi Province in 1982. Through his long hours of hard work, his Changxin Restaurant was highly successful and he was designated a National Outstanding Private-Sector Worker in recognition of his achievements. This was when the trouble began. Bureaucrats and their relatives loved the restaurant but they did not pay the bills. By February 1997 the County Government of Tanying, where the restaurant was located, owed him 80,665 yuan in unpaid bills. On May 20, 1997, burdened by his losses, Huang closed his restaurant.

While this is only one example of petty corruption closing a business, broader calculations offer a quantitative measure of the concrete costs to domestic investment. Using the BI index on corruption, researcher Paolo Mauro (1995) estimated how much domestic investment will be reduced as corruption increases. If we take literally the corruption ratings and point estimates, we conclude that if the Philippines, for example, could reduce its corruption levels to those of Singapore, all other things equal, it would increase its investment/GDP ratio by 6.6 percentage points—quite a substantial increase since the actual ratio was 24 percent in 1997.

Foreign Direct Investment

There is clear evidence that corruption in host countries discourages foreign investment. Using the same methodology as was used above, Wei (1997) estimates that if India, for example, could reduce its corruption level to that of Singapore, the net effect on attracting foreign investment would be the same as reducing its tax rate by 22 percentage points.

Many Asian countries offer substantial tax incentives to lure multi-national firms to locate in their countries. For example, China offers all foreign invested firms an initial two-year tax holiday plus three subsequent years at half the normal tax rate. Wei's (1998) research suggests that these Asian countries would have attracted just as much or even more foreign investment without any tax incentive if they could get domestic corruption under control.

---

2. Reproduced in *New World Times* (in English, circulated in the greater Washington D.C. area) April 24, 1998, p.18, which attributed it to Zhang Shuangwu, *China Youth Daily*, without giving the original date of publication.

When one adds corruption to the mix of factors affecting foreign direct investment, contrary to a cursory reading of the news, China is an underachiever as a host of foreign direct investment. Looking at data from five major source countries (the United States, Japan, Germany, the United Kingdom and France), once one takes into account its size, proximity to some major source countries and other factors, our calculations suggest that high corruption in China may very well have cost China significant foreign direct investment.

Financial Sector

In the WEF executive survey cited above, a series of questions on financial sector performance were correlated against the corruption question described in section 5.2. There is a strong positive correlation worldwide between corruption and bank vulnerability, and between corruption and the poor quality of regulations and supervision of financial institutions. (See figures 5.1 and 5.2.) These findings offer strong evidence supporting the link between transparency and the strength of financial institutions in several important dimensions. Indeed these are two of the dimensions that are most critical to explaining the underlying weaknesses in financial systems in crisis countries: effective government supervision of the banking industry and a healthy banking sector. As can be seen in table 5.2, the list of correlations extends even further into financial infrastructure.

Table 5.2
Composite of correlations between features of the financial markets, and the corruption question from the *Global Competitiveness Report 1998*

	World average
Lack of financial market sophistication	0.83
Bank vulnerability, requiring likely bailout	0.75
Interest rate gap	0.80
Lack of bond market development	0.82
Inadequacy of regulation and supervision of financial institutions	0.81
Government control of deposit or lending rates	0.72
Insider trading pervasiveness	0.75

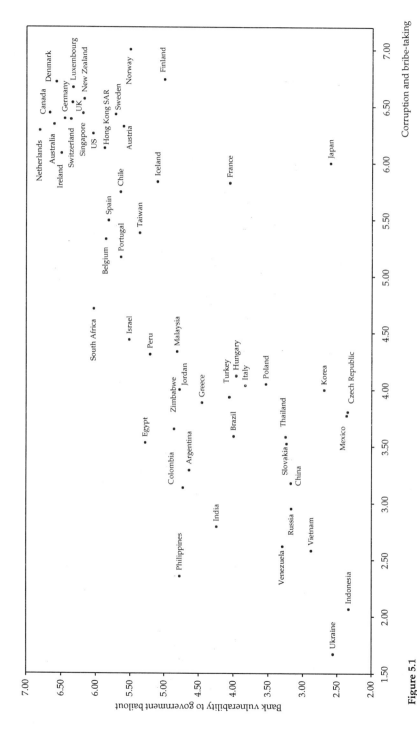

Figure 5.1
Positive correlation between corruption and bank vulnerability. Source: *Global Competitiveness Report 1988.*

Figure 5.2
Positive correlation between corruption and poor quality of regulation and supervision. Source: *Global Competitiveness Report 1998.*

Economic Growth

If corruption reduces domestic investment and reduces foreign investment, one would think that it would also reduce the economic growth rate. Mauro (1995) examined how the conditional growth rate—that is, the growth rate given a particular country's starting point and population size—is affected by corruption. He found a negative relationship between the two variables.

To illustrate the quantitative effect, let us return to the point estimates used in previous calculations. If Bangladesh were able to reduce its corruption to the Singapore level, its average annual per capita GDP growth rate over 1960–1985 would have been higher by 1.8 percentage points. Assuming its actual average growth rate was 4 percent a year, its per capita income by 1985 could have been more than 50 percent higher had corruption been contained.

Government Expenditure

How does corruption change the ways governments spend money? It tends to both increase the size of public investment—at the expense of private investment—and lower the quality of the public investment itself. Many items in public expenditure lend themselves to "manipulations" by high-level officials, which translates into a skewing of public expenditure away from operation and maintenance towards expenditure on new equipment. Corruption also skews the composition of public expenditure away from health and education funds, because these are relatively less easy for officials to manipulate for personal financial gain. Corruption reduces the productivity of public investment and of a country's infrastructure (Mauro 1997). Finally, corruption tends to reduce tax revenue because it compromises the government's ability to collect taxes and tariffs.

Here is an illustration. An increase in corruption from the Singapore level to Pakistan level would increase the public expenditure/GDP ratio by 1.6 percentage points, and reduce the government revenue/GDP ratio by 10 percentage points.

An increase in corruption reduces the quality of roads and increases the incidence of power outages, telecommunication faults and water losses. Specifically, an increase in corruption from the Singapore level to the Pakistan level would be associated with an extra 15-percent increase of roads in bad condition, after controlling for a country's level of development and its public investment to GDP ratio.

Poverty and Urban Bias

The desire to extract bribes distorts the behavior of government officials in a variety of ways. In particular, less "manipulatable" public projects often do not get budgeted, even if they have high social value. Large-scale defense projects are often favored by politicians and bureaucrats because their size and secrecy are often conducive to kickbacks.[3]

Defense contracts are often budgeted at the expense of rural health clinics specializing in preventive care (Gray and Kaufmann 1998). To the extent that rural residents tend to have lower incomes than their urban counterparts, this corruption-induced policy bias may worsen the income distribution and, at the same time, divert the needed resources away from the countryside.

The last example shows that poverty can be made worse and more persistent by corruption. In fact, one can expect that corruption would make poverty worse in cities as well as in rural areas, as poor people have less means to bribe officials and less political power in general. Rose-Ackerman (1998) listed several channels through which poor people are hurt by corruption: (a) The poor receive a lower level of social services; (b) infrastructure investment is biased against projects that aid the poor; (c) the poor may face higher tax or fewer services; (d) the poor are disadvantaged in selling their agricultural produce; and (e) their ability to escape poverty using indigenous, small-scale enterprises is diminished.

Using cross-country regressions over the period 1980–1997, Gupta, Davoodi and Alonso-Terme (1998) show that high and rising corruption, as measured by the ICRG index, increases income inequality and poverty. Several channels have been identified in the paper through which corruption worsens (relative and sometimes absolute) poverty: corruption lowers economic growth, biases the tax system to favor the rich and well connected, reduces the effectiveness of targeting of social programs, biases government policies towards favoring inequality in asset ownership, lowers social spending, reduces access to education by the poor, and increases the risk of investment by the poor.

---

3. In mid-1998 a Taiwanese general in charge of procurement was under investigation for vastly overpaying for a French-made warship in exchange for huge bribes. Similarly, India's arms purchase from Sweden gave birth to one of the most spectacular corruption scandals in both countries.

5.4   Culture: Is Asia Special?

We propose that the "fast-moving envelopes" and the business cultures that condone their exchange are among those factors which have sometimes been prematurely disregarded as not costly to growth and prosperity. Over a longer time horizon, in the context of rapid global integration, these and other previously overlooked inefficiencies (e.g., state-directed bank lending) emerge as unnecessary burdens to national economies.

While there is ample evidence that different people may have different views with respect to bribes versus gifts, or group loyalty versus self-interest, many of these differences may not be inherently cultural. For example, seemingly greater tolerance of bribes in some communities may be a result of the short-term outlooks of officials whose tenures, policies, or budgets are uncertain during times of rapid change (Osborne 1997). These factors, many of which are important features of some of the economies in crisis in Asia and elsewhere, should not be defined as cultural. Further-more, throughout human history, from ancient Greece to Confucian China and Hindu India, one can find repeated expressions of distaste by scholars and ordinary people for corruption and dishonesty. This does not mean that cultural factors are unimportant in the corruption debate, but "Asian culture" can easily be over-used to account for practices which can be more convincingly explained in alternative ways.

In section 5.3 we cited evidence that foreign investors on average invest less in more corrupt countries. Some may suspect that East Asia must be an outlier since it seems such a popular destination for foreign investment. Foreign investment in East Asia has been large, but East Asia is a large market and has been growing faster than the world average. Many East Asian countries also have low wages. Through these factors alone, East Asia naturally attracts more foreign investment. In a study of whether foreign investors are less sensitive to corruption in Asian host countries, Wei (1997) controlled for these factors. Wei found that there is no support for the Asian exceptionalism hypothesis. Investors from the major source countries are just as averse to corruption in East Asia as elsewhere.

5.5   Conclusion

The overall effect of corruption on economic development is negative. This is just as true in Asia as it is elsewhere. There is no evidence to support the notion that corruption in Asia has smaller negative consequences than in other regions of the world.

References

Gray, Cheryl W., and Daniel Kaufmann. 1998. Corruption and development. *Finance and Development* (March), 7-10.

Gupta, Sanjeev, Hamid Davoodi, and Rosa Alonso-Terme. 1998. Does corruption affect income inequality and poverty? IMF Working Paper (May).

Mauro, Paolo. 1995. Corruption and growth. *Quarterly Journal of Economics* 110: 681–712.

Mauro, Paulo. 1997. The effects of corruption on growth, investment, and government expenditure: A cross-country analysis. In Kimberley Ann Elliot, ed., *Corruption and the Global Economy*. Washington, D.C.: Institute for International Economics.

Osborne, Denis. 1997. Corruption as counter-culture: Attitudes to bribery in local and global society. In Barry Rider, ed., *Corruption: The Enemy Within*, pp. 9-34. Hague: Kluwer Law International.

Rose-Ackerman, Susan. 1998. Corruption and development. In Boris Pleskovi and Joseph Stiglitz, eds., *Annual World Bank Conference on Development Economics—1997*. Washington, D.C.: World Bank.

Wei, Shang-Jin. 1997. How taxing is corruption on international investors? The National Bureau of Economic Research Working Paper 6030 (May). Forthcoming in *Review of Economics and Statistics*.

Wei, Shang-Jin. 1998. Foreign, quasi-foreign, and false-foreign direct investment in China. Paper prepared for the Ninth East Asian Seminars on Economics, Osaka, Japan (June 25–28).

World Economic Forum. 1998. *The Global Competitiveness Report 1998*. Geneva: World Economic Forum.

6   Competitiveness in Asia: A Value-Driven Perspective

Thomas G. Lewis

6.1   Introduction

The Asian economic crisis has had an impact on companies as well as countries far beyond the immediate region. Just as Asian countries and companies lost vital economic momentum during the crisis, Western companies investing in the region faced declining stock prices and shaky shareholder confidence that cost numerous multinationals billions of dollars in the short term.

Much of the discussion about what needs to be done has centered on debt and macroeconomic reform. While we agree that reforms are critical to rebuilding confidence in the region's economies, we believe it is equally important to look at the equity side of the equation and the confidence of companies investing in the region. In this section we are delving into the behavior and tactics of companies in the midst of the crisis.

While we discuss many countries of the larger Asian region, including India and China, our focus is primarily on the five countries most affected by the crisis: Thailand, Indonesia, South Korea, Malaysia and the Philippines.

We have adopted a shareholder's perspective in diagnosing pre-crisis competitiveness in the manufacturing sector. The same perspective is used to outline the action we believe must be taken to enhance the future competitiveness of this sector. The most objective measure of shareholder value creation is total shareholder return (TSR), which comprises capital appreciation and dividend yield. The main drivers of TSR are the following.

- Profitability: maximizing returns from existing assets; these returns must be evaluated in relation to the cost of capital.
- Growth: investing in new assets that return more than the company's cost of capital.
- Free cash flow: generating cash and returning it to investors when no profitable investments are available.

Profitability and growth drive a company's capital gains performance. Free cash flow creates value by funding reduction of excessive debt or enabling share repurchases. Management of all three is essential to superior value creation.

In the United States and Europe, increasing numbers of CEOs use TSR as the benchmark for corporate success. At The Boston Consulting Group (BCG), we apply these tools in our work with clients to create increased value for corporate enterprises. An analysis of sector performance and competitiveness in Asia using TSR produces some intriguing results.

6.2   Shareholder Returns in Asia's Manufacturing Sector

Even while the tale of Asia's phenomenal growth was spreading around the world, the underlying weakness of many Asian manufacturers was reflected in their TSRs well before the 1997 financial crisis in East Asia. The share prices of listed manufacturing companies in both South Korea and Thailand were already far off their 1993 and 1994 peaks by the time the devaluation of the baht set off a chain reaction in the currency and stock markets (figure 6.1). Many equity investors apparently observed deterioration in the underlying health of these businesses well before the subject became front-page news around the world.

In addition, from 1987 to 1997 the average TSR of manufacturing companies across several Asian markets was below that of the U.S. equity market, despite consistently high and much discussed real GDP growth rates in the range of 6 to 10 percent annually.

The contradiction requires explanation. Why were Asian manufacturing companies failing to deliver superior returns to investors when their economies were growing at more than twice the rate of growth of the United States and Europe? The answer lies in how these companies allocated capital and managed two of the main drivers of value creation: profitability and growth.

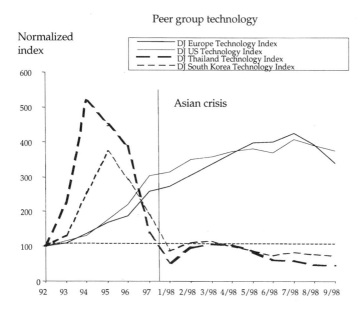

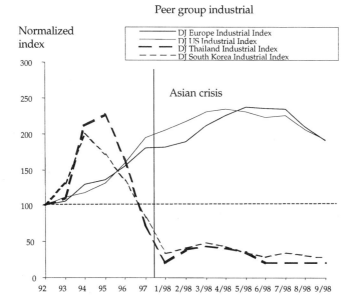

Figure 6.1
Value creation of manufacturing sector—Thailand and South Korea. Dow Jones world technology and industrial indices (1992–9/1998) were chosen as indicators for the performance of the global manufacturing sector. Normalized index = average prices. Source: Dow Jones; Datastream.

6.3   High Growth, Low Profitability

In much of the Asian manufacturing sector, profitability levels before the crisis were below the real cost of capital, and some were in decline. Figure 6.2 illustrates the investment strategies of selected major manufacturers in South Korea and Indonesia, two countries where the crisis has had very serious effects.

Of 15 industrial sectors examined in South Korea, only telecommunications generated profitability[1] above its cost of capital from 1994 to 1997. Annual asset growth for South Korean manufacturers during this time averaged 31 percent. The pattern is similar in Indonesia, where annual growth in four key manufacturing sectors was 42 percent between 1993 and 1996. Yet, the returns earned by the two largest manufacturing sectors fell below the expectations of capital providers.

Profitability is driven by cash flow margins and by asset turnover, or asset productivity. One or both of these measures were declining in most South Korean (figure 6.3) and Indonesian manufacturing sectors well before the onset of the crisis.

6.4   Unsustainable Growth

Weak underlying profitability prevented many Asian manufacturing businesses from financing aggressive expansion plans through internally generated cash flows. Their growth was unsustainable because it could not be financed by reinvesting cash flows without raising new equity or leverage after servicing existing equity and debt holders.

Figure 6.4 shows that, at annual growth rates of 20 percent to 40 percent, almost the entire sample of South Korean and Indonesian manufacturers grew at well beyond a level that would have been sustainable by cash flows from operations during the mid-1990s. According to our analysis, a sustainable growth rate would have been more in the one-digit range. This unsustainable growth, of course, had to be financed by debt.

---

1. Measured as cash-flow return on investment (CFROI).

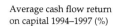

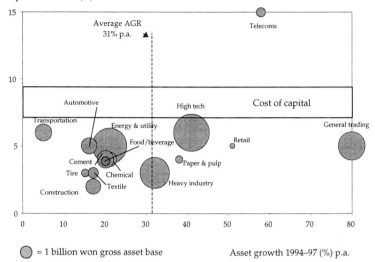

Average cash flow return
on capital 1994–1997 (%)

Selected Korean manufacturing companies

○ = 1 billion won gross asset base   Asset growth 1994–97 (%) p.a.

Selected Indonesian manufacturing companies

Average cash flow return
on capital 1993–96 (%)

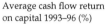

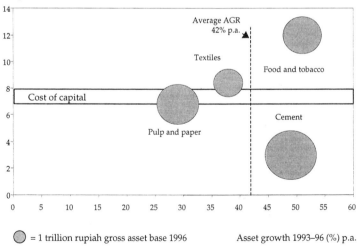

○ = 1 trillion rupiah gross asset base 1996   Asset growth 1993–96 (%) p.a.

Figure 6.2
High two-digit gross investment growth in spite of low levels of profitability. Gross investment = sum of fixed assets at historical cost and net working capital. AGR = asset growth rate. Source: BCG Val database.

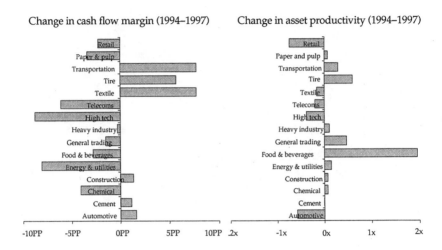

Figure 6.3
Trade-offs between value drivers in South Korean manufacturing (1994–1997). PP = percentage points. "2x" = twofold increase in asset productivity. Source: BCG Val database.

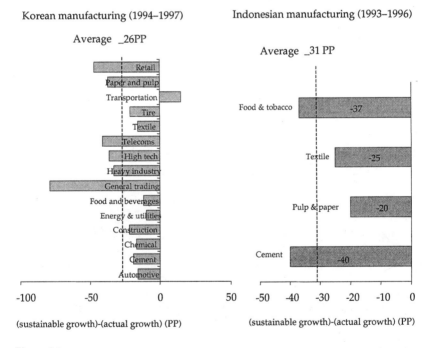

Figure 6.4
Korean and Indonesian manufacturing sectors' actual asset growth rates significantly exceeded sustainable growth rates. Sector data are simple averages of company data. Actual growth is gross investment growth. PP = percentage points. Source: BCG Val database.

6.5 Cheap Debt and Forgiving Investors

In efficient capital markets, the profitability of a company—more specifically, its profitability relative to its cost of capital or "spread"—determines its ability to raise and service debt and equity. The higher the spread, the higher the P/E ratio that equity holders will ascribe to the company, and the greater the potential proceeds from issuing new equity. The greater the value of a company's equity and the higher its cash flows for servicing debt, the more willing are banks to lend money, provided that debt is kept at a prudent proportion of total capital.

This self-reinforcing formula for enterprise economics was inconsistently applied in much of pre-crisis Asia. The cost of funding for many manufacturing businesses did not reflect economic fundamentals and market forces; on the contrary, it was maintained at artificially low levels. This situation was achieved in part by design and in part by circumstance, through a combination of the following factors:

• governments guaranteeing or subsidizing debt;

• governments exerting pressure on banks to extend credit freely;

• deficiencies in banks' credit controls;

• competition among local and international banks to increase their loans to Asia's "booming" businesses;

• corporate structures enabling the syndication of risk across corporate entities; and

• interest rate differentials resulting from currencies being pegged to a rising U.S. dollar relative to the yen.

As a consequence, the estimated pre-crisis cost of capital in South Korea and several ASEAN countries hovered around 7 to 10 percent in real terms.[2] This was above the level of profitability achieved in those countries. Moreover, hindsight reveals that hurdle rates of this order were generous, considering the region's risk profile. In comparison, capital providers were demanding real returns of around 6 to 8 percent in Europe and 4 to 6 percent in the U.S. And in Hong Kong, one of Asia's most developed and transparent capital markets, the required real rate of return was over 10 percent.

---

2. Real cost of capital was derived using a traditional capital asset pricing model (CAPM) methodology.

The cheap funding became more attractive because equity markets tended not to penalize Asian companies when their debt levels rose to above-average levels, particularly when a tangled web of relationships between businesses made it difficult to quantify and assign ownership to debt. In more efficient capital markets, the risk inherent in high debt levels would have typically led to a rise in the cost of capital.

It was therefore perfectly consistent for Asian manufacturing companies to finance their growth agendas by taking on more cheap debt—both in local currency, as was generally the case in South Korea, and as low-interest U.S. dollar denominated debt, as often happened in the ASEAN countries. Under these circumstances, there was no imperative to improve profitability or slow the rate of growth.

In addition to an exacerbated debt burden, the result was an asset bubble that burst as the financial markets lost confidence in the strength of the Asian economies and their overvalued currencies collapsed.

6.6 Manufacturing Conglomerates: Value Creation and Value Erosion

Given a manufacturing landscape characterized by low profitability, high growth and high leverage, it is appropriate to examine the business structures and management models that prevailed when the Asian crisis struck.

Conglomerates control a significant portion of the Asian manufacturing sector, particularly in South Korea, where the chaebols are responsible for some 80 percent of manufacturing output. In Indonesia, the top 20 conglomerates contribute around 20 percent to GDP. In terms of stock market capitalization, conglomerates account for over 80 percent in South Korea, over 40 percent in Indonesia, around 30 percent in Thailand and Malaysia, 25 percent in Taiwan and 20 percent in India. The share is roughly 10 percent in the U.S. and the U.K.

Conglomerates have contributed significantly to the development needs of many economies in the early stages of their growth. In addition, their access to capital, their size, and management experience can accelerate the development of the companies in their portfolios. On their own, such individually independent companies in developing economies would likely have to depend on support from the government, and even then, the resulting development rate could still be lower.

To be successful in the long run, a conglomerate must manage its activities in ways that create value for all stakeholders—investors, employees and society. As economies mature, the most stringent test for a conglomerate's longer-term competitiveness is whether it is able to create more value than its various component businesses could achieve in sum on their own, and more value than investors would have received from alternative investments with comparable risk profiles. Conglomerates that pass this test can attract additional capital less expensively and are better placed to strengthen the competitive positions of their businesses.

Our work with conglomerates around the world has shown that the most successful ones aggressively and effectively manage four key levers:

• Value management: focusing on value creation to ensure that capital allocation optimizes the long-term value of the group.

• Performance enhancement: implementing systematic programs (generally directed from the corporate center) designed to improve productivity and efficiency in the business units.

• Portfolio management: managing the shape and constituents of the portfolio through acquisitions, divestments and strategic alliances.

• Human resource development: ensuring that the highest quality management talent is attracted, retained and developed.

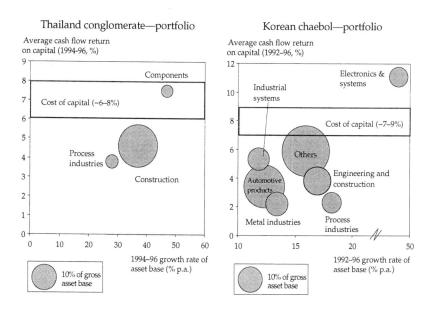

Figure 6.5
Unsustainable conglomerate portfolios—major revenue sources have low profitability.
Sources: KIS Line financial data; BCG analysis.

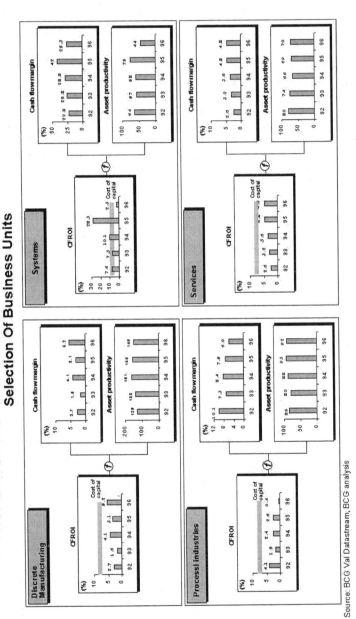

FIGURE 6: KOREAN CONGLOMERATE FACED DECLINING CASH FLOW MARGIN AND STAGNATING ASSET PRODUCTIVITY
Selection Of Business Units

Source: BCG Val Datastream, BCG analysis

CFROI = cash flow return on investment.

Few of the many Asian conglomerates we observed were actively managing all four levers. For example, analysis of a Thai conglomerate and a South Korean chaebol revealed several problems, particularly with respect to the first three levers.

First, in building huge, seemingly successful companies, they placed insufficient emphasis on value management (reflected in low TSR relative to the market). Growth, financed by excessive debt levels of up to 90 percent of total capital by 1997, was the primary objective, and profitability appeared to be of secondary concern. As part of their growth agenda, these companies invested in existing as well as new businesses, and built capabilities without rigorous assessment of whether a proposed new business could generate an adequate return on investment. Figure 6.5 shows the portfolios of these conglomerates; most of their investments achieved returns well below the estimated cost of capital.

Second, scant attention to performance was often exacerbated by corporate structure. The typical Asian conglomerate is an array of associated businesses, usually linked by complicated cross-shareholdings and off-balance-sheet debt. This situation is often a function of the corporate legal environment and the avenues available for financing new business development. In South Korea for instance, holding companies are not provided for in corporate law. The family-controlled chaebols are therefore only loosely linked at the corporate center. Moreover, shareholder and security regulations have facilitated loose financing and ownership disciplines across group companies. As a result, responsibility for business strategy and performance at the operating level is often obscure or diluted, making it easy to lose sight of underlying performance problems in the existing operating units and to focus instead on new businesses.

Figure 6.6 shows the financial profiles of several of a South Korean conglomerate's businesses before the currency crisis. Each generated low profitability, driven by varying combinations of weak cash flow margins and stagnating asset productivity.

Third, portfolio management in Asian manufacturing conglomerates also ran a poor second to growth. In an environment that discouraged decisive action from the corporate center, resources were not always allocated to the most profitable businesses. Similarly, obvious cash "sinkholes" were not divested. In the South Korean conglomerate, for example, as much as 75 percent of the investment in the early 1990s was allocated to under-performing businesses growing at unsustainable rates.

FIGURE 7: VALUE CREATION OF MANUFACTURING INDUSTRY
Taiwanese Manufacturing 1995–1998

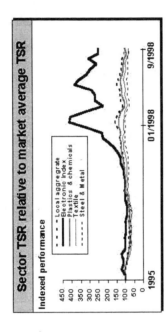

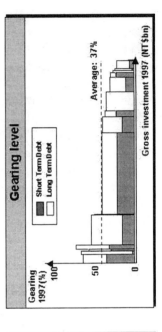

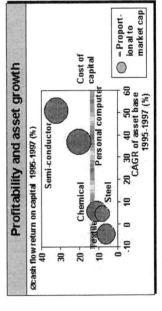

Despite these major failings, manufacturing conglomerates in Asia have accomplished much for the region and themselves. They have used their scale and commercial instincts to marshal the resources necessary to develop businesses and industries. In particular, conglomerates have added value to the labor pool. They have helped millions of people acquire industrial skills and have provided advanced training for middle and top management. The South Korean chaebols, especially, have excelled in people development, infusing top management teams with tremendous entrepreneurship and a strong work ethic.

Leading chaebols have set up production facilities and distribution networks in neighboring countries and around the world, spreading country risk and creating global brands. They have established strong global positions in several industries, including semiconductors, consumer electronics, automobiles and construction.

The challenge ahead for Asian conglomerates will be to leverage their distinctive qualities and regain the confidence of international capital markets. Their ability to aggressively restructure business portfolios around assets with the greatest potential for long-term value creation will be key. Greater transparency and more streamlined corporate structures are also likely to be prerequisites for building an effective platform for restoring international competitiveness.

We turn now to Taiwan, India and China, nations with manufacturing sectors that, in different ways, have been somewhat insulated from the Asian financial storm.

6.7   Taiwan: Calm in the Face of the Storm

In terms of absolute size, Taiwanese manufacturing ranks equally with India as third in the region. Within Taiwanese manufacturing, electronics is the highest growth sector, with increases of over 10 percent per year since 1991. It has consistently outperformed the rest of the industry since the early 1990s.

Taiwanese manufacturing has mostly avoided the debilitating effects of the Asian crisis. Its expected 4–5 percent GDP growth ranked fifth highest worldwide in 1998. The stock market declined a moderate 4 percent compared to the average 1997 performance, but remained a comfortable 34 percent above the average 1996 level. However, as shown in figure 6.7, not all sectors were able to match the outstanding performance of the electronics industry, e.g., steel and metal, plastics and chemicals, and textiles.

Like many other firms in neighboring countries, Taiwanese companies grew strongly through the late 1980s and the 1990s, *but within the limits that cash flow levels could sustain.* Asset growth in the electronics sector, for example, has been at well over 30 percent since 1995 without straining debt levels and has been accompanied by relatively high levels of profitability. Even severe competitive pressure in the semiconductor industry did not push cash flow returns below the cost of capital. Taiwanese companies were responding quickly and effectively to worldwide overcapacity and price pressures, closing production facilities to streamline asset intensity and improve asset productivity. In sectors such as steel and metal, textiles, and chemicals, a generally lower profitability was matched by significantly lower growth rates.

As a result, Taiwanese manufacturers have relatively low debt to total capital or gearing ratios: around 25 percent in electronics, slightly above 30 percent in chemicals and textiles, and around 50 percent in the steel sector. Overall, the average gearing of all listed companies in Taiwan is 30 percent (slightly lower than for the sampled manufacturing sector), compared to more than 80 percent in Indonesia, around 60 percent in Thailand and South Korea, and around 40 percent in Malaysia.

The flexibility of Taiwan's strong small and medium-sized enterprises contributes to its strength. These companies employ 75 to 80 percent of the workforce and contribute 47 percent to GDP. Their sheer number has enhanced competition and reduced the risk of distorted economic relations with governments and banks. They are also more flexible than larger companies in responding to changes in demand and the operating environment. For example, when Taiwan's rising labor costs threatened its competitiveness with neighboring countries, thousands of companies moved their manufacturing operations offshore to Mainland China and other ASEAN countries.

The outlook for Taiwanese competitiveness is bright, provided it can sustain its management of value drivers and organizational flexibility. Taiwan has a strong starting position in many industries in terms of global competitiveness. It is, for example, the world's leading producer of computer notebooks, and has a very strong position as a supplier of computer peripherals as well as in some less well-known consumer goods categories.

6.8   India: A Mixed Outlook

During the 1990s, much of the web of regulations in India was dismantled. But the still significant state-owned portion of the economy escaped much of the reform. Not surprisingly, domestic companies that formerly operated in a highly protected environment found themselves threatened by international competition. The natural source of competitive advantage in the liberalized economy was in lower value-added products, where India enjoyed significant labor-cost advantages. Reduced import duties have not only increased imports, but have also reduced the prices of many products, putting downward pressure on domestic production costs. The result is that Indian companies have been restructuring their operations, and value creation has become a useful indicator of competitiveness.

While Indian GDP has grown on average at 6 percent, India's stock market as measured by the BSE SENSEX[3] has remained flat since 1992. As in East Asia, India's overall GDP growth has not been translated into proportional value creation. This appears to be the case particularly for the manufacturing sector. Our analysis shows that India's five major manufacturing sectors have under-performed the market-average BSE SENSEX. Only the fairly small pharmaceutical and drugs sector and the non-commercial automotive sector have created value relative to the rest of the Indian economy.

Further analysis reveals that growth rates were typically in excess of 20 percent in the major manufacturing sectors and profitability in most of these industries remained below cost of capital in the 1990s. Gearing has remained at below the levels reached in South Korea and Thailand.

The large sector of the economy operated by public sector undertakings does not really lend itself to our definition of competitiveness, but an analysis in terms of value creation is possible for much of the private sector that comprises listed companies.

As in East Asia, many Indian companies are family-controlled conglomerates. India's now-defunct Monopolistic Trading Practices Act effectively meant that companies wishing to grow had to do so in new and unrelated fields, often with diluted ownership on the part of sponsoring companies or families. As a result, Indian conglomerates are, in several ways, similar to chaebols: They are disparate businesses connected by ownership ties but without clear corporate management

---

3.   Indian market aggregate: Bombay Stock Exchange Index.

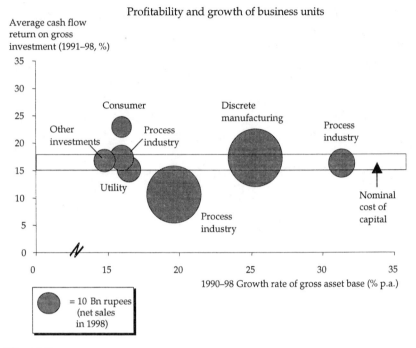

Figure 6.8
An Indian conglomerate's performance (1990–1998). Sources: BCG analysis; Prowess.

structures and lines of responsibility and accountability. There is also the same lack of emphasis on the primary levers of value creation, and the same phenomenon of the rates of return of many businesses being below the cost of capital. Figure 6.8 illustrates a relatively typical situation of an Indian conglomerate in the mid-1990s. Only two of the seven businesses shown actually achieved above market-average shareholder returns.

In the aftermath of the Asian crisis, international investors are much less sanguine about emerging markets, including India. Thus it may be difficult for Indian corporations to meet their capital requirements unless they can convince investors that they are serious about embracing transparency in corporate structure, protection of shareholder rights, and modern, professional management practices.

6.9   China: Preparing for Prosperity in the New Millennium

With manufacturing output of US$400 billion, China represents about half of the Asian manufacturing sector outside Japan. With an annual growth rate of 18 percent,[4] manufacturing has been a driving force in the Chinese economy. China leads the world in the size of several of its industrial sectors, such as printing machines and trucks. Unlike smaller Asian economies, it also offers a unique combination of large potential domestic demand and low-cost labor. This is a promisingly competitive environment, but, similar to the Indian manufacturers, competitiveness is a relatively recent requirement.

Because China's capital market is at an early stage of development and there is too little transparency about the profitability of Chinese enterprises, we cannot easily apply our model of financial viability and value creation as a key indicator of competitiveness. The following analysis extrapolates from the limited available data and our experience working with Chinese companies.

The success of China's industrial, financial and political reform effort will be an important indicator of the country's future competitiveness. The Chinese government's much discussed reform of the industrial sector has been in progress for at least 10 years. This has had significant effects on the structure and, almost certainly, the underlying competitiveness of Chinese industry.

In 1985, 65 percent of China's manufacturing output was generated by state-owned enterprises (SOEs). The figure today is closer to 25 percent, and at the same time foreign-invested and shareholder companies have increased from 3 percent to about 32 percent. In addition, there appears to be a slight trend from lower to higher value-added industries. Equipment manufacturing and food/tobacco are the fastest growing industrial sectors, while lower-value sectors such as textiles and clothing and non-chemical processing industries are the slowest growing (figure 6.9).

The Chinese government's restructuring of the remaining SOEs is also likely to boost competitiveness. A leading consumer durable SOE is a successful example of this kind of reform. It has built the strongest service and direct sell-through network in China, outmaneuvering its domestic and foreign rivals with city-specific promotion campaigns. As a result, it leads the market and enjoys a price premium in several

---

4. Growth of manufacturing output in real terms and local currency.

product categories. This company is an exception among SOEs, but clearly demonstrates the potential to succeed in a competitive environment.

One domestic steel tube manufacturer may better exemplify the challenges confronting SOEs: it struggled for survival, crippled by exorbitant debt levels, and was faced with costs 50 percent above market price, low-quality output, and capacity underutilization. The company was also significantly overstaffed. It implemented a turnaround program focused on three tactics: building a market position in its only business with modern-technology production lines, reducing headcount and improving process efficiency, and restructuring for a customer-oriented organization. Factory operations and profitability have significantly improved. Equipment utilization has increased from 20 percent to 50 percent within a year; the new marketing approach has brought a surge in sales; and a partnership with another SOE steel group has enhanced the factory's capabilities and finances. The merged entity, however, must deal with the high debt levels and the social costs associated with the restructuring.

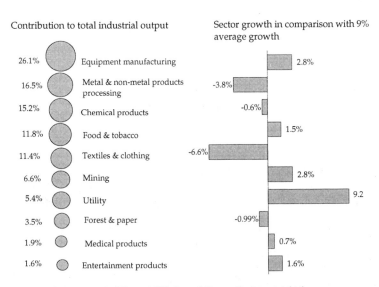

Contribution to total industrial output   Sector growth in comparison with 9% average growth

26.1%	Equipment manufacturing	2.8%
16.5%	Metal & non-metal products processing	-3.8%
15.2%	Chemical products	-0.6%
11.8%	Food & tobacco	1.5%
11.4%	Textiles & clothing	-6.6%
6.6%	Mining	2.8%
5.4%	Utility	9.2
3.5%	Forest & paper	-0.99%
1.9%	Medical products	0.7%
1.6%	Entertainment products	1.6%

Sector growth differential likely to shift contribution weight from low value-added industries to high value-added industries

Figure 6.9
Growth in China's manufacturing sectors. Source: *China Statistic Yearbook 1998*.

The Chinese government's reform efforts focus on the 15,000 largest of 70,000 SOEs. In a "grasp the large, release the small" approach, the smaller enterprises will be successively "released" to operate in free markets. The state will retain about 1,000 of the largest enterprises to preserve its influence in key industries. Many of these more profitable companies are required to drive reform by acquiring less profitable companies, with the objective of leveraging superior management skills and "best practices" and, where the companies are in the same industries, realizing economies of scale and synergies.

Although conceptually simple, in practice the task will be enormous. Many Chinese conglomerates will have to assume responsibility for poorly performing businesses with dated facilities, products and management processes, and, above all, oversized workforces. The massive challenge of restructuring these businesses in a socially responsible way can make the principles of value creation appear irrelevant.

The opening of many manufacturing sectors to foreign companies has made competition as intense as anywhere in the world. China's markets, often overestimated by new entrants, have attracted competition from many countries.[5] This puts further pressure on the Chinese conglomerates to manage according to the four key value levers outlined earlier. They should particularly attempt to avoid the pitfalls that have affected other Asian conglomerates—and to replicate the successes.

6.10   The Outlook is Positive

Despite the severe problems encountered by many Asian manufacturers, a number of factors point to a potentially positive outcome for competitiveness. The region's aggressive growth strategy over recent years has been problematic, but it has also led to the development of a much stronger industrial base. Manufacturing and distribution infrastructure has evolved, labor skills have been fostered, and management capabilities have grown. The future depends on Asia's ability to harness and restructure these valuable assets for overall value creation. Based on our experience, this will involve management efforts along the following four dimensions.

---

5. Very few U.S. businesses, much less those in Europe or Japan, face competition in their home markets from all the major industrial economies. One well-known result is the disappointing levels of profitability achieved by many foreign-owned or foreign-invested enterprises.

• Portfolio restructuring. This is at the top of the agenda for Asian conglomerates. Difficult decisions will have to be made: divesting unprofitable businesses, entering into mergers and acquisitions, and finding
creative ways of ensuring that their businesses earn at least the cost of
capital. Value creation must be the focus and goal of conglomerate
managers.

• Improving profitability of the core. This is not to say that conglomerates should divest themselves of the advantages that their size and
diversity can bring. But managers must address costs and drive up
asset productivity to push profitability to levels that will support
growth. This will involve exploring all possible avenues to create demand as well as making often-painful decisions to rationalize surplus
manufacturing capacity.

• Transparency and decision support systems. To support portfolio
restructuring and value management efforts, Asian corporations must
develop a deep understanding of their businesses. Greater transparency
in the financial performance of individual businesses will be required,
as will more sophisticated decision-making systems that facilitate
portfolio analysis and value management.

• Investor confidence. Asian businesses must regain the trust of the
international investor community. Investors must be convinced that
Asia's corporations are making the appropriate tradeoffs between profitability, growth and risk.

This is a challenging prescription, but considering the success that
Asian manufacturing corporations have had in achieving growth targets,
as well as the determination and ingenuity that they have brought to
the task, we believe a sustained improvement in manufacturing competitiveness is achievable.

There is evidence that a number of Asian manufacturers have heard
the message and are taking action. One example is an Asian electronic
components manufacturer that has created over US$1 billion in share-
holder value during the most severe downturn in the history of Asia's
stock markets. The company, which has its main manufacturing base in
China, had been a global market leader for many years. However, it
experienced a phase of significant value erosion just before the crisis.
From 1994 to 1996, its market capitalization dropped by 30 percent, and
its share price under-performed the local stock market by 13 percent.
Until 1996 the company had implemented much the same growth

agenda as we have witnessed in other parts of Asia. Aggressive capacity expansion programs resulted in asset growth at a rate of 25 percent per annum between 1990 and 1996, but the end result was a significant drop in utilization levels. At the same time, raw materials were stockpiled in an attempt to smooth volatile commodity prices. In spite of increasing cash flows in absolute terms, profitability fell from high levels in 1990 to well below the cost of capital by 1996.

In late 1996 the company began a turnaround process that in two years enabled it to outperform the local stock market by 135 percent. The process involved restructuring the entire company, with programs aimed at increasing cost efficiency, improving asset utilization, and re-vamping the organizational structure to achieve greater customer focus and improved quality control. Asset productivity initiatives improved return-on-investment by increasing inventory turns from two to seven times, halving annual capital expenditures, and increasing capacity utilization levels from 65 to 85 percent. Products were reengineered to reduce the material content and, this, together with improved hedging policies, minimized the impact of volatile commodity prices on margins.

These operational efforts were supported by tools for value-based decision-making. New performance measurement systems were intro-duced to assess the value created by strategic and operational manage-ment. Budgeting and planning processes were redesigned, and executive compensation is being supplemented with performance-based incentives.

This business is now well positioned to continue building its competi-tive position and deliver above-average returns to its shareholders. It is a model that many Asian manufacturers would do well to imitate.

II

Country Profiles: Reform, Recovery, and Growth

7   China: Confronting Restructuring and Stability

Wing Thye Woo

7.1   Introduction

China has been the world's star performer in economic growth for the last two decades. China registered an average annual growth rate of 9.7 percent in the 1978–99 period. However, the growth rates for 1996–99 are not only below the average of the period, they have also declined monotonically from 9.6 percent in 1996 to 7.1 percent in 1999. Naturally, many questions and concerns have arisen about this four-year deviation from the average. How much of the deviation has been due to trend slowdown, how much to the internal economic cycle, and how much to the external shock from the Asian financial crisis? Furthermore, what could be done to offset the decline, and what are the long-term implications of these counter-measures?

In the public pronouncements of Chinese officials, the usual explanation for the slowdown was a drop in consumption and the stagnation of exports caused by the Asian financial crisis. Large-scale infrastructure investment programs were started in 1998 and 1999, and a third round of infrastructure spending is planned for 2000. The rationale is straightforward: infrastructure investment lifts aggregate demand to maintain full capacity usage, and alleviates production bottlenecks to ease inflationary pressures.

The above diagnosis and cure have been rejected by a number of economists. In the opinion of Thomas Rawski (1999):

This diagnosis is mistaken and the policy misconstrued. Weakness in the economy, which pre-dates the Asian crisis of 1997/98, runs much deeper than China's leaders appear to believe. The difficulties are structural rather than cyclical. Short-term pump-priming exacerbates structural problems and undercuts long-term reform objectives.

Table 7.1
China: Pre-crisis situation

	1990–94	1995	1996	1997
Growth rate of real GDP (%)	10.7	10.5	9.5	8.8
CPI growth rate (%)	10.4	16.9	8.3	2.8
Fixed investment (as % of GDP)	31.7	34.2	33.6	33.8
Gross domestic savings (% of GDP)	39.0	42.0	43.9	40.8
Current account balance (% of GDP)	1.4	0.2	0.9	1.2
Reserve money growth (%)	28.8	20.6	29.5	17.0
Narrow money growth rate (%)	30.1	18.8	19.8	25.0
Broad money growth rate (%)	32.8	29.5	25.3	20.7
Government expenditure (% of GDP)	14.6	11.5	11.4	11.8
Government budget balance (% of GDP)	−1.0	−1.0	−0.8	−0.7
Foreign debt (as % of GDP)	17.3	17.2	16.0	n.a.
Debt service ratio for all external debt	12.3	12.8	12.2	n.a.
Exchange rate (vis-à-vis US$)	6.1	8.3	8.3	8.3
Real exchange rate (1995=100, WPI based)	102.0	98.7	85.0	76.2
Real wage index	97.9	95.1	95.1	92.6
Current account balance (US$ million)	5,393	1,618	7,243	29,718
Capital account balance (US$ million)	13,431	38,673	39,966	22,957
Foreign direct investment (US$ million)	16,062	35,849	40,180	44,236
Export value (US$ million)	86,191	148,797	151,197	182,877
Composition of exports, value of highest four exports (1996 ranking, US$ million)				
Articles of apparel and clothing accessories	16,820	24,139	25,920	n.a.
Miscellaneous manufactured articles	7,640	13,962	14,766	n.a.
Textile yarn, fabrics, made-up articles	9,210	14,034	12,696	n.a.
Electrical machinery, apparatus and appliances	3,552	9,535	10,654	n.a.
Import value (US$ million)	83,298	129,113	138,944	142,189
Composition of imports, value of highest four imports (1996 ranking, US$ million)				
Textile yarn, fabrics, made-up articles	10,416.3	16,744.8	18,644.7	n.a.
Electrical machinery, apparatus and appliances	6,283.2	12,269.2	14,173.6	n.a.
Specialized machinery	9,786.2	12,960.6	14,094.0	n.a.
Artificial resins, plastic materials	5,500.0	10,590.9	10,947.2	n.a.
Exports' dependence on unaffected markets (%)	26.7	32.8	34.1	n.a.
International reserves minus gold (US$ million)	33,221	74,721	106,404	142,165

Table 7.1 (continued)

	1990–94	1995	1996	1997
Value of total foreign debt (US$ billion)	74.9	118.1	128.8	135.0
Short-term foreign debt (US$ billion)	13.3	22.3	25.4	n.a.
DS Stock Market Index ($)	446.9	260.1	472.9	628.1
DS Stock Market Index (local currency)	509.4	398.5	723.1	958.3
Shanghai Composite Index	638.7	555.3	917.0	1,194.1
Nominal lending rate (%)	9.7	12.1	10.1	8.6
Nominal deposit rate (%)	9.1	11.0	7.5	5.7

Table 7.2
China: Changes in labor employment and output composition

	Composition of output		Composition of labor force	
	1986	1996	1970	1990
Agriculture	27.1	18.1	78.3	72.2
Industry	44.0	54.2	10.1	15.1
Services	28.9	27.7	11.6	12.7

Table 7.3
China: Forecasts for the 1999–2001 situation

Forecasting institution and date of forecast	GDP growth (%)			CPI inflation (%)		
	1999	2000	2001	1998	1999	2001
International Monetary Fund, October 1999	6.6	6.0	—	−1.5	1.5	—
HSBC Asia Economic Weekly, January 2000	7.1	7.9	7.4	−1.3	1.0	2.9
Economist Intelligence Unit, 2000:1Q	7.1	7.5	7.6	−1.3	1.5	3.0

Nicholas Lardy (1998a), while not offering an explanation for the slowdown, also deemed China's reflation program to be a mistake:

China's leadership has made its short-term growth objective its highest priority. Longer-term structural reform of state-owned banks and enterprises is being postponed. Ironically, even if the program increases the rate of growth, ultimately, the costs of postponed reforms will be even greater, meaning it likely will fail to alleviate social unrest.

We agree with some elements in the above analyses, but we differ in emphasis and sometimes have drawn different conclusions. The following points will be argued:

(a) The structural flaws in China's economy in 1995, if left uncorrected, would surely cause growth to slow down in the future, say within a decade, but these structural flaws were not responsible for the significant slowdown in 1996–99.

(b) The slowdown in 1996–97 was largely the result of the austerity program that Zhu Rongji had implemented since mid-1993 to wring inflationary pressures out of the economy and to restructure the economy simultaneously.

(c) The further slowdown in 1998–99 reflected the export decline caused by the Asian financial crisis.

(d) The reflation program of 1998–99 did not represent a wavering of commitment to restructuring; its emphasis on infrastructure investment (as opposed to a generalized increase in investment) was a sensible response to a temporary external shock.

Thomas Rawski and Nicholas Lardy are correct that radical restructuring of the state enterprise sector and the state banking system is absolutely crucial to avoiding a drastic drop in the trend growth rate in the future. The maintenance of the 1996 status of the state enterprises and state banks is not a viable option in the long run, because the economy will be unable to support the growing burden from these two sectors.

The Chinese view that under-consumption (high saving) has made macroeconomic management more difficult is correct (and we will develop this point later), but we do not consider larger state spending, even in infrastructure, to be the optimum policy response. The correct response is restructuring, not stabilization; financial restructuring is needed to create financial institutions that would quickly channel the additional saving to investments with the highest rates of return.

The general view of this paper is that the short-run costs of economic restructuring may have been overstated. Restructuring state-owned enterprises (SOEs) could worsen short-term growth while improving long-term growth prospects, but restructuring state-owned banks could improve both short-term and long-term growth. Financial restructuring is a win-win reform activity because it will eliminate the liquidity trap that now exists in credit creation and will neutralize the short-run deflationary effects of higher saving. Finally, the macroeconomic record suggests the interesting possibility that a clear commitment to a restructuring strategy based on promoting the convergence of China's economic institutions to the norms of modern market economies improves the short-term tradeoff between growth and inflation.

This paper is organized as follows. Section 7.2 presents the case for economic restructuring. Section 7.3 analyzes the macroeconomic record. Section 7.4 evaluates the post-1997 reflation package. Section 7.5 takes up the question of the susceptibility of China to the type of financial crisis that had hit Asia in 1997–98. Section 7.6 examines the issue of under-consumption and the need for financial restructuring, especially in the rural sector, if China's high growth is to be prolonged. Section 7.7 discusses the issues surrounding the reform of the SOEs. Section 7.8 contains brief concluding remarks.

7.2 The Restructuring Imperative

The successful completion of the bilateral U.S.–China negotiations in November 1999 over the conditions of China's entry into the World Trade Organization (WTO) marks a watershed on many fronts for China. First and foremost, admission into the WTO marks an important improvement in the economic security of China. Trade and foreign investment have constituted an important engine of growth since 1978. The requirement for annual renewal by the U.S. Congress of China's normal trading relationship with the United States made China's economic growth vulnerable to the vagaries of American domestic politics. Through WTO membership, this engine of growth could no longer be unilaterally shut off by the United States without the action being a major violation of international law.

WTO membership also marks a watershed in China's public recognition of the primary source of its impressive growth in the last two decades. The WTO is an international economic organization that specifies and enforces broadly similar economic policy regimes on its membership. China's willingness to join such an institution reflects more than a desire to protect itself from potential blackmail by the United States; it also reflects China's realization that the active ingredient in Deng Xiaoping's recipe for growth was the convergence of China's economic institutions to the economic institutions of modern capitalist economies, particularly of East Asian capitalist economies.

At the early stages of China's reform, when most of the intelligentsia did not know the full extent of the economic achievements of their capitalist neighbors, and when most of the top leaders were ideologically committed to Stalinist-style communism, it was important for the survival of the reformist faction of that time that the changes to China's economic institutions were comfortingly gradual, conveniently located in areas far from Beijing, and cloaked in the chauvinistic rhetoric of "experimentation to discover new institutional forms that are optimal for China's socialist system and particular economic circumstances." After 20 years of evolution in economic institutions, of rotation in political leadership, and of tectonic change in the political fortune of the communist parties in Eastern Europe and the former Soviet Union, the only organized opposition today to the continued convergence of China's economic institutions to international forms comes from a few sentimental Stalinists such as Deng Liqun.[1] The social and political landscape in China has changed so much that the political leadership now incurs only minimal ideological liability when they introduce more capitalist incentives (e.g., differentiated pay, leveraged buy-outs, and stock options for managers) and capitalist tools (e.g., joint-stock companies, bankruptcy laws and unemployment insurance). The leadership is hence confident that its explicit embrace of capitalist institutions under WTO auspices would be seen by the general Chinese public (and the Chinese elite) as a step forward in the reform process rather than as surrender of China's sovereignty in economic experimentation.[2]

---

1. For recent warnings from this faction against perceived suicide by the Communist Party, see "Elder warns on economic change," *South China Morning Post*, January 13, 2000, and "Leftists make late bid to slow reforms," *South China Morning Post*, February 10, 2000.
2. Unfortunately, this de facto public recognition by the government that the *deus ex machina* of China's impressive growth since 1978 is the convergence of its economic institutions to those of market economies will not end the academic debate on this issue. Many China specialists have waxed eloquently about how China's experimentation has created economic institutions that are optimally suited for transition economies in general; see Sachs and Woo (forthcoming) for a survey of this debate.

It must be underscored that WTO membership will involve considerable costs to China. China has agreed to reduce its industrial tariffs
from an average of 24.6 percent to 9.4 percent by 2005, and its agricultural tariffs from an average of 31.5 percent to 14.5 percent by 2004.
China has also agreed to liberalize trade in many services, including
telecommunications, insurance and banking. Compliance with WTO
rules will create substantial dislocation in China, albeit for the sake of a
better future. China is a natural food-importer and a natural factory-
oriented society given its low land-man ratio. The agricultural sector
employs over 332 million people, which amounts to over two-thirds of
the rural labor force. China's SOEs employ over 40 percent of the urban
labor force, but most of these firms survive only because of various
forms of subsidies and import barriers, and such instruments contravene WTO regulations. The agricultural sector and the state sector
together employed 60 percent of the total labor force in 1998. Conservatively, a fifth of China's workers may have to change jobs, and this
could be a politically destabilizing process if not handled adeptly, and if
external shocks were to slow down economic growth.

The tradeoff between stability and restructuring that is so starkly
brought to the forefront by China's (forthcoming) admission into the
WTO is not a new tradeoff. China's WTO membership has accentuated
an existing dilemma rather than introduced a new one. The government
has always realized that the soft budget constraint of the inefficient
state-owned enterprise sector is a constant threat to price stability, and
the diversion of resources to keep this sector afloat is a drag on economic growth. But serious restructuring of SOEs means much more than
facing higher urban unemployment, it also means confronting the
politically powerful industrial-military complex and the industrial-
bureaucratic complex. Economic rents now pose a bigger obstacle to
restructuring than ideological sentimentality, and the rents, unlike the
ideology, will not lose their power with the mere passing of time.

Luckily for China, the job of restructuring had been made easier
because China's economic structure could allow growth to occur without much restructuring in the early years of the reform. This is because
China, in 1978, was still an undeveloped economy dominated by self-
subsistence peasant agriculture, unlike the urbanized Central European
and Russian economies in 1989, which had an overabundance of heavy
industries. This meant that the introduction of market forces caused
economic development in China but economic restructuring in Poland

and Russia, which translated, respectively, into output growth and output decline.[3]

The movement of Chinese labor from low-productivity agriculture to higher-productivity industry, and from the poor inland provinces to the richer coastal provinces, produced an average annual growth rate of 10 percent in 1978–95. The Chinese state sector certainly did not wither away in this period; it employed 18.6 percent of the workforce in 1978 and 18.0 percent in 1995, and there were 38 million more state workers in 1995 than in 1978.[4] There was reallocation of labor from agriculture to industry, but not reallocation of labor from state to non-state enterprises. China in 1978 was thence very different from Russia in 1991: extensive growth was still possible in China, but it had run its course in Russia.[5]

Since China was in the fortunate situation of being able to postpone most of the pain of restructuring, it was quite understandable that China did so. The result is that after two decades of "reform and open-ing," the job of economic restructuring is far from done. The following are some of the many daunting problems that remain:

• a government sector that is still too large (despite recent reductions in the central bureaucracy), too intrusive, and susceptible to corruption;

• a state-owned enterprise system that has proved itself resistant to numerous efforts to increase its efficiency and profitability;

• a state-dominated financial system in which the banks lack the ability to assess the economic merits of proposed projects, and, worse, have shied away from lending to non-state enterprises, the most dynamic component of the economy; and

• lack of established institutional infrastructure that allows smooth running of a market economy; for example, an efficient commercial court system, speedy bankruptcy procedures, independent mechanisms to mediate labor conflict, uniform accounting standards, and social safety nets.

---

3. This argument is developed in Sachs and Woo (1994).
4. The 18.0 percent for 1995 is calculated from the *China Statistical Yearbook 1996* because the total workforce data from 1990 onward was revised upward in the China Statistical Yearbook of the succeeding years by increasing the size of the rural workforce. The revised data are inconsistent across time. The growth in labor force between 1989 and 1990 is now 15.5 percent (!), while the old data show an increase of 2.5 percent. Using the revised data, the SOEs employed 17 percent of the total labor force.
5. Easterley and Fischer (1994) showed that extensive growth came to a quicker end in Russia than would have occurred in capitalist market economies because the elasticity of substitution between capital and labor in Russia was much lower.

It was only after the ascent of Zhu Rongji to the prime ministership in early 1998 that a decisive program of restructuring was implemented. The size of the central government was cut by a third, and the process of privatizing many small and medium enterprises was speeded up. Twenty million workers left the payroll of state-owned units in 1998 compared to two million in 1997. This represented an 18-percent reduction in state employment in one year![6] Now that China is entering the WTO, it can no longer postpone the required restructuring of the inefficient components of its economy. However, the restructuring job was made more difficult in the last two and a half years because of negative external shocks. The Asian financial crisis caused Chinese exports to East and Southeast Asia to decline tremendously, and Chinese exports to North America and Western Europe to face increased competition from the Asian countries whose currencies had fallen in value against the renminbi (RMB). Foreign direct investments amounted to $40 billion in 1999, down from $45 million in 1998. The result was a GDP growth rate of 7.8 percent in 1998 and 7.1 percent in 1999, despite the government's vigorous attempts to reflate the economy since mid-1998.

7.3   The Macroeconomic Situation

Figure 7.1 summarizes the growth and inflation record since 1978, when China embarked on the first steps toward a market economy. There have been two episodes of high inflation, 1988–89 and 1993–95, when the inflation rate exceeded 10 percent. It is interesting that the output cost of wringing out inflation was very different in each episode. The drop in inflation from 18.8 percent in 1988 to 3.1 percent in 1990 was accompanied by a 7-percentage-point drop in the growth rate; whereas the drop in inflation from 24.1 percent in 1994 to 2.8 percent in 1997 saw less than a 4-percentage-point drop in the growth rate.

---

6. This is such a large shift that it raises the discomforting thought that some of the shift may be a mere change in employment classification without change in work conditions; however, we cannot go into this issue here.

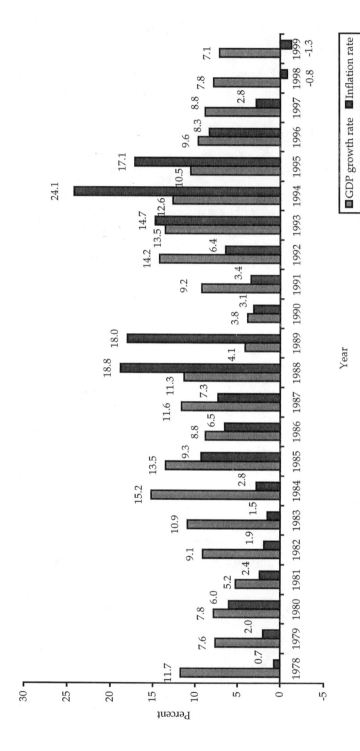

Figure 7.1
Growth and inflation in China (1978–1999)

Table 7.4
China: Tracking economic developments

	1997:Q1	1997:Q2	1997:Q3	1997:Q4	1998:Q1	1998:Q2	1998:Q3	1998:Q4	1999:Q1	1999:Q2
Growth rate of real GDP (%)	9.4	9.6	8.1	8.4	7.2	7.0	7.4	9.1	8.3	7.1
Exchange rate (against US$)	8.3	8.3	8.3	8.3	8.3	8.3	8.3	8.3	8.3	8.3
Real exchange rate (1990 = 100, WPI based)	80.3	81.4	79.1	76.2	74.1	73.1	74.2	74.2	76.9	77.5
International reserves minus gold (US$ million)	113,349	122,211	135,420	142,165	143,390	143,367	145,016	149,188	150,497	150,565
Reserve money growth (%)	28.9	33.5	30.6	17.0	8.9	11.2	0.1	2.8	0.8	-4.7
Narrow money growth rate (%)	27.5	29.5	26.1	25.0	13.0	10.3	14.3	12.7	12.2	12.0
Broad money growth rate (%)	24.8	23.0	20.7	20.7	15.8	14.3	16.2	14.9	16.3	16.3
CPI growth rate (YOY%)	5.2	2.9	2.1	1.0	0.0	-0.9	-1.4	-1.1	-1.4	-2.2
Nominal lending rate (%)	10.1	10.1	10.1	8.6	8.0	8.0	6.9	6.4	6.4	5.9
Nominal deposit rate (%)	7.5	7.5	7.5	5.7	5.2	5.2	4.8	3.8	3.8	2.3
Export value (US$ million)	35,585	45,360	48,173	53,759	40,072	46,488	47,190	49,839	37,290	45,727
Import value (US$ million)	28,804	33,998	35,370	44,017	29,453	34,834	34,386	41,632	33,022	41,980
DS stock market index ($)	596.7	608.6	578.6	628.1	615.3	575.3	498.7	517	517	818
DS stock market index (national currency)	912.2	929.8	883.3	958.3	938.8	877.8	760.9	788.7	788.8	1,247.9
Shanghai Composite Index	1,234.6	1,250.3	1,097.4	1,194.1	1,243.0	1,339.2	1,242.9	1,146.7	1,158.0	1,689.4

Table 7.5
Sources of aggregate demand in China in reform period, 1978–1998. Percentage point contribution to GDP growth rate by each expenditure category

	Annual GDP growth rate	Rural household consumption	Urban household consumption	Government consumption	Fixed capital formation	Change in inventory	Net exports	Total household consumption
1979–98	9.8	2.4	2.3	1.2	3.3	0.3	0.2	4.7
1988	11.3	3.1	4.1	0.4	3.2	1.7	-1.2	7.2
1989	4.1	0.7	1.3	1.1	-4.0	5.2	-0.1	2.0
1990	3.8	-0.8	0.7	0.4	0.5	-1.0	4.0	-0.1
1991	9.2	0.9	2.2	2.2	4.7	-1.3	0.4	3.2
1992	14.2	2.5	4.0	2.1	8.8	-1.6	-1.7	6.5
1993	13.5	0.5	2.9	1.3	10.5	1.5	-3.3	3.4
1994	12.6	2.1	2.7	1.4	3.0	-0.1	3.5	4.7
1995	10.5	2.9	3.4	-0.2	2.2	1.6	0.5	6.3
1996	9.6	3.7	1.9	1.2	2.7	-0.4	0.6	5.5
1997	8.8	1.3	2.2	1.2	2.4	-0.4	2.0	3.6
1998	7.8	0.6	2.7	1.2	4.5	-1.4	0.3	3.3

What accounted for the drastically more favorable tradeoff between growth and inflation in the second episode? In statistical analysis not reported here, we found that the differences in the inflation and growth performance across the two episodes could not be systemically linked to differences in the credit polices that started and then ended the two periods of high inflation. My hypothesis for the different tradeoffs in these two episodes is that consumers' confidence and investors' confidence about China's future were very different in the two stabilization programs. The 1989–90 stabilization occurred amid widespread doubt about whether the movement toward a market economy would continue, if not reverse. Following the unfortunate Tianamen tragedy in June 1989, economic policy-making returned to the hands of the central planners, and numerous announcements were made about reining in capitalist tendencies. The implementation of the 1994–97 stabilization, in contrast, occurred after the 14th Party Congress in 1992 had pledged to build "a socialist market economy with Chinese characteristics." This denial of a universal norm for socialism was correctly read as renewed commitment by the Communist Party toward convergence to a market economy.

Our hypothesis is that this difference in anticipation about the future direction of China's economic policy had very different effects on the behavior of consumers and investors. The heightened confidence in a prosperous future was responsible in large part for why fixed capital formation contributed over 2 percentage points to GDP growth in 1996–97, compared to –1.7 percentage points in 1989–90, and why consumption spending contributed an average 4.5 percentage points to growth in 1996–97 versus 1 percentage point in 1989–90 (see table 7.5).

Since inflation in 1996 was down to 8.3 percent from 24.2 percent in 1994, and the 1996 growth rate of 9.5 percent almost equaled the average 10-percent growth rate of the 1978–95 period, one could say that the Chinese stabilization program that started in mid-1993 had achieved a soft landing in 1996. Some observers have used this reasoning to describe the continuation of tight macroeconomic policies until early 1998 as a case of "macroeconomic policy overkill." While the precipitous plunge in money (M1) growth from an inflationary 43 percent in 1993 to 20 percent in 1996 was desirable, the further drop to 10 percent in 1998:2Q was an overkill, as evidenced by the fall in the level of retail prices since October 1997.[7]

---

7. Prices fell except in August and September 1998, when severe flooding disrupted supplies in several heavily populated parts of the country.

We do not dispute the macroeconomic consequences of the tight monetary policies and the tight controls over investment spending before mid-1998, but we note that these restrictive policies had succeeded in forcing considerable restructuring in the inefficient SOE sector. Because most loss-making SOEs did not receive their accustomed allotments of credit to continue production (a large portion of which went straight into inventory), the default outcome was that many were taken over by new owners[8] who reorganized the firms and changed the output mix. Our point is that a temporary slowdown in growth is often necessary to force resources to move to a new growth path that will lead to a more competitive economy. We also should recognize in the so-called "macroeconomic policy overkill" the audacity of the top Chinese leadership: they boldly chose dislocating reforms, which would produce sustained dynamic growth in the future, over Brezhnev-style maintenance of the comfortable status quo, which would ensure a dismal future.

In short, the "macroeconomic policy overkill" from 1997:1Q to 1998:2Q reflected a deliberate decision to accept growth rates that were lower than the 10-percent average growth rate of the 1978-95 period in order to ensure an acceptable rate of economic restructuring and to moderate the boom-bust cycles of the last two decades. The implicit growth range that policy makers appear to regard as compatible with achieving the restructuring and stabilization objectives seems to be about 7.0 to 8.0 percent. When the Asian financial crisis hit in 1998, causing China's exports to fall, and hence rendering growth lower than intended, it was only natural that the government undertook stimulation of domestic demand to reflate the economy.

7.4   Responding to the Post-1997 Deflation

The government responded to the onset of price deflation in 1997:4Q by cutting the average lending rate from 10.1 percent to 8.6 percent. However, the anticipated surge in credit expansion did not occur. This is largely because of the newfound reluctance of the state commercial banks to extend more credit to its traditional clients, the SOEs (especially the loss-making SOEs). This "liquidity trap" phenomenon will be discussed below.

---

8. In many cases, the new owners were employees of the firms.

By early 1998, in the wake of the collapse of several important Pacific Asian economies, Chinese policy makers recognized that stronger reflation was required to offset the coming collapse in external demand. Furthermore, the SOE reform program announced at the 15th Party Congress in September 1997 was beginning to take effect, and firms would soon begin to shed excess workers. So, stronger reflation was also desirable to induce the establishment of new urban enterprises to soak up the newly released SOE workers.

The reflation program sought to boost aggregate demand by trying to:

- increase investment by approving faster the backlog of investment applications,
- increase government spending,
- loosen monetary policy, and
- stimulate private spending through housing reform.

Faster Approval of Investment Applications

The State Planning Commission was literally put on an overtime schedule in early 1998 to speed up the approval of investment projects. "Increased economic openness" was a fortuitous by-product of this measure. Approval was given to a number of large foreign projects that had been held up for several years because of concern either about the possible domination of these particular lines of business by foreign firms or about the possible competition that they might provide to domestic firms of national strategic importance.

One unexpected check on approval acceleration as a reflation tool was that many local governments had not bothered to turn in local investment plans for 1998 because of the across-the-board rejection of local investment plans since the earnest implementation of the stabilization program in 1994. However, the greatest obstacles to the effectiveness of investment approval as an economic stimulus are conditions or events that interfere with actual investment. The translation of approval of investment into realization of investment is usually low in times of declining aggregate demand. Hence, not surprisingly, many foreign and domestic firms postponed their actual investment until sustained economic recovery seemed imminent. Actual foreign direct investment (FDI) was US$40 billion in 1999, 10 percent down from US$45 billion in 1998, despite the "increased economic openness" noted above, in part because of the low aggregate demand in China and abroad, but mostly because of panic in international credit markets.[9]

Expansionary Fiscal Policy

In July 1998, the government announced the issuance of RMB100 billion in bonds to finance *new* infrastructure investment by the central and local governments. (It seems that these bonds had been purchased mainly by state banks.) This announcement was quickly followed by new spending plans on telecommunications, railways and roads. The economy continued to slow steadily throughout 1999, so the government implemented a new fiscal stimulus package of RMB60 billion in August 1999. In March 2000, the government announced that it would soon issue RMB100 billion of bonds to finance additional infrastructure investment, especially in the interior provinces.[10]

A natural question raised by the recent expansionary fiscal policy is whether the public debt in China is still at a level that will not impose too heavy a burden in the future. The issue is what should be counted as "public debt," when so much of the economy is still state owned. If public debt is defined to be the stock of government bonds that has been issued to finance budget deficits (and held by both domestic and foreign agents), then the public debt-GDP ratio was 7.3 percent of GDP in 1996 and 8.1 percent in 1997.

It has been argued, however, that since the government is the guarantor of the state banks, the non-performing loans of the state banks ought to be counted as public debt. Estimates of the extent of non-performing loans range from 20 to 50 percent of total bank loans.[11] If we take the NPL ratio to be 33 percent, then the broader definition of public debt would put the "broader public debt"-GDP ratio at 37.0 percent of GDP in 1996 and 41.1 percent in 1997.

What about the debt of SOEs and other state institutions (for example, the regional trust and investment companies, TICs)? The government could be construed as being responsible for these bad debts, just

---

9. "Foreign capital off the rails," *South China Morning Post*, February 16, 2000.
10. "Zhu pledges to keep cash flowing," *South China Morning Post*, March 6, 2000.
11. This range reflects our selection of credible estimates (e.g., a missed interest payment does not necessarily mean that the loan is bad), so this range does not encompass all estimates that have been reported in the press. For example, Bloomburg News has reported that some analysts believed bad loans to be 70 percent of bad loans ("China hopes to sell bad loans at discount," *New York Times*, January 5, 1999).

as they were construed to be responsible for the bad debts held by the banks. Since the bulk of the *domestic* borrowing of SOEs and state institutions is from the state banks, the inclusion of non-performing loans of the state banks in the broader definition of public debt has already taken into account the bad debts of SOEs and state institutions that are owed to domestic agents.

Foreign debts of SOEs and other state institutions may deserve different treatment than their domestic debts because of the government's great concern about China's continued access to international financial markets at favorable interest rates. To arrive at the "broadest" definition of public debt, we took into account all the bad debts that SOEs and other state institutions could *potentially* owe to foreigners. We constructed the "maximum" public debt as the sum of the broader public debt plus the entire foreign debt of SOEs and public institutions. The "maximum public debt"-GDP ratio was 50.1 percent of GDP in 1996 and 55.1 percent in 1997.[12]

Is a debt-GDP ratio of 55.1 percent too low or too high? The Italian, Swedish and U.S. central government debt (after deducting intra-governmental debt) to GDP ratios were, respectively, 117.6 percent in 1995, 70.8 percent in 1995, and 50.5 percent in 1996. Thus, it might appear that there is still substantial room for the Chinese government to increase its borrowing to finance its expansionary fiscal policy without causing serious debt problems in the future. However, such a conclusion would be overly optimistic, because China raises much less state revenue (as a share of GDP) than these other countries, and hence has a much lower capacity to service its public debt. The revenue-GDP ratio was 11 percent for China in 1995, 30 percent for Italy in 1995, 38 percent for Sweden in 1995, and 21 percent for the U.S. in 1996. The point is that until China increases its tax collection, there is a real tradeoff between restructuring the state financial sector and increasing infrastructure investment to stimulate the economy. In addition, it is important to note that increasing tax collection is as much a political challenge as it is an administrative challenge.

---

12. The terms "broader public debt" and "maximum public debt" are from Fan (1998). He differs from my calculations in that he assumes a NPL ratio of 25 percent.

Easier Monetary Policy

The People's Bank of China has cut interest rates several times since price deflation became obvious. For example, the bank lending rate has been reduced steadily from 10.1 percent in September 1997 to 5.9 percent in September 1999. Furthermore, the bank reserve ratio has been lowered twice: from 13 percent to 8 percent in March 1998 and then to 6 percent in November 1999. However, the money (M1) growth rate continued its downward course from 25 percent in 1997:3Q and 1997:4Q to 13 percent in 1998:1Q, and then to 10 percent in 1998:2Q, prompting some Chinese economists, like their Japanese colleagues, to postulate the existence of liquidity traps.

This reluctance by banks to extend credit has its origin in the determined efforts of Zhu Rongji to improve the balance sheets of the state banks and to promote restructuring in the SOE sector since he took over as economic czar in mid-1993. By the end of 1997, the twin facts that Zhu Rongji would be promoted to become the Prime Minister in 1998 and that he had peremptorily dismissed bank managers when the proportion of NPLs in their banks had gone up had instilled a new sense of prudent lending in the entire state banking system. Until the typical bank manager faced personally severe consequences from an increase in the ratio of NPLs, he never had to respond to the knowledge that the demand for credit by bankrupt SOEs was always high because they really do not expect to repay any of their debts. The loss-making SOEs were engaging in the gamble of the desperate; new loans offered the only chance of a lucky investment that would pull them out of their seemingly hopeless financial straits. This new behavior by bank managers is the reason that money growth continued to drop in line with the decline in GDP growth, despite additional reductions in interest rates and required reserve ratios by the central bank.

This slowdown in loans to the SOEs has unfortunately not been replaced by an increase in loans to non-state enterprises, the primary engine of growth in China's economy. The state banks are reluctant to lend to the non-state enterprises, partly because the latter's non-standard accounting makes risk assessments difficult. More importantly, a banker knows that while an NPL to an SOE is financially undesirable, an NPL to a private enterprise is more than that: it is politically undesirable. The banker feared that the NPL to a private firm could result in him being accused afterward of working with capitalists to embezzle the state. Thus, we have the present situation where the loans that state banks are most willing to make are infrastructure loans guaranteed by the central government.

Money growth increased to 14 percent in 1998:3Q only after the central bank implicitly assured the banks in mid-1998 that new NPLs incurred in support of SOEs that were producing saleable goods would be overlooked. But then caution reasserted itself as bank managers were rightly skeptical about the government's assurance that the new NPLs would not count against them in the future. The result was that money growth, after the 14 percent spurt in 1998:3Q, declined steadily to 11.3 percent in 1999:3Q.

Hence, the practical short-run solution to this "liquidity trap" is for the government to undertake *new* infrastructure spending financed by the state banks (and ultimately by new reserves from the central bank). However, a larger sustained increase in credit is possible only if the state commercial banks use the new deposits (new reserves) to extend new loans, i.e., only if banks act according to the standard "money multiplier" process. As the banks' willingness to lend depends now on finding economically viable projects, the government has sought to create new safe-lending opportunities to the banks by announcing housing reforms, including privatization of the housing stock. The hope is that the banks would then expand mortgage lending, because the household debt would be fully (and, presumably, also safely) backed by a marketable asset, and hence lead to a boost in aggregate demand.

Housing Reform as a Short-Run Stimulus

Until very recently, the majority of the urban population has lived in virtually free housing supplied by their employers.[13] In early 1998, the government announced that SOEs and other state institutions would stop providing free housing after July 1 and the housing stock would be privatized.[14] To compensate for the loss of free housing, and to encourage their workers to buy the houses that they are presently staying in, many local governments are giving subsidized mortgages to civil

---

13. Of course, housing and other subsidies are in fact largely paid for by the employees themselves; this is why their take-home pay is so low.
14. The practical method of privatizing the housing stock is to offer the houses to the existing tenants at prices which approximate the present discounted value of the stream of low rent payments. By giving the existing tenants the right of first refusal, this method makes explicit whatever existing inequality there is in housing allocation. This method does not create new inequalities.

servants. By the end of 2000, government workers had purchased 60 percent of the public housing stock.[15] The marketization of housing is now in full swing, marking another significant milestone on the way to a market economy. The marketization of housing will enhance labor mobility and free the SOEs to focus on production and distribution of goods.

China Macroeconomic Analysis (1998:3Q issue) estimated that, with a functioning mortgage system in place, the marketization of housing would increase the annual demand for housing by 20 to 30 percent. Since housing investment is presently about 4.3 percent of GDP, the housing reform would increase GDP growth by 1 percentage point.[16]

However, in our assessment, the short-run result of the housing reform was a decrease in aggregate demand, even though the new steady-state level of housing demand under the market regime is higher than the old steady-state level of housing demand under the entitlement regime. Several reasons account for the decrease in aggregate demand. First, the demand for new residential construction by SOEs stopped abruptly on July 1, 1998, and because it takes time for private agencies to appear to intermediate between the builders and the millions of disparate buyers, the immediate impact was more likely to have been a drop in housing demand than an increase. Second, the mortgage system is not yet in place. The banks need time to build up expertise in mortgage lending, and the certification/registration system of house ownership is usually not standardized province-wide. More importantly, at the moment, only the richest 5 to 10 percent of the urban population can qualify for mortgage loans; and these well-to-do folks are likely to have already acquired most of the housing that they want.

Results of the Reflation Package

The reflation package has worked much better than was expected by most observers. When the negative effects of the Asian financial crisis started hitting in early 1998 and slowed China's GDP growth, most observers steadily revised their forecasts of 1998 growth downward.

---

15. "Civil servants own 60% of public housing," *The Straits Times*, February 24, 2000.
16. The Minister of Construction has claimed that the housing reform contributed 1.5 to 2 percentage points to the 1999 growth rate; see "Civil servants own 60% of public housing," *The Straits Times*, February 24, 2000. The construction of housing might contributed this amount, but the relevant question is whether the housing reform had actually increased the amount of construction. We doubt this claim for the reasons given in the paragraphs below.

For example, the Economist Intelligence Unit's (EIU) Country Report on China predicted a 1998 growth rate of 7.3 percent in the 1998:1Q issue, 6.7 percent in the 1998:2Q issue, and then 6.1 percent in the 1998:3Q issue. The credit spurt and investment splurge in the last half of 1998 disappointed all these forecasts by lifting GDP growth to 7.6 percent in 1998:3Q and 9.6 percent in 1998:4Q, to produce an annual growth rate of 7.8 percent for 1998. The decomposition of aggregate demand in table 7.5 shows that fixed capital formation added 4.5 percentage points to the 1998 growth rate.

However, given the widespread expectation that the Asian financial crisis would be long-lasting, and the skepticism about China's ability to undertake sustained fiscal stimulus, the EIU continued to predict low growth rates for 1999 despite the falsification of its gloomy forecasts for 1998. The 1999:3Q issue predicted a 1999 growth rate of 6.7 percent. The actual 1999 growth rate turned out to be 7.1 percent, partly due to the additional fiscal and monetary stimulus in the last quarter, and partly due to the rapid recovery of exports in response to the end of the Asian financial crisis.

Several observers believe that the official growth numbers are wrong, and that actual growth in 1998 was between 3 and 5 percent. The basis of this skepticism is the low usage of electricity, the low volume of goods being transported, and the continued fall in the level of retail prices. The well-known Chinese economist, Mao Yushi, was quoted as saying: "The GDP figure is still dubious. ... There must be some local government trying to please the central government by reporting inflated statistics." [17] Mao Yushi's statements are credible because Premier Zhu had criticized provincial leaders in early December for having reported their provincial growth rates to be greater than 10 percent in the first half of 1998, when the national growth rate was only 7.2 percent. [18]

The 1999 growth rate of 7.1 percent, low as it is, also deserves skepticism for the same reasons. First, only two provinces, Shanxi and Sichuan, have reported growth rates below 7.1 percent. Second, the sum of all individually reported provincial GDP figures exceeded the official national GDP by 7 percent. [19]

---

17. "China just misses 8 percent growth rate," *South China Morning Post*, December 30, 1998.
18. "China admits to cooking the books: editorial," *Agence France Presse*, December 23, 1998.
19. "Beijing has $546b chasm in key data," *South China Morning Post*, February 29, 2000.

Table 7.6
Export earnings (fob, in US$ million)

	Q1	Q2	Q3	Q4	Year total
1996	28,249	35,803	39,979	47,166	151,197
1997	35,585	45,360	48,173	53,759	182,877
1998	40,072	46,488	47,190	49,839	183,589
1999	37,290	45,727	54,201	n.a.	n.a.

In Woo (1998), we found that the annual GDP growth rate in the 1985–93 period could have been overstated, on average, by as much as 2 percentage points; and, after taking various factors into account, we suggested a downward correction of about 1 percentage point. The overstatement is less serious, however, when the inflation rate is low. In light of our work, the negative inflation, and the skepticism expressed in the two preceding paragraphs, we think that the actual GDP growth rate could plausibly be about 7 percent in 1998 and around 6.5 percent in 1999.

Table 7.6 compares exports in each quarter to the level in the same quarter of the previous year. It shows that the negative effects from the Asian financial crisis reached their peak in the 1998:3Q to 1999:2Q. With the recovery of the Asian crisis economies in 1999, China's exports leaped to $54 billion in 1999:3Q. Since the Asian crisis countries are expected to continue their economic expansion in 2000, China now has more room to undertake continued restructuring.

7.5 Susceptibility of China to a Financial Crisis

The Asian financial crisis was typified by a collapse of the exchange rate because of heavy capital outflow, and a collapse of the domestic financial system causing a shortage of working capital that, in turn, caused output to collapse. So how vulnerable is China to a meltdown scenario of this type?

A dramatic speculative attack on the renminbi can be ruled out, simply because the renminbi is not convertible for capital account transactions in financial assets. It is difficult for an individual to borrow renminbi from a Chinese bank to buy U.S. dollars to speculate against the exchange rate, because the purchase of U.S. dollars requires documentation to prove that the transaction is trade-related.

Capital outflow by foreign private agents has not occurred because most of the foreign private investments in China are foreign direct investments, and there is very little short-term foreign debt. At the end of 1999, short-term foreign debt was less than 20 percent of the total foreign debt of US$168 billion. The fact that China also had US$155 billion in foreign exchange reserves made defense of the exchange rate feasible even if all short-term foreign debts had been recalled.

Furthermore, foreign participation in the Chinese stock markets is limited to transaction in B-shares. Only foreigners can own B-shares, and B-shares are denominated in U.S. dollars and transacted using U.S. dollars. In short, an abrupt withdrawal by foreigners from the Chinese stock markets can affect the value of the yuan-dominated A-shares (which only Chinese can own) only if such withdrawal would cause Chinese speculators to revise their expectations of future Chinese growth downward.

Of course, capital flight can occur through channels such as over-invoicing of imports and under-invoicing of exports. A successful speculative attack on the renminbi via large and pervasive mis-invoicing is theoretically possible, but it would be difficult to prove because the paper trail would point to trade imbalance rather than portfolio adjustment as the cause of the exchange rate collapse. An exchange rate collapse from mis-invoicing of trade requires that the government be rigidly committed to current account convertibility, but this is not credible. Any government (e.g., China's) that has in place a comprehensive administrative system that processes every import application to buy foreign exchange (to prevent capital movements) can easily defend the exchange rate by delaying approvals of import applications. So imports could be compressed to a significant degree whenever a trade deficit threatens to materialize.

We turn now to the issue of whether China's banking system would collapse spectacularly as in the countries experiencing the Asian financial crisis. When the won, baht and rupiah went into free fall, many Korean, Thai and Indonesian banks were rendered insolvent through a combination of the following channels: the sudden increase in the value (measured in domestic currency) of their foreign liabilities; the default on bank loans by domestic corporations bankrupted by the soaring of their external debts; and the default on bank loans by exporters who could not get short-term credit from their foreign suppliers of inputs. Many of the Korean, Thai and Indonesian banks were already financially fragile before their collapse because of under-capitalization, and because of considerable NPLs that had been hidden by accounting gimmicks. The exchange rate shock pushed these fragile banks over the brink.

Much alarm has been raised in recent months about the amount of NPLs in China's banking system, with estimates for NPLs ranging from 20 to 50 percent of total bank loans. Some analysts have suggested as a serious possibility that a run by depositors is almost inevitable, causing a banking collapse that would trigger a general output decline.

We find the likelihood of either bank runs or a collapse of the banking system to be minimal. Admittedly, there have been bank runs in China since 1978, e.g., in 1988. But these bank runs were motivated by anticipations of high inflation caused by imminent lifting of price controls, and not by anticipations of bank failures. Whenever the government began indexing interest payments to the inflation rate, the bank runs reversed themselves. In the present time of falling prices, inflation-induced bank runs will not occur.

Admittedly, there is no depositor insurance in China, but this in itself is unlikely to cause a bank run induced by fear over the large amount of NPLs. This is because all but one of the banks are state owned and the government has repeatedly pledged to honor all deposits in the state banks. This pledge is credible because the government is in a position to make good its promise. As pointed out earlier, the government can easily borrow to cover the NPLs; and assuming an NPL ratio of 33 percent, the borrowing would raise the public debt-GDP ratio to just 40 percent. Alternatively, the government could always raise taxes to cover the NPLs.

Even if a bank run does occur, there need not be a collapse in bank credit, because the central bank could just issue currency to the state banks to meet the withdrawals. This expansion of high-power money cannot be easily translated into a loss of foreign reserves because capital controls are in place. This expansion of high-power money will also not have much impact on inflation because this is mainly a shift out of bank deposits into cash, and not a shift into goods.

Simply put, even if the state banks are truly insolvent, as has been alleged, and even if the insolvency does induce bank runs, a collapse in bank credit does not have to follow. It is well within the technical ability of the government to accommodate the bank runs, and it is also well within the financial ability of the government to recapitalize the state banks. Furthermore, these two government actions would not cause much (if any) damage to the economy, such as lower growth and higher inflation.

While China can prevent the NPLs of the state banks from maiming the payments system and crippling production, we recognize that the NPLs have imposed real costs on the economy. With NPLs accounting for a third of total bank loans (our estimate), bank loans accounting for about a fifth of fixed investments since 1985, and fixed investments at about 35 percent of GDP, this means that about 2.3 percent of GDP has been wasted annually in the last decade. Moreover, since most of the bank loans are extended to SOEs, with little going to the more efficient non-state sector, the performing loans are not in investments with the highest rates of return. In short, the productive capacity of the economy could be higher than it is.

Of course, we also recognize that the NPL problem might be even worse at the non-bank financial institutions (NBFIs) such as the regional TICs.[20] However, because NBFIs constitute only a small part of the national credit system, their failure is not capable of bringing down the payments system. The biggest dangers from the collapse of NBFIs are social instability (especially when the base of NBFIs is small depositors) and reduction in foreign credit.

After the 1998 closure of the financial arm of the Guangdong International Trust and Investment Company (GITIC), the central government assumed responsibility for all properly registered foreign debt. Since trade-related credit with maturity of less than three months and foreign debts of GITIC's branch in Hong Kong did not require official Registration, it is likely that a very substantial amount of GITIC's foreign debt will not be assumed by the Chinese government. In October 1999, GITIC's liquidation committee reported that, after rejecting illegal contingent guarantees issued by GITIC, the total liabilities had been reduced from US$4.7 billion to the range of US$1.7 billion to US$2.7 billion. The value of recoverable assets was put at US$0.9 billion.[21]

---

20. According to the *Far Eastern Economic Review* ("Tic Fever: China's shaky trust and investment houses start to fall," October 22, 1998), "most of the country's 243 Tics are on the rocks." Lardy (1998b) reported the claim that 50 percent of the assets of the non-bank financial sector was non-performing.

21. "Illegal Gitic deals delay payout," *South China Morning Post*, October 23, 1999.

Table 7.7
Consumption shifts in China in reform period, 1978–1998

Part A: Expenditure category as proportion of GDP, 1978–1998

	Rural household consumption	Urban household consumption	Government consumption	Fixed capital formation	Change in inventory	Net exports	Total household consumption	Rural share of population
1978	30.3	18.5	13.3	29.8	8.4	-0.3	48.8	82.1
1988	30.4	21.5	11.7	31.4	5.9	-1.0	51.9	74.2
1998	22.1	24.1	11.9	35.3	2.8	3.8	46.2	69.6
Period 1: 1979–83	32.6	19.0	14.4	27.6	6.1	0.4	51.6	79.7
Period 2: 1984–88	31.9	19.5	13.1	30.7	6.3	-1.5	51.4	75.5
Period 3: 1989–93	26.5	22.2	12.9	30.0	7.7	0.7	48.7	73.0
Period 4: 1994–98	22.8	23.3	11.9	34.8	4.7	2.6	46.1	70.5

Part B: Decomposition of the change in the consumption-GDP ratio

	Change in consumption-GDP ratio	Percentage point change in consumption-GDP ratio due to:		
		Rural-urban shift	Consumption shift	Interaction effects
Rural sector				
Change between 1978 and 1998	-8.2	-4.6	-4.2	0.6
Change between periods 1 and 4	-9.7	-3.8	-6.7	0.8
Urban sector				
Change between 1978 and 1998	5.6	12.9	-4.3	-3.0
Change between periods 1 and 4	4.2	8.7	-3.0	-1.4

As discussed earlier, this assumption of all the properly registered debt of state institutions and SOEs would raise the public debt-GDP ratio to 55 percent, which is still a very low level when compared with the public debt-GDP ratios of most Western European countries. As a general principle, the government's decision to let NBFIs fail is important to reducing the moral hazard problem inherent in supervision of the financial sector. Both domestic depositors and foreign creditors have to be encouraged to assess and manage risks better.

As things stand at the beginning of 2000, it looks unlikely that China will succumb soon to a financial crisis marked by bank runs, capital flight, a severe shortage of working capital, and a deep recession.

7.6　The Importance of Financial Intermediation for Stabilization and Growth

Part A of table 7.7 shows that total household consumption has declined steadily as a proportion of GDP. It dropped from an average of 52 percent in 1979–83 to 46 percent in 1994–98. However, this fall in consumption is not seen in all sectors. While rural consumption fell from 33 percent of GDP in 1979–83 to 23 percent in 1994–98, urban consumption rose from 19 percent to 23 percent. However, because the proportion of the population living in urban areas has gone up from 20 percent in 1979–83 to 30 percent in 1994–98, it is not surprising that urban consumption has risen relative to GDP, while rural consumption has fallen. The important analytical issue is whether urban consumption increased relative to GDP, once the rural-urban shift has been controlled for.

Part B of table 7.7 presents a decomposition of the change in rural and urban consumption behavior after taking the rural-urban movements into account. The decomposition follows from

$$(C_i/GDP) = [L_i/L] * [(C_i/L_i)/(GDP/L)], \tag{7.1}$$

where

C_i = consumption in sector i,

L_i = population in sector i, and

L = total population.

The decomposition in equation (7.1) can be described as:

(consumption in sector i as share of GDP) = (share of population living in sector i) * (normalized per capita consumption in sector i).

Taking differences, equation (7.1) becomes

$$\Delta(C_i/GDP) = [(C_i/L_i \: / \: (GDP/L)] * \Delta[L_i/L] + [L_i/L] * \Delta[(C_i/L_i)/(GDP/L)]$$

$$+ [\Delta(L_i/L)] * [\Delta\{(C_i/L_i)/(GDP/L)\}]. \qquad (7.2)$$

The decomposition in equation (7.2) can be described as:

Percentage point change in consumption in sector i as share of GDP

= percentage point contribution from the shift in the share of population in sector i

+ percentage point contribution from the shift in normalized consumption in sector i

+ percentage point contribution from interaction of the two shifts.

We note that the normalized per capita consumption in sector i can in turn be decomposed into

$$[(C_i/L_i)/(GDP/L)] = (C_i/Y_i) * [(Y_i/L_i)/(GDP/L)]$$

(C_i/Y_i) = average propensity to consume in sector i

$[(Y_i/L_i)/(GDP/L)]$ = [(per capita income in sector i)/(per capita GDP)]

= normalized per capita income in sector i.

We now have a natural definition of chronic under-consumption: it means a secularly declining average propensity to consume.

Since per capita income in China's urban sector has risen faster than per capita GDP over the entire reform period, the normalized consumption in the urban sector would increase if the average propensity to consume in the urban sector remained unchanged. A drop in normalized consumption in the urban sector could only mean that the average propensity to consume among urban residents has gone down, i.e., that there is chronic under-consumption in the urban sector.

A drop in normalized consumption in the rural sector would be consistent with a drop or a rise in the average propensity to consume of rural dwellers. The ambiguity arises because growth in per capita income in rural areas has lagged behind growth in per capita GDP.

Part B of table 7.7 shows that there is unambiguous chronic underconsumption in urban China, and that this is also likely to be the case in rural China. There has been a downshift of 3 percentage points in the normalized consumption of urban residents between period 1 (1979–83) and period 4 (1994–98), and a downward shift of 6.7 percentage points in the normalized consumption of rural residents during the same periods. This much bigger downward shift in rural normalized consumption suggests that the rural average propensity to consume is likely to have fallen also.

Keynes pointed out in his paradox of thrift that a rise in the saving rate could, in the short run, depress aggregate demand and cause the economy to produce below capacity. Only if financial markets were informationally perfect, would the increased saving be translated instantaneously into investments and the level of aggregate demand be maintained. The paradox of thrift is a result of coordination failure between savers and investors, and the minimization of its occurrence requires highly sophisticated financial intermediation. In a centrally planned economy, the paradox of thrift would not exist because the planner controls both the amount of saving and the amount of investment; however, for well-known reasons, a large portion of the saving would be wasted on value-subtracting projects.

China's marginally reformed financial system contains the worst aspects of the preceding two financial systems: the coordination failure of the market financial system and the allocation irrationality of the command financial system. China's high saving rate is also partly a reflection of this serious problem in financial intermediation. The steady liberalization of the economy has increased the number and range of profitable investment opportunities, but the state banks have refused to lend to private entrepreneurs. Consequently, the private entrepreneurs have to engage in self-financing, and this requires high saving to accumulate the required threshold of capital.[22] In short, the convergence of financial intermediation in China to the level of financial sophistication in the United States would lower China's saving rate, as well as ensure the full employment of saving and its allocation to the most profitable projects.

---

22. A formal model and testing of this argument is in Liu and Woo (1994).

Table 7.8
Investment and output by ownership forms

	Fixed investment (as % of GDP)		Share of fixed investment (%)		Share of industrial output (%)	
	1987	1997	1987	1997	1987	1997
All ownership forms	30.4	33.4	100.0	100.0	100.0	100.0
SOEs	19.2	17.5	63.1	52.5	59.7	25.5
TVEs	8.9	7.7	29.1	23.0	32.5	47.6

Most analysis of China's financial sector has focused on its urban banks. This neglect of rural financial intermediation is most unfortunate, because rural enterprises (popularly known as township and village enterprises, TVEs) have been the main source of China's economic growth since 1984.[23] It has been clear since the 15th Party Congress in September 1997 that China has decided to reduce the importance of SOEs by sharply accelerating the diversity of ownership forms. The amendment of the constitution in March 1999 to accord private ownership the same legal status as state ownership is a logical development from the 1997 policy decision. Implicitly, TVEs are expected to become an even more important engine of growth in the future.

In Woo (1999) we argued that this expectation of continued high TVE growth may be unrealistic, however, given recent investment trends. TVE investment in the 1990s has declined relative to both GDP and total fixed investment, in a period in which total investment went from 30 percent of GDP in 1987 to 33 percent in 1997.

So far, the TVEs have increased their output share not only without getting any of the investment share released by the shrinking SOE sector but doing so with a decreased investment share, e.g., from 29 percent in 1987 to 23 percent in 1997(table 7.8). This is unlikely to be a sustainable situation. It is hard to see how the TVEs could move up the value-added chain in production without significant capital investments in the near future. If China's capital markets continue to not allocate sufficient investment funds to the most dynamic sector of the economy, China's high growth rate is unlikely to continue in the medium run.

23. The industrial output alone from rural enterprises accounted for about 31 percent of the increase in GDP between 1984 and 1993; calculated from Woo (1998).

The Agricultural Bank of China (ABC) was established in 1955 to provide financial services to the rural sector and to channel funds for grain procurement. Small-scale collectively owned rural credit cooperatives (RCCs, *Nongcun Xindai Hezuoshe*) were started in the early 1950s, under the supervision of the ABC, to be the primary financial institutions serving the rural areas. RCCs operate an extensive network of branches, savings deposit offices, and credit stations in market towns and remote areas. The number of RCC units rose from 389,726 in 1981 to 421,582 in 1984, and then fell steadily to 365,492 in 1995.[24] This decline in the number of RCC units after 1984 is important because it implies a decrease in the effort to mobilize rural saving and less access of the rural community to investment financing.

In our opinion, the primary reason for the drop in TVE investment (as a share of GDP and as a share of total domestic investments) is that TVEs suffer from two big disadvantages in investment financing. First, the still heavily regulated financial system is directing too much of the investment funds to the SOE sector, thus starving the TVEs sector of investment funds. Second, because of political discrimination against private ownership, TVEs generally have vague, collective forms of property rights that cannot attract market-driven investment funds.

The deregulation of financial intermediation will allow the appearance of new small-scale local financial institutions that will mobilize local savings to finance investments in local TVEs. Our expectation is based on the impressive growth of folk finance (*minjian rongzhi*) since 1978, despite the absence of legal recognition and legal protection. According to Liu (1992), folk finance was the source of the development of TVEs in Wenzhou City in Zhejiang Province:

Ninety-five per cent of the total capital needed by the local private sector has been supplied by "underground" private financial organizations, such as money clubs, specialized financial households and money shops..."[25]

---

24. The number of RCC units is the number of RCCs plus the number of branches, savings deposit offices and credit stations.
25. The competition from the new rural financial institutions is likely to force the ABC-RCC system is improve its operations. This expectation is again based on Wenzhou's experience: "In order to compete with [the new folk finance institutions] ... , as early as 1980 a local collective credit union, without informing the superior authority, abandoned for the first time the fixed interest rate and adopted a floating interest rate which fluctuated in accordance with market demand but remained within the upper limit set by the state. Despite the dubious legality of the floating interest rate, the local state bank branches and all the credit unions in Wenzhou had already adopted it before the central state officially ratified it in 1984." (Liu 1992.)

It is crucial that financial deregulation is accompanied by the introduction of adequate banking supervision and of prudential standards that comply with international norms. The rash of banking crises in Eastern Europe in the early 1990s and in East and Southeast Asia recently should serve as warnings of what could result from financial deregulation without adequate improvement in the government's ability to monitor the activities of the financial institutions.

Besides deregulating rural financial intermediation, it is also important that the property rights of rural enterprises are clearly defined, protected legally, and freely tradable like the property rights of shareholding firms. The present trend of restructuring TVEs into shareholding cooperatives by dividing their assets among the workers (sometimes, among the original inhabitants of the community) is a natural convergence to an enterprise form which, international experiences have shown, assures investors that managers have the incentives to maximize profits in a prudent manner.

7.7   The Many Disappointments of State Enterprise Reform

When China started its SOE reform two decades ago, it followed the principles of market socialism to motivate the SOE manager to maximize profits. The state entered into a profit-sharing arrangement with the firm, and gave increasing operational autonomy to the manager. The official conclusion is that the decentralization of decision-making to the firms has failed to improve their performance.

The current problems of SOEs are: excessive investments in fixed assets with very low return rates, resulting in the sinking of large amounts of capital; and a low sales-to-production ratio, giving rise to mounting inventories. The end result is that the state has to inject an increasing amount of working capital through the banking sector into the state enterprises. (Vice-Premier Zhu Rongji, 1996.) [26]

The situation as regards the economic efficiency of [state] enterprises has remained very grim.... And the prominent feature is the great increase in the volume and size of losses. (Vice-Premier Wu Bangguo, 1996.) [27]

---

26. "*Guo you qiye sheng hua gaige ke burong huan,*" (No time shall be lost in further reforming state-owned enterprises), speech at the 4th meeting of the 8th People's Congress, *People's Daily*, overseas edition, March 11, 1996.

27. "Losses of state-owned industries pose problems for China's leaders," *The Washington Post*, November 3, 1996.

SOE losses have steadily increased since additional decision-making powers were given to SOE managers in 1985.[28] The three most commonly cited reasons for this development are the emergence of competition from the non-state enterprises, the failure of the SOEs to improve their efficiency, and embezzlement by SOE personnel.

The competition explanation is perhaps the weakest explanation because the profit rates of SOEs in the sectors of industry that experienced little entry by non-SOEs showed the same dramatic drop as the profit rates of SOEs in sectors with heavy penetration by non-SOEs. Fan and Woo (1996) compared the SOE profit rate and the proportion of output sold by SOEs in different sectors of industry in 1989 and 1992. In four of the five cases where the degree of SOE domination was unchanged, the profit rates were lower in 1992; e.g., the profit rate of the tobacco industry dropped 82 percentage points, and that of petroleum refining dropped 13 percentage points. The 1992 profit rates were lower in six of the seven cases where the degree of SOE domination had declined by less than 5 percentage points.

The failure-to-improve explanation has generated a heated debate in the academic literature. Analysts have derived a wide range of total factor productivity (TFP) estimates, going from large negative to large positive, and these disparate estimates could be due to an array of factors such as the possibility of Potemkin data sets, the functional form, the estimation method, and the choice of price deflators.[29] Our reading of the evidence is that any improvements in TFP were minor and, most likely, temporary.

The attribution of China's SOE losses to embezzlement of profits and asset-stripping by employees (managers and workers) is reminiscent of the relentless escalation of SOE losses during the decentralizing reforms in pre-1990 Eastern Europe. With the end of the central plan and the devolution of financial decision-making power to the SOEs, the key sources of information to the industrial bureaus regarding the SOEs

---

28. Recent evidence suggests that past reports on SOE losses (e.g., two-thirds of SOEs make zero or negative profits) may be understated. A national audit of 100 SOEs in 1999 found that 81 falsified their books and 69 reported profits that did not exist. An audit of the Industrial and Commercial Bank of China and the China Construction Bank found accounting abuses involving RMB400 billion, of which RMB200 billion was overstatement of assets ("China: Finance ministry reveals widespread accounting fraud," *Financial Times*, December 24, 1999). In January 2000, auditors in Hebei caught 67 SOEs covering up losses of RMB600 million ("Beijing moving to improve quality of statistics," *South China Morning Post*, February 29, 2000).

29. For a review of the empirical findings, see Huang, Woo and Duncan (1999).

were reports submitted by the SOEs themselves. This reduction in the monitoring ability of the state in a situation of continued soft-budget constraint meant that there was little incentive for state-enterprise managers to resist wage demands because their future promotion to larger SOEs was determined in part by the increases in workers' welfare during their tenure. The reduction in the state's monitoring ability, combined with the steady reduction in discrimination against the private sector, also made it easier for the managers to transfer state assets to themselves.[30]

Besides creating a fiscal crisis for the state, the "disappearing profits" at the SOEs have also contributed to social instability. The increasing public outrage over the inequity of the informal privatization of the SOE sector is well captured in a recent book by He Qinglian who wrote that the SOE reform has amounted to:

a process in which power-holders and their hangers-on plundered public wealth. The primary target of their plunder was state property that had been accumulated from forty years of the people's sweat, and their primary means of plunder was political power. [31]

There can be little doubt that the Chinese leadership recognizes the increasingly serious economic and political problems created by the agency problem innate in the decentralizing reforms of market socialism. This is why the debate between the conservative reformers and the liberal reformers has progressed from whether privatization is necessary to the question of the optimal form and amount of privatization. The emerging consensus is that all but the thousand largest SOEs and the defense-related SOEs are to be corporatized, with part of their shares sold to employees and the general public. The preferred privatization method for small and medium-sized SOEs has been employee (insider) privatization. Even for the larger SOEs that are to be corporatized, the state need not be the biggest shareholder.

The thousand largest SOEs will be given preferential financing to develop into business groups (like the Japanese *zaibatsus* and the Korean *chaebols*) that allegedly will enjoy enormous economies of scale. The truth is more prosaic. Given the coexistence of conservative and liberal reformers, any SOE reform package will have to contain a

---

30. It is hence not surprising that of the 327 cases of embezzlement, bribery and misuse of public funds that were tried in Beijing in 1999, " 76 percent took place in SOEs," "Judicial attention to SOEs pledged," *China Daily*, February 19, 2000.
31. The translated quote is from Liu and Link (1998), p. 19.

component that appeases each group. The upshot is dual-track SOE reform: state-sponsored conglomerates for the conservative reformers, and publicly traded joint-stock companies for the liberal reformers. However, in light of the 1997–98 external debt crisis in South Korea, which was caused by imprudent borrowing by the chaebols, one should question the wisdom of creating such large state business groups.

The key to SOE reform is not privatization per se, but a transparent, legal privatization process that society at large can accept, at the minimum, as tolerably equitable. An adequate privatization program must compensate retired workers and those who have been laid off, permit takeover by core investors, and respect the rights of minority share-holders, so it is important that legal reforms be carried out simultaneously. Without a transparent, equitable privatization process (overseen by an adequate legal framework), China is likely to repeat the mistakes of the Russian privatization program implemented by Premier Cherno-myrdin. Just as the creation of the new *kleptoklatura* in Russia has robbed the Yeltsin government of its political legitimacy, its occurrence in urban China could be socially explosive.

7.8   Concluding Remarks

We want to highlight one possible negative long-run result of the present reflation package. There is strong evidence that the larger credit growth in the third and fourth quarters of 1998 was achieved only after implicit assurances were given to bank managers that they would not be held responsible if their NPL ratios were to increase. A temporary deviation from the firm policy of cleaning up the balance sheets of the state banks may be defensible in the midst of the Asian financial crisis, but a prolonged deviation would undermine the credibility of the commitment to reform the state banks and would mean a return to the traditional socialist boom-bust cycle.

The long-term solution to the NPL problem goes beyond punishing bank managers who experienced increases in NPL ratios. The answer lies in changing both the supply side and the demand side of the credit market. The most fundamental changes include the transformation of the state banks and the SOEs into shareholding corporations to make profit maximization their primary objective, the establishment of a modern legal framework to promote transparency and reduce transaction costs, and the creation of a prudential regulatory body to reduce excessive risk-taking by banks.

These complex institutional changes that are necessary to deal with the NPL problem illustrate that most of China's economic problems cannot be individually addressed: success depends on systemic reform. This brings us to the basic point that while President Jiang and Premier Zhu deserve much credit for their competent handling of the current macroeconomic problems so far, their position in Chinese history will depend more on their success in addressing the many and varied long-term development challenges facing China. These challenges include the slowdown in agricultural productivity growth, the decline in job creation in the rural enterprise sector, the acceleration of losses by SOEs, the relentless growth in NPLs at the state banks, the inability of the legal system to meet the demands of an increasingly sophisticated economy, and the inadequacy of social safety nets to cope with the temporary dislocations that are characteristic of a fast-growing economy. Whether China will maintain its international competitiveness after the Asian financial crisis is over depends on the resolution of the above problems.

China's forthcoming accession into the WTO reveals that the top leaders recognize that convergence of China's economic institutions to the institutional norms of modern market economies offers China the only chance to achieve sustained high growth, and, more importantly, it shows that the top leaders are committed to ensuring that convergence will occur.

References

Easterley, William, and Stanley Fischer. 1994. The Soviet economic decline: Historical and Republican data. Working paper no. 4735, National Bureau of Economic Research, May.

Fan, Gang. 1998. Fiscal stimulus and debt-financing: Potential and constraints. Manuscript, September.

Fan, Gang, and Wing Thye Woo. 1996. State enterprise reform as a source of macroeconomic instability, *Asian Economic Journal* 10(3): 207–24.

Huang, Yiping, Wing Thye Woo and Ron Duncan. 1999. Understanding the decline of the state sector in China, *MOCT-MOST: Economic Policy in Transitional Economies* 9(1): 1–15.

Lardy, Nicholas. 1998a. China chooses growth today, reckoning tomorrow, *Asian Wall Street Journal*, September 30.

Lardy, Nicholas. 1998b. Financial reform: Fast track or back track. Global Emerging Markets, Credit Lyonnais Securities Asia, November.

Liu, Binyan, and Perry Link. 1998. China: The Great Leap Backward? *The New York Review of Books*, October 8.

Liu, Liang-Yn, and Wing Thye Woo. 1994. Saving behavior under imperfect financial markets and the current account consequences, *Economic Journal* 104(424): 512–27.

Liu, Yia-Ling. 1992. Reform from below: The private economy and local politics in the rural industrialization of Wenzhou, *China Quarterly* no. 130 (June): 293–316.

Rawski, Thomas. 1999. China's move to market: How far? What next? Manuscript, October 25.

Sachs, Jeffrey, and Wing Thye Woo. 1994. Structural factors in the economic reforms of China, Eastern Europe, and the former Soviet Union, *Economic Policy* 18: 101–45.

Sachs, Jeffrey, and Wing Thye Woo. (forthcoming) Understanding China's Economic Performance, *Journal of Economic Reform*.

Woo, Wing Thye. 1998. *Zhongguo Quan Yaosu Shengchan Lu: Laizi Nongye Bumen Laodongli Zai Pei Zhi de Shouyao Zuoyong* (Total factor productivity growth in China: The primacy of reallocation of labor from agriculture), *Jingji Yanjiu* 3: 31–39.

Woo, Wing Thye. 1999. Some observations on the ownership and regional aspects in financing the growth of China's rural enterprises, translated into French as *"La croissance des entreprises rurales selon les regions et la propriete"* in *Revue d'Economie du Developpement*, Juin, no. 1–2.

8   Indonesia: A Troubled Beginning

Steven C. Radelet and
Wing Thye Woo

8.1   The Economic Consequences of Political Failure

Indonesia is still in the maelstrom set off by the Asian financial crisis. The political situation is unstable and the economic situation is depressed. However, in a sense, this is the worst of times and the best of times for Indonesia. Constitutional democracy has reappeared after its suppression in 1957 because, this time, the social dissatisfaction with political authoritarianism has spiraled beyond the control of the army and the bureaucracy. If constitutional democracy can survive its troubled beginning, and go on to establish responsive political institutions and implement effective economic strategies, Indonesia will finally achieve the aspirations of its founding fathers in 1947, and attain the international standing that it deserves.

It is hard to have a more obvious indicator of extreme economic distress than a 36-percent collapse in real fixed investment in one year and a further 21-percent drop in the following year. Such was the dismal economic picture in Indonesia in 1998 and 1999. The financial system is dysfunctional: the seven state banks that dominated the financial system before the crisis are now insolvent. The corporate sector is mired in debt, and owners of bankrupt firms are reluctant to embrace formal bankruptcy or to engage in debt-equity swaps because of the possible loss of control over the firms. The hope is that the rupiah will appreciate when political stability is restored, thence the debt-servicing problem will be greatly diminished. However, without a marked improvement in the economy, and with it the generation of economic rents to co-opt political opposition, it is unlikely that political normalcy will return any time soon.

Table 8.1
Indonesia: Pre-crisis situation

	1990–94	1995	1996	1997
Growth rate of real GDP (%)	7.3	8.2	8.0	4.7
CPI growth rate (%)	8.6	9.4	8.0	6.2
Fixed investment (as % of GDP)	33.6	31.9	30.8	32.1
Gross domestic savings (% of GDP)	32.3	32.3	33.2	n.a.
Current account balance (% of GDP)	−2.2	−3.5	−3.4	−3.6
Reserve money growth (%)	16.9	17.8	35.8	38.3
Narrow money growth rate (%)	15.3	13.7	9.6	33.2
Broad money growth rate (%)	24.4	27.2	27.2	25.2
Government expenditures (% of GDP)	17.2	14.7	14.6	18.0
Government budget balance (% of GDP)	0.4	2.2	1.2	−0.7
Foreign debt (as % of GDP)	63.4	64.6	59.7	n.a.
Debt service ratio for all external debt	14.4	13.2	16.6	n.a.
Exchange rate (vis-à-vis US$)	2,053	2,308	2,383	4,650
Real exchange rate (1990=100) WPI based	95.7	91.3	80.4	126.3
Nominal minimum wage index	109.7	138.4	140.2	n.a.
Real wage index	92.6	90.3	84.7	n.a.
Value of total foreign debt (US$ billion)	86.9	124.4	129.0	137.4
Current account balance (US$ million)	−2,985	−6,431	−7,663	−4,890
Capital account balance (US$ million)	5,158	10,259	10,847	−603
Foreign direct investment (US$ million)	1,693	4,346	6,194	4,677
Export value (US$ million)	33,132	45,417	49,814	53,443
Composition of exports, value of highest four exports (1996 ranking, US$ million)				
Petroleum and petroleum products	6,587	6,444	7,390	n.a.
Articles of apparel and clothing accessories	4,029	4,824	5,321	n.a.
Cork and wood manufactures (excl. furniture)	4,110	4,664	4,944	n.a.
Gas: natural and manufactured	4,027	4,024	4,595	n.a.
Import value (US$ million)	27,059	40,630	42,929	41,694
Composition of imports, value of highest four imports (1996 ranking, US$ million)				
Specialized machinery	2,956	4,016	4,281	n.a.
General industrial machinery and equipment	2,075	2,760	3,154	n.a.
Road vehicles	1,409	2,639	2,505	n.a.
Petroleum and petroleum products	1,609	2,173	2,453	n.a.

Table 8.1 (continued)

	1990–94	1995	1996	1997
Exports' dependence on unaffected markets (%)	31.4	33.1	32.9	n.a.
Volume of exports (index)	138.2	170.6	179.2	230.3
Volume of imports (index)	133.9	196.9	218.0	n.a.
International reserves minus gold (US$ million)	10,112	13,708	18,251	16,586
Short-term foreign debt (US$ billion)	16.2	26.0	32.2	n.a.
DS Stock Market Index ($)	48.7	63.5	75.4	20.6
DS Stock Market Index (local currency)	54.9	79.6	97.6	61.9
Jakarta Composite Index (average)	399.6	513.9	637.4	401.7
Nominal lending rate (%)	21.7	18.9	19.2	21.8
Nominal deposit rate (%)	17.5	16.7	17.3	20.0
Non-performing loans (% of total loans)	8.3	10.4	8.8	9.0

Table 8.2
Indonesia: Changes in labor employment and output composition

	Composition of output		Composition of labor force	
	1986	1996	1970	1990
Agriculture	24.3	16.3	66.3	55.2
Industry	33.8	42.7	10.3	13.6
Services	41.9	41.0	23.4	31.2

Table 8.3
Indonesia: Forecasts for the 1999–2001 situation

Forecasting institution and date of forecast	GDP growth (%)			CPI inflation (%)		
	1999	2000	2001	1998	1999	2001
International Monetary Fund, October 1999	−0.8	2.6	—	22.7	5.7	—
HSBC Asia Economic Weekly, January 2000	0.2	4.0	5.0	20.4	2.0	7.0
Economist Intelligence Unit, 2000:1Q	−0.7	4.6	4.3	20.4	7.0	6.8

Economic management has been frequently paralyzed since 1998. The last six months of Soeharto's reign was characterized by futile attempts to shore up the business empires of his children and close associates, and the abortive attempt to set up a currency board to stabilize the value of the rupiah. After Bacharuddin Jusuf Habibie took over from Soeharto in May 1998, economic policy was often neglected and sometimes subordinated to Habibie's political needs. The pressures on Habibie were immense. First he had to mobilize his widely despised Soehartoist party, Golkar, to win a respectable share of seats in the parliamentary elections in June 1999, and then he had to engage in political horse-trading to try to clinch the presidency in October 1999. Habibie's reputation as an advocate for industrialization based on high-tech sectors, and the advocacy of his close economic advisor, Adi Sasono, for an economy organized on cooperative ownership, helped to undermine the efficacy of the various market-oriented reform programs being implemented. Habibie's management of the economy became more difficult from August 1999 onward, when foreign aid was suspended after the military-supported rampages against the East Timorese, who had voted overwhelmingly for independence in elections supervised by the United Nations.

The surprise election of the blind Abdurrahman Wahid (widely known as Gus Dur) to the presidency resulted in the formation of a large cabinet that encompassed the wide range of interests that the coalition partners represented. The head of the economic team, Kwik Kian Gie, is from Partai Demokrasi Indonesia-Perjuangan (PDI-P), a secular nationalist party. PDI-P is headed by Megawati Sukarnoputri, and it received the highest share of popular votes, 34 percent, in the parliamentary elections. However, the Muslim parties and Golkar cooperated to elect Gus Dur, who headed a Muslim party that won 13 percent of the popular votes.[1] In the wake of violent protests by Megawati's followers, she was elected vice-president. She is constitutionally poised to succeed the sickly Gus Dur, who suffered two strokes recently, if he does not finish his five-year term. The discord within the ruling coalition is so deep that the speaker of parliament, Amien Rais, has proposed amending the constitution to prevent automatic succession to the presidency. Because many important ministers within the economic team are from parties opposed to a Megawati presidency, Kwik Kian Gie has found it difficult to assert leadership in economic policy, to coordinate the work of the various economic ministries, and to formulate a coherent development strategy out of the disparate economic programs.

---

1. Golkar won 22 percent of the popular votes.

Nevertheless, despite the continued confusion over economic policy and the lack of significant progress on economic reform and economic restructuring, the Indonesian economy is on the mend after the precipitous drop in GDP of over 13 percent in 1998.[2] GDP growth in 1999 is widely expected to be in the range of zero to half a percent. This economic rebound is similar to the economic rebounds in Malaysia, South Korea and Thailand, albeit weaker: the financial panic has run its course, enabling the currency to strengthen and interest rates to fall, developments that will improve the balance sheets of the banking and corporate sectors.

The larger output loss and slower recovery in Indonesia compared with its neighbors should be regarded as more of a political failure than an economic failure. In the three-decade-long rule of Soeharto, he relied upon satisfactory economic growth as the justification for his stewardship of the country. Regularization of the political process was neglected, possibly because Soeharto believed such regularization would lead to a reduction in his power. So, instead of establishing political institutions and channels to resolve important socio-political issues about regime legitimacy, political succession, administrative transparency, regional concerns, ethnic disputes and religious tensions, Soeharto resorted to political manipulation, co-optation, and occasional violence to minimize discussions of these issues. The result was that beneath the façade of stable rule, buttressed by support from the armed forces, social dissatisfaction with the Soeharto regime was rising in step with the expansion of the middle and professional classes, and in step with the growth of the economic power of Soeharto's children.

As Soeharto entered his seventies, and as his health showed signs of decline, the tensions associated with political succession became impossible to contain, and fissures within the army appeared. The fissures multiplied and widened when Soeharto promoted his son-in-law, General Prabowo Subianto, over several more senior generals to be the head of the most powerful military command based in Jakarta (Kostrad)—the post that Soeharto held when he made his bid for political power in 1965. Soeharto's increasing tendency toward an "all-in-the-family" approach to economic and political matters discredited him considerably within his core constituencies, the army and the bureaucracy. When the Asian financial crisis, which brought financial insolvency to the business elite and economic difficulties to the urban professionals, had revealed that the aging Soeharto had become an incompetent manager, there was massive withdrawal of

---

2. Most sectors of the economy started recovering in the second quarter of 1999.

political support by the upper and middle classes, and the factionalism within the army and the civilian bureaucracy spun out of control. The Indonesians, unlike the Malaysians, the South Koreans and the Thais, did not have the option of expressing their outrage at gross incompetence through the ballot box, so they expressed their outrage in the only form available to them—a social explosion that produced the economic meltdown.

8.2   The Economic Meltdown

After economic growth that had averaged 7.7 percent per year during the early 1990s and declined to 4.7 percent in 1997, the economy contracted by 13.2 percent in 1998. This single-year reversal in growth of almost 18 percentage points is one of the most abrupt one-year slides recorded anywhere in the world in recent economic history. Hundreds of firms are insolvent, and the banking system is all but moribund. Tens of thousands of Indonesians, many of whom had lived just above the poverty line, have lost their jobs. The crisis was compounded by a severe drought in 1997 that disrupted food production, and by low world commodity prices (partially due to the crisis itself) that substantially reduced export earnings.

Indonesia's turnaround was a stunning blow, because the economy had performed well for many years. Until the 1990s, Soeharto had left the bulk of economic management to a group of technocrats (known as the Berkeley Mafia) who saw to it that the budget was kept in balance, inflation remained low, and the agricultural sector was healthy.[3] For 30 years, many well-managed and competitive manufacturing firms were established that produced a wide range of labor-intensive goods for world markets. Employment opportunities had expanded for the huge workforce, wages grew steadily, and millions were lifted out of poverty. For these reasons and others, by the mid-1990s Indonesia had become a favorite destination for foreign investors.

As with Thailand, Korea and Malaysia, the crisis in Indonesia resulted from a combination of weaknesses in the domestic economy, flaws in global financial markets, and mismanagement in the early stages of the crisis. Three crucial changes within Indonesia planted the seeds of the problem. First, Indonesia introduced a series of financial and banking reforms in the late 1980s that led to a very rapid expansion of the financial

---

3. See Woo, Glassburner and Nasution (1994) for an account of economic management from 1965 to 1990.

sector.[4] Private banks were allowed to open and compete with the large state-owned banks; all banks were given much greater leeway in their lending decisions; and the stock market began to grow and develop. These changes brought many benefits, such as reducing financial intermediation costs, providing more options for Indonesians to save, and reducing the direct role of the state in allocating credit. However, the government did not develop the regulatory and supervisory capacity needed to ensure strong and sustainable financial development, and basic prudential banking standards were not enforced. Many banks, both private and state-owned, were undercapitalized or were allowed to violate other prudential regulations without penalty. A growing number of major business groups owned their own banks, and many simply used the banks as lending vehicles to support their own activities, with the result that the banks had a substantial exposure to affiliated companies. In the early 1990s, non-performing loans rose quickly, and although they began to decline again starting in 1994, they remained at relatively high levels, especially in the state-owned banks. The financial sector came under growing stress, and despite the efforts of some government officials, little was done to redress the situation.

Second, the Soeharto family (particularly his children) and the family's close allies expanded their business interests rapidly in the late 1980s and early 1990s. The children became involved in a growing range of business activities, first in natural resource-based ventures, then in manufacturing for the domestic market, and later in a range of services (such as construction, operation of toll roads, and financial services). There seemed to be few constraints on family business activities, especially during the heyday of rapid growth in the early 1990s. Corruption and cronyism were not new in Indonesia; in the past, substantial economic activity had been channeled to the military and a small circle of private businessmen close to Soeharto. However, whereas during difficult economic times in the past Soeharto has been willing to make tough decisions that required some sacrifice by these chosen entities, he seemed increasingly unwilling to do so when his children's business interests were at stake.

Third, Indonesian corporations, and to a lesser degree banks, borrowed heavily from foreign creditors utilizing loans with short maturity structures. Short-term foreign debt outstanding grew rapidly from $19 billion in 1994 to $35 billion in June 1997, the latter figure being far greater than the $20 billion in foreign exchange reserves available at the time to meet these obligations.

---

4. See Nasution (forthcoming) for a full discussion.

To compound the problem, very little of this debt was hedged against the risk of exchange rate movements, since (according to the World Bank) hedging would have added about 6 percentage points to the cost of borrowing. Of the total debt (short and long-term) of $59 billion owed to foreign banks in June 1997, $40 billion was borrowed by Indonesian corporations, $12 billion by Indonesian banks, and just $7 billion by the government, as shown in table 8.4. Moreover, corporations borrowed substantial amounts in foreign currencies from *Indonesian* banks, so the data in table 8.4 actually understate the total amount of foreign currency corporate debt.

Corporations found short-term loans attractive because of the lower interest rates on such loans and because they assumed that they would be able to roll the loans over as the economy continued to expand. Foreign lenders happily complied, often not undertaking adequate appraisal of the investments. Many of these loans went to solid, competitive firms, but a substantial portion went to companies that were closely associated with Soeharto, and that the lenders believed would not be allowed to fail. Note that Indonesian banks were much less exposed than corporations, in part because of government borrowing policies adopted in 1991 that successfully limited the amount that banks could borrow.

In the weeks that followed the depreciation of the Thai baht in July 1997, foreign creditors began to reduce their exposure to Indonesia, putting pressure on the rupiah. In August, Bank Indonesia widened the trading band within which the rupiah was allowed to float, and the currency began to depreciate quickly. Unhedged Indonesian borrowers jumped into the market to try and cover their positions, propelling the rupiah further downward. Domestic capital began to flee for safer havens offshore, adding to the pressure.

Table 8.4
Debt outstanding to foreign commercial banks (billions of dollars)

| | Debt by sector | | | | | Foreign reserves (excl. gold) |
	Total	Banks	Public	Non-bank private	Short-term debt	
June 1997	58.7	12.4	6.5	39.7	34.7	20.3
Dec. 1997	58.4	11.7	6.9	39.7	35.4	16.6
June 1998	50.3	7.1	7.6	35.5	27.7	17.9

Sources: Debt data are from the Bank for International Settlements. Reserves data are from the International Monetary Fund.

In the early stages of the crisis, Indonesia was widely praised for reacting swiftly and appropriately to the unfolding events by not spending down its foreign exchange reserves, allowing the rupiah to float, and by quickly loosening rules on some types of foreign investment. Many observers believed that Indonesia would be less affected than other countries in the region. But it was not to be. Mismanagement of the crisis by the International Monetary Fund and by Soeharto turned the situation into a full-fledged panic and made the resulting economic contraction much deeper than was necessary. A major mistake was the demand by the IMF to close 16 commercial banks on November 1, 1997. There is little doubt that these banks, as well as others, were in poor shape and needed to be closed. The problem was that the banks were closed very abruptly in the midst of very volatile capital withdrawals and without a comprehensive and well-thought-out financial restructuring plan in place. The IMF's initial program failed to include provisions for establishing deposit insurance, a plan for managing the performing and non-performing assets of these and other banks, or a strategy for strengthening the rest of the banking system. Deposits began leaving Indonesian private banks in August, but after the abrupt closures these withdrawals turned into full-fledged bank runs that seriously undermined the rest of the banking system, including healthy banks. In the months that followed, the central bank aggravated the problem by providing huge lines of credit to keep certain banks open, especially those owned by well-connected businessmen. These credits added to the money supply and helped fuel inflation during the height of the crisis.

The World Bank (1998), among others, was very critical of the bank closures mandated in the first IMF program, and tied them to the later monetary expansion. In its 1998 country report on Indonesia, the World Bank concluded:

[the bank closures] led to a loss of confidence in the banking system. Large deposit withdrawals from private banks prompted the central bank to issue emergency credits in ever increasing amounts to ensure these banks did not go under. ... rather than instilling fresh confidence in the banking system, it caused panic withdrawals of deposits from most private banks.

The crisis was mishandled in other important ways by both the government and international agencies. For example, the IMF program initially mandated overly-austere fiscal policies, and demanded that banks recapitalize too quickly. The international community strongly, and incorrectly, criticized the government for its proposed new budget in January 1998, sending the financial markets into a nosedive. Soeharto waffled on key reforms, e.g., by allowing his son to open a new bank within a week after another bank owned by the son had been closed. He first cut back on investment projects, then reversed himself and announced that he planned to allow several to proceed, all of which were controlled by his close associates. For several weeks, he publicly flirted with the ill-advised notion of establishing a currency board, further undermining his credibility and his relationship with the IMF and the international community. Finally, the focus of the initial program was simply misplaced. Both the IMF and the government gave very little attention to the two most pressing problems underlying the panic—the collapse of the banking system and the withdrawal of short-term foreign debt—until it was too late. The result was substantial doubt about the capacity of Soeharto and the IMF to manage the crisis. Enormous uncertainty developed over the direction of economic policy. Investors fled, and by early 1998 the economy was in a tailspin.

The economic crisis quickly evolved into a political crisis, beginning with Soeharto's illness in December 1997, and reaching a peak in May 1998 with several bloody riots that culminated in Soeharto's resignation. Many shops and homes were destroyed in the riots, and substantial economic activity was disrupted. Many Indonesians of Chinese descent fled the country because their businesses bore the brunt of the violence. Both internal and foreign trade was disrupted for several weeks after the rioting. Some foreign buyers temporarily stopped placing orders for Indonesian exports.

The depth of Indonesia's crisis was also partially due to simple bad luck, and the global price effects of the financial crisis. The drought in mid-1997, brought on by the effects of El Niño, reduced food production and rural incomes. Fortunately, the rains were better in 1998, and food production rebounded. World prices for oil and gas, which remain Indonesia's largest exports, plummeted with the collapse of Asian demand. Indonesian oil sold for around $12/barrel, well below the average of about $18/barrel that prevailed between 1995 and 1996. On an annual basis, weak oil prices resulted in about $4 billion in lost foreign exchange earnings and government revenue to support the budget in 1998. Prices for a wide range of other export products fell as well, including plywood, copper and rubber, which on an annual basis cost the economy an additional $3 billion in lost revenues. Total losses of $7 billion was the equivalent of about one-seventh of total export earnings in 1997. The lost foreign exchange earnings were surely an important factor in keeping downward pressure on the rupiah. This factor alone would have caused a substantial depreciation of the rupiah, even in the absence of the collapse of the banking system and the panicked withdrawal of foreign credits.

Table 8.5
Indonesia: Tracking economic developments

	1997:Q1	1997:Q2	1997:Q3	1997:Q4	1998:Q1	1998:Q2	1998:Q3	1998:Q4	1999:Q1	1999:Q2
Growth rate of real GDP (%)	8.5	6.8	2.5	1.4	-7.9	-16.5	-17.4	-17.7	-8.0	3.1
Exchange rate (vis-à-vis US$)	2,419.0	2,450.0	3,275.0	4,650.0	8,325.0	14,900.0	10,700.0	8,025.0	8,685.0	6,726.0
Real exchange rate (1990 = 100, WPI based)	74.7	77.8	98.1	126.3	172.6	266.6	163.0	132.7	132.3	103.0
International reserves minus gold (US$ million)	19,011.8	20,336.3	20,275.2	16,586.9	15,770.0	17,949.9	19,650.0	22,713.4	25,160.7	26,318.6
Reserve money growth (%)	13.9	36.6	27.8	38.3	66.1	70.1	80.8	59.7	27.6	1.3
Narrow money growth rate (%)	21.5	24.8	11.3	33.2	53.7	55.4	52.0	26.9	3.9	-2.6
Broad money growth rate (%)	27.2	25.7	27.3	25.2	52.6	81.5	67.4	63.5	34.3	9.2
CPI growth rate (YOY%)	4.5	4.9	6.4	9.2	29.9	52.1	79.7	77.5	56.0	30.9
Nominal lending rate (%)	19.0	18.7	23.4	26.2	26.3	32.2	34.9	35.2	34.1	30.3
Nominal deposit rate (%)	16.7	16.1	21.3	26.1	24.7	34.3	44.9	52.3	39.5	30.9
Export value (US$ million)	12,405.0	13,155.0	13,942.0	13,941.0	12,516.0	12,053.0	12,680.1	11,598.3	10,165.8	11,503.0
Import value (US$ million)	10,675.0	10,737.0	10,389.3	9,892.0	7,205.7	6,097	6,857.7	7,176.6	5,557.3	5,977.0
Volume of exports (index)	199.5	214.2	241.6	265.8	236.0	200.0	207.4	212.7	197.4	—
DS stock market index ($)	75.1	79.6	46.3	20.6	18.0	9.1	11.0	23.2	21.8	42.3
DS stock market index (national currency)	98.8	105.9	83.0	61.9	85.2	73.4	42.6	101.2	103.7	159.3

Table 8.6
Indonesia: Decomposition of growth in 1998 and 1999

	1998:Q1	1998:Q2	1998:Q3	1998:Q4	1998	1999:Q1	1999:Q2	1999:Q3[a]	1999:Q4[b]	1999[c]
A. Growth in GDP by sector, % real change on year										
Agriculture	-0.87	-1.79	-4.52	13.17	0.81	4.01	6.21	-4.54	-2.01	0.94
Mining	-2.13	-5.97	-4.50	0.31	-3.09	0.11	0.22	0.62	-0.41	0.13
Manufacturing	0.60	-15.70	-14.02	-18.01	-11.87	-7.87	7.91	-0.40	7.8	1.53
Utilities	7.14	1.47	0.00	0.00	1.82	-25.93	8.7	9.34	35.42	7.53
Construction	-34.84	-45.30	-43.15	-38.47	-40.48	-10.55	9.85	3.37	2.26	0.76
Trade, hotels, restaurants	0.17	-17.01	-24.38	-28.96	-18.05	-18.21	-0.41	3.86	15.21	-0.91
Transport and communication	-0.63	-14.27	-21.84	-23.29	-15.10	-17.88	-3.15	8.39	11.29	-1.41
Financial and business services	-6.92	-24.78	-25.76	-44.18	-26.62	-22.80	-7.80	-5.51	4.9	-8.77
Other services	-3.94	-2.13	-3.66	-3.02	-3.14	2.55	3.04	3.30	2.69	2.89
GDP	**-3.97**	**-14.61**	**-16.11**	**-17.72**	**-13.20**	**-7.95**	**3.10**	**0.54**	**5.74**	**0.12**
Non-oil GDP	-4.40	-15.50	-17.50	-19.16	-14.26	-8.60	3.42	0.84	6.59	0.29
B. Growth in GDP by expenditure, % real change, year on year										
Private consumption	3.98	1.86	-7.19	-10.95	-3.32	-3.34	-1.93	6.42	5.54	1.55
Government consumption	-14.32	-7.28	-19.01	-19.93	-15.36	-3.93	5.14	16.20	17.21	8.39
Fixed investment	-25.56	-37.83	-36.93	-41.70	-35.54	-27.85	-23.64	-22.78	-8.25	-21.24
Exports of goods and services	57.55	21.83	22.66	-40.38	11.18	-44.33	-37.48	-39.93	11.43	-32.51
Imports of goods and services	23.40	8.70	4.39	-46.41	-5.29	-52.95	-48.86	-49.26	-19.79	-45.32
GDP	**-3.97**	**-14.61**	**-16.11**	**-17.72**	**-13.20**	**-7.95**	**3.10**	**0.54**	**5.74**	**0.12**

a. Preliminary.
b. Forecast derived from first three quarters' data and official full-year forecast.
c. Official forecast.
Source: Economist Intelligence Unit, Country Report on Indonesia, issue 1999:4Q.

Table 8.7
Sectors affected by trade and investment deregulation

Import tariffs reduced	Non-tariff import barriers removed	Export taxes reduced	Domestic trade regulations liberalized	Foreign direct investment restrictions eased
Chemicals Steel Metals Fishery products	Dairy products New and used ships Sugar Wheat Soybeans Garlic	Forestry products Leather Cork Ores	Livestock Cloves Vanilla Cashews	Retail trade Wholesale trade Banking Listed companies Plantations

8.3   The Situation at the End of 1999

Table 8.6 shows GDP growth in 1998 and 1999 decomposed according to economic sector and expenditure type. The collapse in 1998 was generalized and relentless throughout the year. The construction sector was hit particularly hard: it experienced a 40-percent drop in activity level. The next biggest losers were in the service sector: financial and business services (–26 percent), trade, hotel and restaurants (–18 percent), and transport and communication (–15 percent). The only bright spot in 1998 was the export sector, which grew 11 percent thanks to the over-devaluation.

Although the full economic performance in 1999 is still not clear, we do know that the economy bottomed out in the first quarter. GDP grew 8 percent in 1999:2Q, 0.5 percent in 1999:3Q, and (expected) 5.7 percent in 1999:4Q. The only sector expected to decline more than 2 percent in 1999 is financial and banking services (–9 percent)—confirming that the banking sector is in very poor shape. The big negative development is the (expected) 32-percent drop in exports.

The widespread economic distress has translated into rising formal sector unemployment, a great concentration of employment in informal activities, and falling real wages. The World Bank estimated that real wages have fallen about 50 percent. Not surprisingly, the number of Indonesians living below the poverty line has jumped sharply, after many years of hard-fought efforts to reduce poverty.

The rupiah, which depreciated to over Rp/$16,000 in the aftermath of the May 1998 riots, appreciated to Rp/$8,025 at the end of 1998 and then to Rp/$7,085 by the end of 1999. The appreciation has provided some welcome relief on import prices, and has given some hope that foreign debts can be restructured, as discussed in more detail below. By 1999:2Q, the Jakarta stock index had returned to its level in 1997:1Q. Inflation, which had soared to 82 percent on an annual basis in September 1998, dropped to an annualized 1.6 percent in November 1999, as the rupiah appreciated. The combination of the appreciation of the rupiah and the dramatic drop in inflation enabled interest rates to fall from prohibitively high levels. The call money rate fell from 81 percent in August 1998 to 33 percent at the end of 1998, and then dropped to 12 percent at the end of 1999.

To encourage exports and investment, Indonesia introduced sweeping trade and investment deregulation measures in 1998, which should help Indonesian firms to become even more competitive in the future. As summarized in table 8.7, tariffs were reduced on a wide range of products, many non-tariff import barriers were removed, export taxes were reduced, restrictions on domestic trade (between provinces and islands) were lifted, and foreign investment regulations were liberalized. Several of the deregulation measures affect sectors that effectively had been off-limits to investors, such as forestry products, sugar, wheat and cloves, because they were under the control of associates of former President Soeharto.

8.4   The Three Big Challenges

The key problem currently facing Indonesia is political uncertainty. The big question is whether Indonesia will survive as one country or as several countries. This is a very serious issue, given the strong separatist movements in Aceh and Irian Jaya, and the severe Christian-Muslim clashes in the Maluku islands. Until the political situation stabilizes, Indonesia is unlikely to attract widespread investment outside of export activities. Political and social leaders must face the daunting tasks of simultaneously rebuilding the economy and redesigning the political system, a challenge that that will take years to surmount.

Beyond politics, the two most important economic problems that Indonesia faces are the malfunctioning banking system and the huge debt burden on private corporations. The Indonesian banks are severely undercapitalized, hold a large amount of non-performing assets, and have been very reluctant to extend new credit. For all intents and purposes, the banking system is moribund.[5]

The government's initial reaction to the panic that overtook the banking system in late 1997 after the initial closure of banks was to introduce

---

5. See Woo (1995) for a discussion of the Indonesian financial sector before the Asian crisis.

sweeping guarantees on all bank deposits and most other liabilities.[6] It also provided substantial amounts of liquidity assistance (Rp130 trillion through June 1997) to support banks facing large credit withdrawals, including some very weak banks controlled by the political elite that were later shut down. The government established the Indonesian Bank Restructuring Agency (IBRA) in January 1998 to oversee the bank restructuring process. IBRA has the authority to close, manage or oversee troubled banks, and to transfer assets of closed banks to its own Asset Management Unit (AMU) for eventual disposal.

In the beginning, much of IBRA's efforts focused on recovering the liquidity credits that Bank Indonesia had lent to support ailing banks that were eventually frozen. Progress has been made with some of the biggest banks, including Bank Central Asia, Bank Danamon, and Bank Dagang Nasional Indonesia. Since these banks (and several others) could not repay their liquidity credits, they agreed to swap the debts for shares in a plethora of affiliated companies. While this provides some comfort that the government will eventually be able to recover at least some of the funds, the mechanism for disposing of these assets has been hotly disputed.

In December 1998 the government completed an audit to separate the banks into sound banks, salvageable banks and bad banks. The banks were classified according their capital asset ratios (CAR):

Category A banks: CAR > 4 percent   Sound banks
Category B banks: −25 percent < CAR < 4 percent   Salvageable banks
Category C banks: CAR < −25 percent   Bad banks

There were 74 banks in category A, and the seven state banks that dominated the industry before 1998 were all in category C.[7] According to the government, category B banks would be eligible to participate in a state-sponsored recapitalization program, and category C banks (except for state-owned banks) would be closed unless they could raise enough capital to push themselves into category B.

In March 1999, the government announced that it would close 38 domestic private banks, nationalize 7 domestic banks, and recapitalize 9 banks. The government recapitalization program works as follows. For every one rupiah of new capital that the owners of the bank inject into the

6. Many thanks to Susan Baker for providing much of the information on which the section is based.
7. The best state bank, Bank Rakyat Indonesia, had a CAR of −35 percent, and the worst state bank had a CAR of −136 percent.

bank, the government will add 4 rupiah. In other words, the government will take on 80 percent of the cost of recapitalizing these banks. The owners of the bank will have the option of repurchasing the government's shares within three years, and the right of first refusal to buy the shares for three to five years. In addition, the government will allow these banks to swap some of their non-performing loans for government bonds. Banks will be allowed to continue to try to collect these bad loans, and if successful, they may use the proceeds to buy back part of the government's capital share. The proposal is attractive to many banks, since the government is providing the recapitalization funds on very generous terms. Moreover, the government will voluntarily restrict its voting rights within the banks, and not insist on replacing bank management, since these are considered to be relatively good banks.

This plan, if implemented without too many exceptions, should go a long way towards recapitalizing banks and returning some rationality to the banking system. However, it provides little incentive for the banks to either restructure debts owed by corporations or make new loans. In this way, Indonesia's recapitalization plan differs from Thailand's, which ties some of the government's capital injections to the amount of corporate debt the bank writes down and the amount of new lending it undertakes. As it stands, even with the capital injections, it will be some time before Indonesian banks begin to expand their lending operations again. The recovery of the banking sector will depend on the speed with which the recapitalization plan proceeds, and the degree to which the government can introduce new measures to encourage banks to begin lending.

The second major economic challenge is the enormous amount of outstanding corporate debt. Corporations have large amounts of both foreign and domestic debt, and apart from exporters, apparently few firms are servicing their debts. Table 8.4 shows Indonesian debt owed to foreign commercial banks between June 1997 and June 1998.

The government made its first move on the debt issue in January 1998 by suggesting a voluntary freeze on debt servicing for firms that were unable to service their loans. In June 1998, Indonesia reached agreement (the "Frankfurt agreement") with a group of private creditors on restructuring three classes of debt, as follows:

• **Trade credits.** Indonesian commercial banks would repay all trade credits that were in arrears, and in return, foreign banks would make their best efforts to maintain trade credits at the April 1998 level. Bank Indonesia would guarantee new trade credits. A substantial portion of these arrears was paid in June 1998.

• **Inter-bank debt.** Foreign banks would exchange new loans of maturity between one and four years for obligations owed by Indonesian commercial banks maturing by March 31, 1999. The new loans would be guaranteed by Bank Indonesia. This mechanism has been used widely, and is generally seen as successful.

• **Corporate debt.** The government created the Indonesian Debt Restructuring Agency (INDRA) as an institutional mechanism for facilitating repayment of restructured corporate debt. Debtors and creditors must agree to restructure foreign currency payments over eight years, including a three-year grace period for principal payments. INDRA acts as an intermediary by receiving rupiah payments from the debtor and making dollar payments to the creditor. INDRA is designed to provide protection for the debtors against the risk of further real depreciation of the rupiah (i.e., if the rate of depreciation exceeds the rate of inflation), and to give assurance of foreign exchange availability for debt repayments. INDRA does not provide commercial risk protection if debtors do not make payments in rupiah.

While the first two elements of this agreement have been relatively successful, only one corporate restructuring had taken place through INDRA as of March 1999. One reason is that even with the exchange rate guarantee, current exchange rates are simply too unfavorable for most corporations to repay the debt. The plan provides little actual cash relief for debtors, since they still must make regular rupiah payments to INDRA. Moreover, many creditors have been unwilling to substantially write down the value of their loans. Japanese banks hold about 38 percent of the loans outstanding to Indonesia, and because of their own fragile condition they were in no position to offer significant debt relief. Essentially, with both creditors and debtors in such weak financial positions, they have been unable to agree on how much debt the creditors are willing to write off, and how much the debtors are willing to repay.

The INDRA facility is available after a restructuring agreement has been reached, but does not actually provide any sort of a framework for the restructuring negotiations themselves. To further encourage restructuring, the government announced the "Jakarta Initiative" in September 1998. The initiative offers guidelines on the formation of creditor committees, standstill arrangements, exchange of information, subordination of old loans to new credits, and other restructuring issues. However, the initiative does little to address the fundamental problem of making progress on burden sharing between the creditors and debtors. The result is that of the 234 debtors registered with the Jakarta Initiative in July 1999, only 16 had reached restructuring agreements with their creditors.

A further complication undermining both domestic and foreign debt workouts has been problems in implementing Indonesia's new bankruptcy law, which was adopted in April 1998. The inexperience of both judges and lawyers involved in the cases has led to very few cases being decided so far. Many of the decisions that have been reached have been highly criti- cized. For example, of the 55 companies brought to the court in 1998, only 16 of them were declared bankrupt. At best, given the enormous number of distressed firms, case-by-case bankruptcy proceedings for all affected firms will take many years to sort out. Given the delays and the unpredictability of the outcomes, many firms are likely to pursue out-of-court settlements.

Despite these problems, some individual restructurings have taken place. For example, in December, Bakrie & Brothers was able to swap $250 million in debt owed to Chase Manhattan Bank and American Interna- tional Group for $152 million in shares in Iridium, its wireless communi- cations company. In another deal, PT Trakindo Utama, the Indonesian agent for Caterpillar heavy machinery, restructured $171 million in over- due loans to Chase Manhattan. The company agreed to pay $81 million of the amounts outstanding immediately, in return for restructuring the additional $90 million over three years. Several other similar deals have either been completed or proposed. But these are just small steps forward in dealing with a huge problem. Ultimately, given the exposure of Japanese banks to Indonesia, a resolution of Indonesia's debt problem probably will depend on assistance from the Japanese government (perhaps through the $30 billion promised to the region as part of the Miyazawa Plan) and a strengthening of the Japanese banks themselves.

8.5   Concluding Remarks

One could be tempted to conclude from the combination of the debt over- hang, the weaknesses of the banking system, and the political uncertainty in Indonesia, that a return to a sustained 7-percent annual growth may not occur in the very near future. Such a conclusion would not be justified by the economic history of Indonesia. The political and economic situation in 1965–66 was at least as bad as the present time, and sustained growth took hold from 1968 onward.[8] We think that as long as civil war is absent, that

---

8. See chapters 3 and 6 in Woo, Glassburner and Nasution (1994).

foreign aid continues at existing levels, and that the policies of economic deregulation and economic restructuring are pursued vigorously, we may see an economic recovery like the one that began in 1968. The recent loosening of restrictions on foreign investment and the elimination of rent-induced trade barriers will allow Indonesia to once again reap the fruits of integration into the international economy.

For sustained economic progress to take root, one big difference between today's economy and the Indonesian situation of 1965 must be realized. The difference is that Indonesia today must "get its institutions right" in addition to "getting its prices right." Specifically, Indonesia must establish political institutions that will provide legal outlets for the expression of social dissatisfaction, so that such problems can be addressed. The freedom to vote for change in the political arena is now as important as the freedom to buy and sell in the market place. Democracy was the vehicle that enabled South Korea to move quickly on to new leaders who will make the changes required for continued prosperity.

Finally, Indonesia must also establish high-quality academic institutions at all levels before it will benefit fully from the new information age and the global economy.

References

Nasution, Anwar. (forthcoming). The meltdown of the Indonesian economy: Causes, impacts, responses and lessons. *ASEAN Economic Bulletin.*

Woo, Wing Thye, Bruce Glassburner and Anwar Nasution. 1994. *Macroeconomic Crisis and Long-Term Growth: The Case of Indonesia,1965–1990.* World Bank Press.

Woo, Wing Thye. 1995. "Indonesia," in Stephen Haggard and Chung Lee (eds.) *Government, Financial Systems, and Economic Development: Allocation and Efficiency.* Cornell University Press.

World Bank. 1998. Indonesia in crisis: A macroeconomic update. July.

9

Japan: The World's Slowest Crisis

Richard P. Mattione

Compared to the speed with which the Asian crisis broke in the summer and fall of 1997, Japan's economic troubles merit the title of "The World's Slowest Crisis." Even with the rebound of 1999, equity market indices are at less than half of the peak reached in 1989. Land prices have not yet begun to recover, and are now at roughly 25 percent of their peak. Yet it was not until November 1997 that the average Japanese citizen woke up to the fact that there was a crisis in Japan—not just a temporary period of slow growth, but a situation that required changes in the way business had been done. That month the bankruptcies of Yamaichi Securities and Hokkaido Takushoku Bank drove home most forcefully the existence of a crisis. Each failure ran counter to the expectations of the average Japanese citizen about how Japan was supposed to operate.

The decision by the Fuyo group, one of the six main bank-centered *keiretsu* (business groups) in Japan, not to support one of its key members violated the rules under which most Japanese expected their economic system to work. Indeed, Yamaichi Securities' own employees, junior and senior, seemed stunned when related companies would not bail them out. Ultimately, it was Yamaichi's decision to hide over $2 billion of *tobashi* losses[1] in shell companies in the Caribbean—and then deny the existence of such a maneuver—that provided a convenient excuse for the group to cut off support to a key member.

---

1. *Tobashi* (flying) was a practice in the early 1990s of buying stocks back from clients at an agreed, non-market price, and then keeping the stocks "flying" between accounts so as not to recognize the losses. The tobashi losses at Yamaichi Securities eventually flew to the Caribbean, where they were not under any regulator's review. The buybacks themselves were legal until the early 1990s, when they were outlawed after a scandal. Hiding the losses on the buybacks was never legal.

Table 9.1
Japan: Pre-crisis situation

	1990–94	1995	1996	1997
Growth rate of real GDP (%)	2.2	1.5	3.9	0.9
CPI growth rate (%)	2.0	–0.1	0.1	2.1
Exports (% of GDP)	9.0	8.6	8.9	10.0
Fixed investment (% of GDP)	30.4	28.5	29.7	28.3
Gross domestic savings (% of GDP)	32.5	30.0	31.3	30.8
Current account balance (% of GDP)	2.5	2.2	1.4	2.2
Reserve money growth (%)	2.2	7.8	8.5	7.3
Narrow money growth (%)	5.8	13.1	9.7	8.6
Broad money growth (%)	3.2	2.7	2.3	3.1
Government expenditure (% of GDP)	20.5	—	—	—
Government budget balance (% of GDP)	–0.7	–3.7	–4.1	–2.9
Exchange rate (vis-à-vis US$)	119.2	102.8	116.0	130.0
Real exchange rate (1990=100, WPI based)	89.1	85.8	95.2	94.9
Nominal wage index	105.0	110.7	111.8	114.0
Real wage index	100.6	103.4	104.3	104.2
Current account balance (US$ billion)	97.3	111.0	65.9	94.4
Capital account balance (US$ billion)	–78.6	–66.2	–31.4	–122.1
Foreign direct investment (US$ billion)	1.4	0.0	0.2	3.2
Export value (US$ million)	340,300	443,116	410,900	420,957
Composition of exports, value of highest four exports (1996 ranking, US$ million)				
Road vehicles	76,637	78,057	74,724	n.a.
Electrical machinery, apparatus and appliances	42,323	73,102	66,552	n.a.
Office machines and automatic data processing	27,592	33,895	32,560	n.a.
General industrial machinery and equipment	20,321	28,602	27,748	n.a.

Table 9.1 (continued)

	1990–94	1995	1996	1997
Import value (US$ million)	244,494	335,882	349,151	338,753
Composition of imports, value of highest four imports (1996 ranking, US$ million)				
Petroleum and petroleum products	21,553	34,991	41,412	n.a.
Electrical machinery, apparatus, and appliances	10,064	20,683	22,146	n.a.
Articles of apparel and clothing accessories	11,677	17,630	18,831	n.a.
Office machines and automatic data processing	6,894	15,249	18,762	n.a.
Exports' dependence on unaffected markets (%)	52.4	46.2	45.3	n.a.
Volume of exports (index)	102.2	106.6	107.2	117.5
Volume of imports (index)	107.1	136.2	140.9	144.7
International reserves minus gold (US$ million)	89,313	183,249	216,648	219,648
DS Stock Market Index ($)	1,076.4	1,258.3	1,046.8	765.8
DS Stock Market Index (local currency)	422.5	430.6	403.1	330.4
Nikkei 500 index	384.8	409.1	383.7	305.4
Nominal lending rate (%)	5.8	3.4	2.7	2.4
Nominal deposit rate (%)	3.0	0.9	0.3	0.3
Non-performing loans (% of total loans)	3.3	3.3	3.4	n.a.

Table 9.2
Japan: Changes in labor employment and output composition

	Composition of output		Composition of labor force	
	1986	1995	1970	1990
Agriculture	3.0	1.9	n.a.	7.0
Industry	40.3	38.0	n.a.	34.0
Services	56.7	60.0	n.a.	59.0

Table 9.3
Japan: Forecasts for the 1999–2001 situation

Forecasting institution and date of forecast	GDP growth (%)			CPI inflation (%)		
	1999	2000	2001	1998	1999	2001
International Monetary Fund, October 1999	1.0	1.5	—	−0.4	0.0	—
Economist Intelligence Unit, 2000:1Q	0.6	0.7	1.4	−0.3	0.0	0.8

Closing the doors of Hokkaido Takushoku Bank probably left an even greater impression on the average Japanese. Other cases of banks closing their doors in the postwar period had involved institutions other than the city banks, trust banks, and long-term banks that were considered to be the core of the Japanese financial system.[2] The few institutions deemed unquestionably safe saw huge deposit inflows in succeeding months—a banking near-panic not previously seen in the postwar period.[3]

Succeeding months have continued to hammer home the point that the rules are changing. Banks let a large food wholesaler fail in December 1997, despite debts of a size that previously would have made it "too big to fail"—or, at least, too big to fail without a lot more effort over years, not months. Long-Term Credit Bank became the first bank nationalized in the postwar period, handing itself over to the government in October 1998 once the new Financial Revitalization Law made possible such a resolution. Other recognizable names, such as the copier company Mita, have also found their way into bankruptcy court. Besides banks, the only sector with institutions deemed too big politically to fail

2. For example, Hyogo Bank closed in August 1995, but the Kobe earthquake in January of that year had provided the convenient fiction that Hyogo Bank would have survived but for the extraordinary damage wrought by the earthquake. In fact, at the time of its closing, bad loans were estimated to account for more than half of the total portfolio at Hyogo Bank.
3. November's closures also led to a fear of holidays. With Sanyo Securities closed on Culture Day (November 3) and Yamaichi Securities closed on Labor Thanksgiving Day (November 24, since the normal holiday fell on Sunday), the market was beset by rumors for the next several holidays about which institution's closure was imminent. So far, however, no other closures of listed institutions have occurred on holidays.

is the construction sector, and even there the bankruptcy filing of Japan Development Corporation in December 1998 raised the threshold that a firm must exceed to be considered "safe."

While the sense of crisis only developed in late 1997, the seeds of Japan's current difficulties go back at least to the mid-1980s. With the Plaza Accord of 1985, the yen began to appreciate rapidly against the U.S. dollar (as did most European currencies). Japanese exports had been an important driver of growth during the first half of the 1980s, and Japan's policy makers felt the need to replace that engine of growth. Government spending programs provided something of a boost, but monetary policy was forced to bear most of the adjustment burden. From 1987 to 1990, money supply growth (as measured by M2 + CDs) grew at double-digit rates, reversing a policy of decelerating money supply growth that had been in place for over a decade. Yet consumer price inflation peaked at a relatively mild 3.3 percent in 1991, in part because of the competitive pressures that resulted from an appreciating yen. Thus the bulk of the monetary stimulus flowed into asset-price inflation—both stocks and real estate. This generated a number of famous anomalies: the land under the emperor's palace was supposedly worth more than the entire state of California, and the market capitalization of Nippon Telegraph and Telephone (NTT) was worth more than the capitalization of entire markets such as Germany.

One key difference between Japan and the rest of Asia is that Japan's asset price bubble was deflated for many years without triggering more than a "growth recession." The Nikkei stock market index peaked at 38,916 at the end of 1989, fell back several times to lows just above 14,000, and hit a low for the 1990s of 12,880 on October 9, 1998. Land prices are barely one quarter of the peaks recorded at the top of the bubble. Bankruptcies have risen and growth has been anemic, but Japan managed to record an increase in real GDP every year of the 1990s until fiscal year 1997 (ending March 1998).

9.1   State of the Economy

Growth and Inflation

Superficially, the statistics argue against Japan's inclusion in a discussion of Asia's crisis countries. Fiscal year 1998 (ending March 1999) posted the second consecutive year of negative real GDP growth. The cumulative decline of 3 percent is modest compared to the disastrous fall experienced by many of Japan's neighbors, especially when one takes into account the virtual absence of population growth in Japan.[4] It is expected, however, that growth will remain below the economy's long-run potential despite further economic measures approved in early 1999. Moreover, fears about the future of Japan's economy and weakness in asset values have brought an increase in the savings rate in Japan that has exacerbated the recession.

Deflation has accompanied the downturn. This might at first sound like good news, and it is certainly preferable to a ravaging inflation. But, in fact, slow deflation has turned out to be at least as much a problem as slow inflation. The proclivity to raise savings rates is further stoked by the fact that goods are likely to be cheaper if bought later, and consumers are usually choosing to delay discretionary purchases, especially of durables.

Trade and Capital Flows

The absolute volumes of capital flowing out of Japan have been no smaller than those experienced by its neighbors in Asia. The key difference, however, is that Japan's current account was already in substantial surplus, and thus the government had no balance-of-payments reason to pursue a weak currency strategy in attempting to reflate its economy. Japan had a current account surplus on the balance of payments of ¥11.4 trillion ($98 billion) in 1997, which widened to ¥15.8 trillion ($121 billion) in 1998. Foreign exchange reserves maintained an almost relentless rise except for the brief period of extreme yen weakness in early 1998, and hit $272 billion at the end of November 1999. The currency, however, weakened until the summer of 1998 because outflows on the capital account were even larger—¥15.9 trillion in 1997, for example. Those outflows slowed to a trickle by early 1999, however, as domestic investors held back on overseas securities purchases, and as foreigners discovered a renewed enthusiasm for Japanese equities.

Some portion of those outflows stemmed from the fact that, until late in 1998, it seemed all too easy in the capital markets to bet against the yen. For example, one major hedge fund technique was the yen carry trade—borrowing short-term yen at an interest rate close to 0 percent to invest in long-term U.S. Treasury bonds yielding in excess of 5 percent,

4. One full percentage point can be blamed on timing effects from the hike in the consumption tax effective April 1, 1997.

and bearing the exchange rate risk. The weakness of Japan's economy and the apparently inexhaustible strength of the U.S. economy reinforced the notion that this was nearly a risk-free trade.

Domestic investors also looked beyond the yen in recent years. Life insurers, which over-promised and under-delivered on their pension fund contracts, pursued overseas investments as a way of meeting the return promises they made to their customers. Individuals invested in foreign bond funds, which promised much better yields than the measly amounts available on domestic bank deposits or government bonds, at a time when they remained reluctant to return to the domestic stock market. Bankruptcy risk considerations reinforced this tendency. Even when they kept money in yen, some Japanese moved their deposits and savings to foreign institutions, such as Citibank.

While many investors in Japan were growing more interested in overseas investments, bad loan problems were forcing Japanese banks gradually to withdraw from overseas activities. The earlier notion that all Japanese banks were among the world's best credit risks was soon replaced by the fear that all Japanese banks were among the (industrialized) world's worst credit risks. The "Japan premium" for funding to Japanese banks in overseas markets (that is, the amount by which the cost of funds for Japanese banks exceeded the average for their competitors) rose rapidly, cresting in late 1997 at 125 basis points; it held at around 80 basis points until early 1999 before finally falling back to around 10 to 20 basis points. This makes overseas operations unprofitable. Banks have begun to unwind these activities, close foreign branches, and even sell parts of overseas operations. In addition, Japanese manufacturers have sharply reduced the pace of direct investments into Asia, which had been concentrated in areas such as automobiles and electronics, as existing capacity dwarfs the now-shrunken size of regional demand for those products.

Japan's trade surpluses are again generating friction, but they are not the direct cause of problems in Asia. Conflicts have appeared on three fronts. First, Japan's weak economy has stifled the growth of Japanese imports, which shrank 5.4 percent in volume terms in 1998. That hampered Japan's ability to act as an engine of growth for the rest of Asia during its economic crisis. Second, there has been an underlying current of discontent directed at Japan's exports. Continued economic expansion in the United States has kept that discontent under control so far, and both Japan and the United States remain sensitive to any such trade complaints. Third, there have been accusations that Japanese goods are

unduly competing with other Asian exports in third markets, such as
the United States and Europe. On closer examination, however, Japan's
heavy concentration on automobiles and electronic goods, where it has
strong competitive advantages vis-à-vis its Asian neighbors, suggests
that the competition from Japanese exports has not been a major factor
in worsening the outlook for the rest of Asia. The nation most affected
has probably been South Korea, where there is significant overlap in
such areas as steel, chemicals and low-end consumer electronics.

Bank Loans

The seeds of Japan's present bad loan problems were sown in the mid-
1980s when the Bank of Japan eased domestic credit conditions to smooth
adjustment to the yen's rapid appreciation after the Plaza Accord. When
the manufacturing sector no longer required significant amounts of new
credits, the banks turned to the "bubble sectors" of construction, real
estate and non-bank finance to build their loan book. Loans to the
bubble sectors accounted for 27 percent of the loan portfolio at city,
trust and long-term banks as of March 1998, against only 16 percent in
March 1986 before the bubble really took off. Loans to all three sectors
were backed primarily by land as collateral.

The cost of the bubble period is finally being paid. Banks, of course,
are rarely in any hurry to recognize bad loans, but in this case the
Japanese regulators also felt no particular sense of urgency—and were
in any case understaffed for the task. Historically, loan losses had been
very small, as lenders had helped almost all borrowers through tough
times. In the previous worst case, the land bubble of 1973–74, banks had
been rescued in nominal terms by double-digit inflation that eventually
brought collateral values in line with the principal amounts of the bank
loans. Such a rescue was not forthcoming, however, under the 1990s
environment of low inflation (2 percent or less) modulating to outright
deflation.

Japanese banks and officials have a mixed record with respect to
implementation of the capital adequacy rules of the Bank for International Settlements (BIS). Banks have been forced to hold capital equivalent to at least 8 percent of risk assets, as previously agreed, but
regulators have used a variety of mechanisms to be generous in the
measurement of capital.

Table 9.4
Japan: Tracking economic developments

	1997:Q1	1997:Q2	1997:Q3	1997:Q4	1998:Q1	1998:Q2	1998:Q3	1998:Q4	1999:Q1	1999:Q2
Growth rate of real GDP (%)	3.8	1.0	1.7	-0.8	-3.6	-1.8	-3.5	-1.7	0.1	1.0
Exchange rate (against US$)	124.1	114.4	121.0	130.0	132.1	140.9	135.3	115.6	120.4	121.1
Real exchange rate (1990 = 100, WPI based)	98.8	88.9	92.0	98.8	99.1	107.3	109.0	97.0	—	—
International reserves minus gold (US$ million)	218,180.8	221,127.8	224,411.8	219,648.3	222,460.5	204,744.8	211,163.1	215,471	221,371	245,245
Reserve money growth (%)	7.0	5.8	7.2	7.3	11.2	8.1	—	3.8	4.1	5.2
Narrow money growth rate (%)	5.9	5.3	6.3	8.6	7.1	7.2	—	5.0	7.8	10.5
Broad money growth rate (%)	1.5	1.4	1.6	3.1	3.2	3.0	—	4.2	4.5	4.7
CPI growth rate (YOY%)	0.6	2.0	2.1	2.1	2.0	0.3	-0.2	0.5	-0.1	-0.3
Nominal lending rate (%)	2.5	2.5	2.4	2.4	2.4	2.3	—	2.3	2.2	2.2
Nominal deposit rate (%)	0.3	0.3	0.3	0.3	0.3	0.3	—	0.2	0.2	0.1
Export value (US$ million)	99,467.4	105,823.6	107,196.7	108,469.3	97,968.5	93,918.9	—	98,160.0	93,830.0	92,950.0
Import value (US$ million)	87,615.7	84,839.8	85,004.0	81,294.1	75,200.7	66,895.8	—	63,550.0	64,180.0	64,340.0
Volume of exports (index)	110.4	116.5	118.2	124.8	113.0	114.3	—	115.6	108.7	—
Volume of imports (index)	142.6	142.7	147.6	145.8	140.4	134.1	—	139.8	143.3	—
DS stock market index ($)	918.5	1,130.0	964.0	765.8	785.9	744.7	648.6	867.0	975.3	1,080.8
DS stock market index (n.c.)	377.3	429.0	386.1	330.4	347.7	342.9	292.9	324.5	383.2	433.9
Nikkei 500 Index	359.2	405.6	361.4	305.4	327.8	322.3	275.0	286.5	337.1	379.9

Some would argue that generous assessments of capital have been the rule since the day the BIS Accords were agreed, as a concession had already been made to allow Japanese banks to count 45 percent of unrealized gains on listed securities toward secondary (Tier II) capital. Then capital was stretched by slowing the recognition of bad loans. More recently it has been done by creative accounting schemes, such as writing up the value of a bank's own real estate (such as headquarters buildings) and allowing securities to be valued at the higher of cost or market.

But new capital has also been raised. Some came from group companies; another significant portion came from foreigners enticed by structured products that seemed to eliminate much of the downside risk that investors faced in holding bank stocks. When market sources of new capital ran low in early 1998, the Japanese Diet passed a package that provided interim funding from the government to banks. Then in October 1998 the government implemented a much bigger package that provides ¥60 trillion in funds to bail out banks. The legislation included ¥25 trillion for help prior to bankruptcy, ¥18 trillion for cleaning up after bankruptcy, and ¥17 trillion to protect depositors (the latter portion reiterated an amount already set aside in 1997).

Restructuring is slowly trimming the number of banks. There were 20 "major" banks at the end of 1994, before any sizable write-offs began.[5] As of the end of 1999, three of those 20 have been closed, one was bailed out by its keiretsu, one has recently agreed to sell its crown jewel (the pension business), and many are pulling back from overseas operations.[6] Mergers announced during the second half of 1999 would consolidate ten of the remaining 17 "major" banks into four new institutions, for a grand total of 11 major banks.[7] Substantial bad loan problems exist outside the listed bank sector, especially among cooperatives, that will also have to be resolved.

---

5. This is adjusted for the merger of Bank of Tokyo and Mitsubishi Bank into Tokyo-Mitsubishi Bank. Both components were in relatively good shape as regards bad loans prior to the merger.
6. Hokkaido Takushoku Bank, Long-Term Credit Bank, and Nippon Credit Bank have been closed. Nippon Trust Bank was bailed out by Mitsubishi Bank. Yasuda Trust plans to transfer its pension business to a joint venture that also incorporates Fuji Bank and Dai-Ichi Kangyo Bank. Almost all have made some sort of announcement about overseas cutbacks.
7. Some of the mergers propose the use of a holding company structure, but overall management would be vested into a board at the holding company level, making it appropriate to count these as only four banks.

Social Dimensions

Japan's traditional social system is holding together, perhaps so well that it generates excuses for not dealing with the deeper issues the country faces. The overall unemployment rate hit 4.9 percent in the summer of 1999, and among young people the rate is probably over 10 percent. These are record highs for the postwar period, but are strikingly low when compared with other Asian countries caught up in the crisis. Only recently have companies done more in the way of job cuts than to speed attrition by lowering the retirement age from 55 years to 50 years. Though Japan faces the need for a sharp adjustment in industrial structure that will likely raise the unemployment rate over the next several years, few economists have been so brave as to suggest a figure much above 5 percent for the peak unemployment rate.

9.2   Policies So Far

The Japanese government has been consistently half-hearted in its attempts to deal with the problems of the 1990s. Monetary ease was accompanied by usually modest spending programs, while little was done until recently to deal with the problem of reconstructing the financial system. More recently, however, the economic situation has become politically intolerable, making the government more amenable to broader initiatives to deal with the problem.

Monetary Policy: Caught in a Liquidity Trap?

The Bank of Japan (BOJ) raised short-term rates to 6 percent in the summer of 1990 to burst the asset-price bubble of the late 1980s. The BOJ succeeded beyond its wildest expectations in the fight against asset price inflation: land prices are somewhat less than 30 percent of the peak, and stock prices bottomed out at less than 40 percent of the peak attained 10 years before. Having dealt with asset price inflation, however, the BOJ was slow to deal with the economic slowdown of the 1990s. The first cut in interest rates occurred in 1991 as the BOJ moved slowly and deliberately to eradicate all traces of asset-price inflation from the economy. The monetary authorities underestimated the amount of real economic adjustment that would be required to work off the excess plant and equipment investment of the 1980s, and they were therefore surprised by the persistence of slow growth into 1994. The financial market's continuing interest in holding yen assets until 1995, when it took less than 80 yen to buy one dollar, increased the deflationary pressure on the Japanese economy.

The economy turned up in 1995, and was temporarily reinforced in 1996 by consumers' decisions to move purchases forward to beat the hike in the consumption tax. Throughout this period there were hints that the next move in interest rates was up, not down. But when the BOJ discovered that bad loans and excess capacity meant that the economy was not yet ready to launch into self-sustaining growth, the BOJ had to cut interest rates to virtually 0 percent. Bankruptcies of major financial institutions in late 1997 led consumers to move deposits to the safest of institutions, requiring further injections of liquidity. The limited success so far in restarting the economy has kindled fears that Japan has entered a liquidity trap, a situation not experienced by a major industrial country since the Great Depression of the 1930s.

Fiscal Policy: Are the Coffers Running Empty?

The fiscal authorities have been immobilized for much of the 1990s by the contradictions inherent to the various problems they are trying to deal with through fiscal policy. As a result they have occasionally proposed initiatives on one front, only to pull back and seek another battleground.

Since the 1980s the government has focused on the coming Social Security crisis—a large number of elderly citizens will have to be supported by a relatively small working-age population. The problem is hardly unique to Japan, though the magnitude of the demographic difficulties appears to be slightly greater than in several of the major continental European economies. Fiscal policy has attempted to deal with this impending demographic problem through a mix of spending cuts and tax hikes.

The longer-term demographic problem has made the Ministry of Finance and the ruling Liberal-Democratic Party reluctant to use either tax cuts or spending initiatives in a significant way to deal with the economy's current slowdown. The Japanese budget process has always left the true status of fiscal policy rather obscure. The government and the press compare proposed spending not to the actual level of spending in the previous year, but to the budget initially submitted, which leads to an overstatement of the fiscal stimulus being provided. Thus the press calculates spending programs equivalent to around 70 trillion yen during the 1990s (excluding the programs now under discussion), while the actual boost is figured at closer to roughly 23 trillion yen.[8]

The most unfortunate aspect of fiscal policy was the timing of the increase in the consumption tax from 3 percent to 5 percent, effective April 1997, without permanent income tax cuts. Consumers went on a buying binge just before the hike was implemented, but have been on strike ever since because the tax increase exacerbated the feeling that disposable income will be pinched in coming years.

Having spent years stuck in old ruts on the fiscal front, the central government now faces a new problem—many regional governments are themselves teetering somewhere between illiquidity and insolvency. The wealthier suburban regions have been caught in this trap first, because the slow economy has decimated corporate profits, their main source of funding. (The more rural prefectures tend to rely on construction spending rather than on their pro rata share of tax revenues.) This will further erode the efficacy of supplemental spending programs, since regional governments may have difficulty raising their share of the funds. Tokyo governor Ishihara recently dropped a bombshell on the banks and the central government by proposing "external taxation" for large banks' operations in Tokyo; that is, taxation not based on corporate earnings. Political opportunity rather than economic efficiency was the obvious driver behind a proposal that targets so narrow a tax base, but politicians and bureaucrats quickly decided to look into an expansion of the concept to all firms nationwide.

Restoring the Financial System: How Much is Enough?

At the bleakest moments it seemed that no amount, not even the ¥60 trillion package approved in October 1998, would be enough to deal with the rot in the financial system. Is that plausible? The recently voted funds are equivalent to around 15 percent of Japanese GDP. That exceeds the cost of solving the savings and loan crisis of the United States during the 1980s and 1990s. It is low, however, when compared to the cost of reconstruction of some emerging markets' financial systems, such as Argentina and Chile in the 1980s.[9]

---

8. See Adam S. Posen, "Restoring Japan's Economic Growth," published by the Institute for International Economics in 1998, for further discussion.
9. See "Swamps and Crocodiles!" Tim Condon and John Hobson, Morgan Stanley Dean Witter, October 16, 1998.

Overall, however, Japan seems to have put most of the mechanisms and necessary funds in place, but it is essential to follow through promptly. A former Justice Ministry official took charge of the new Financial Supervisory Agency (FSA), and seemed to pursue a course independent of those who had failed to admit that a bank problem existed. The FSA also has a mandate to collect the real facts about the bad loans, in particular, to clarify the status of Class II loans (impaired, but being serviced). Those are two prerequisites for solving the problem, and results for the last two reporting periods (March 1999 and September 1999) show more loans being written off than had been expected. Mechanisms are in place for bridge banks and other temporary funding mechanisms, and the funding behind them appears to be of the same order of magnitude as the bad loans themselves. The present financial crisis is manageable as long as those funds and mechanisms are used vigorously and without delay. Some improvements may be needed in the legal system to liquidate problem loans more promptly, but even the U.S. authorities did not have everything that they needed in place when they started to rectify the mess in the savings and loan institutions.

Overall, one is forced to conclude that the Japanese government has done what was necessary to get the main constituents of the regular banking system ("major" banks and regional banks) functioning again. Japanese consumers seem to have agreed, because funds returned from the super-safe members of that group to the others. There remains the task of straightening out other segments of the financial system.

9.3   What Still Needs to be Done

It is conceivable that patience alone will be enough to get Japan back on a slow growth track. But time alone is unlikely to do the trick, and a vibrant Japan is hard to imagine without further policy initiatives. There are a number of fronts that seem most promising.

Monetary Policy

The Bank of Japan will simply have to keep supplying reserves until near-term liquidity needs are met and the economy recovers to a consistent real GDP growth rate near 2 percent. Deflation must be stopped, since it exacerbates the difficult labor force adjustment process that Japan faces. An inflation rate of around 1 percent would seem to be consistent with underlying price stability, given the often documented ways in which official statistics can overstate inflation. However, the BOJ should not adopt suggestions that inflation be targeted at higher figures, such as 3 percent per year, in an attempt to restart private consumption spending. Such a policy would generate substantial losses on the banks' holdings of government securities, and could renew the banking crisis.

Fiscal Policy

This observer's view will seem heretical: freeze the consumption tax at 5 percent, and instead make substantial cuts in corporate and individual income taxes in Japan. This is heretical to the extent that the hike in the consumption tax in 1997 clearly cut the legs out from under the economy, and because the political maneuvering on the tax has contributed to a freezing of the political debate in Japan. However, the consumption tax has already been implemented and, most importantly, it does address future fiscal needs in Japan. Permanent abolition is not all that credible in any case, given the efforts the Liberal Democratic Party has put into implementing the consumption tax over decades. And temporary cuts followed by a rapid return to the 5 percent rate now in force (the proposal of the Liberal Party) seem likely to exacerbate the stop–go cycles in which the economy has found itself mired during the 1990s, without boosting long-term growth.

But if the consumption tax stays, other taxes need to be lowered considerably. The proposed cut to around 40 percent in the effective corporate tax rate is a good start. If implemented at a time when profitability is low in the corporate sector, the loss of revenues may not be as noticeable over the short run, while it could spawn renewed economic vigor for the long run. The government needs to cut income tax rates for individuals on a permanent basis, rather than as mere extensions of the temporary tax cut. But it is extremely disappointing that the government seems to have postponed the introduction of consolidated accounting because this measure, if combined with changes in certain expense allowances, could speed up corporate restructuring.

Reconstructing the Financial Sector

The key is to turn the promises inherent in recent legislation into reality. The FSA will have to take a moderately hard line on the gray area of

Class II loans to give the process credibility; fortunately, the early signs are that the agency is pursuing this harder line, at least with the larger banks. Banks also need to force more of their problem borrowers, especially from the bubble sectors, into bankruptcy. The bankruptcies of several retailers in February 2000 might indeed signal such a willingness.

The legal status of collateral must be clarified, and large-scale sales of real estate (direct or securitized) must begin soon. This argues against the proposal of the Economic Strategy Council that the government buy up land; such a policy would merely prolong the overhang.

The government has been fairly quick to sell off some of the larger failed institutions. A consortium with significant foreign participation looks set to buy the remnants of LTCB from the government, while a domestic group looks set to take over Nippon Credit Bank. Now, however, reconstruction must extend past listed institutions to the credit unions and cooperatives, and loans to the "third sector" (joint public–private development corporations) will also have to be resolved. To speed up this process, Japan needs to implement the "payoff" proposal, which would shut bad banks (and credit unions and cooperatives) and pay off their depositors, rather than force mergers of these entities with other banks.

Finally, if Tokyo should implement "external taxation" of banks it might be necessary to provide extra capital to some of the banks, since the proposal threatens to reduce operating profits by around 12 percent (net profits remain in the red because of loan write-offs). The ultimate outcome of that proposal is unclear at this time, however, and most of the larger institutions should emerge intact, though with their long-run profitability reduced.

Reconstructing the Corporate Sector

Tax cuts will help, but more radical reconstruction is needed. Too many companies have weak balance sheets, and even those with strong balance sheets often have too much of their assets tied up in cross-holding of stocks. A tax holiday on gains from the sale of crossholdings, as proposed by the Keidanren, could give a further boost to restructuring efforts. Such a tax holiday would be far preferable to the proposal by the 21st Century Public Policy Institute that the government purchase shares. Government purchases would only prolong the overhang in the stock market, and this is especially hard to justify at the moment because the stock market now shows signs of coming to life, at least for

Internet and "new Japan" companies. The bulk of corporate restructuring, however, will depend upon the efforts of individual companies to rationalize, to shut plants and to make the painful decisions inherent in exiting some lines of business. It is unavoidable; too many companies are worth more dead (for their land and stockholdings) than alive (when they constantly run in the red).

Speeding Up the Resolution of the World's Slowest Crisis

So far, progress seems to be made on the basis of "enough is enough – for now." Regulators closed a few banks, but the financial sector has many soft spots outside the major financial institutions. Banks let a few moderate-sized construction companies fail, but have a long list of "bubble" companies that are not strong enough to survive. This situation has led many observers to conclude that *gaiatsu* (outside pressure) is necessary to speed the resolution of Japan's economic crisis. Gaiatsu may sometimes force a decision, especially if it is convenient to certain groups or factions within Japan; however, many times gaiatsu causes wrong decisions to be made for the wrong reasons.

The economic situation remains serious; Japan must make the hard decisions soon so that sustained growth can occur. It is true that Japan's renewed growth will benefit other areas of the world, for instance by absorbing more goods from the rest of Asia and boosting the incipient recovery there. Likewise, by buying more goods from the United States and Europe, a recovering Japan would quiet the renewed stirrings of trade friction with its partners. But the biggest beneficiary of these actions will be Japan, and the greatest losses from inaction will also accrue to Japan. If Japan cannot sustain its recovery, it will hold back the rest of the world. Yet ultimately the rest of the world will probably survive any Japanese economic mistakes much better than Japan will.

10 Korea: Returning to Sustainable Growth?

Kiseok Hong and
Jong-Wha Lee

10.1 Introduction

Two years have passed since the eruption of the Asian financial crisis. As the end of 1999 approaches, Korea is recovering rapidly from the sharp recession that followed the crisis. The initial impacts of the crisis have been more severe than had been predicted. The growth rate plummeted from the pre-crisis average of 7 to 8 percent to −5.8 percent in 1998, while the inflation rate rose to 7.5 percent from 4.4 percent in 1997. Since the second half of 1998, however, Korea has been recovering fast from the worst-ever recession through financial and corporate restructuring and timely macroeconomic policies. The economy is expected to grow by about 10 percent in 1999. It is clear, however, that the rapid rebound is partly attributable to the previous year's low base, and the current pace of recovery cannot be sustained in the future.

Although the crisis was initially triggered by sudden foreign capital outflows and the depletion of foreign reserves, the Korean economy was also destabilized by several structural weaknesses. Despite a relatively low overall external debt level and a moderate and sustainable current account deficit, Korea had high short-term debt relative to its international reserves level, which made it vulnerable to a balance-of-payments crisis. Inefficient management and imprudent lending among financial institutions, and over-investment and low profitability in the corporate sector, increased the economy's vulnerability to financial panic and economic collapse.

Since the onset of the crisis, Korea has initially focused on resolving the immediate liquidity crisis by stabilizing exchange rates and restoring market confidence, assisted by the IMF and other international organizations. It adopted tight monetary and fiscal policies and started implementing comprehensive reforms in the corporate and financial sectors.

Table 10.1
Korea: Pre-crisis situation

	1990–94 (average)	1995	1996	1997	1998
Growth rate of real GDP (%)	7.6	8.9	6.8	5.0	−5.8
CPI growth rate (%)	7.0	4.5	4.9	4.5	7.5
Exports (% of GDP)	27.9	30.2	29.5	34.7	48.7
Fixed investment (% of GDP)	37.1	36.7	36.8	35.1	29.4
Gross domestic saving (% of GDP)	35.4	35.1	33.3	32.9	33.0
Current account balance (% of GDP)	−1.3	−2.0	−4.9	−1.9	12.5
Reserve money growth (%)	14.7	16.3	−12.2	−12.5	−8.1
Narrow money growth (%)	18.2	19.6	1.7	−11.4	1.6
Broad money growth (%)	17.9	15.6	15.8	14.1	27.0
Government expenditure (% of GDP)	10.5	9.7	9.8	9.5	10.0
Government budget balance (% of GDP)	−0.5	0.4	0.3	−1.5	−4.2
Foreign debt (as % of GDP)	21.7	26.0	31.6	33.2	46.6
Exchange rate (vis-à-vis US$)	772.5	774.7	844.2	1,415.2	1,207.8
Real exchange rate (1995=100)	102.9	100	103.9	118	150.7
Nominal wage growth (%)	15.3	11.2	11.9	7.0	−2.5
Real wage growth (%)	7.7	6.4	6.7	2.4	−9.3
Current account balance (US$ million)	−3,428	8,508	23,005	8,167	40,039
Capital account balance (US$ million)	5,720	16,786	23,327	1,314	−3,991
Foreign direct investment (US$ million)	819	1,776	2,325	2,844	5,143
Export value (US$ million)	78,353	125,058	129,715	136,164	132,313
Composition of export, value of highest four exports (1996 ranking, US$ million)					
Electrical machinery, apparatus, appliances	11,789	28,456	25,907	—	—
Textiles, yarn, fabrics, made-up articles	8,364	12,313	12,944	—	—
Road vehicles	4,801	10,115	12,565	—	—
Telecommunications	7,033	8,877	9,047	—	—

Table 10.1 (continued)

	1990–94 (average)	1995	1996	1997	1998
Import value (US$ million)	83,858	135,119	150,339	144,616	93,282
Composition of import, value of highest four imports (1996 ranking, US$ million)					
Petroleum and petroleum products	8,545	14,430	18,930	—	—
Electrical machinery, apparatus, appliances	8,502	14,302	16,000	—	—
Specialized machinery	4,723	7,528	7,803	—	—
General industrial machinery and equipment	4,480	7,188	7,610	—	—
Exports' dependence on unaffected markets (%)	42.1	36.3	32.5	—	—
Volume of exports (index)	66.5	100	119.8	149.6	174.9
Volume of imports (index)	66.1	100	112.6	114.3	90.3
International reserves minus gold (US$ million)	18,296	32,677	33,201	20,369	51,974
Total foreign debt (US$ billion)	—	127.2	164.3	158.1	149.4
Total short-term foreign debt (US$ billion)	—	71.6	93	63.2	30.6
DS stock market index ($)	161.2	197.7	123	39.9	—
DS stock market index (n.c.)	153.8	189.1	128.2	83.3	—
Korea Composite Index (average)	737.0	934.9	833.4	654.5	406.1
Nominal lending rate (%)	9.4	9	8.8	11.9	15.2
Nominal deposit rate (%)	9.4	8.8	7.5	10.8	13.3
Non-performing loans (% of total loans)	2.1	12.1	20	31.2	—

Table 10.2
Korea: Changes in labor employment and output composition

	Composition of output		Composition of labor force	
	1986	1996	1970	1990
Agriculture	11.2	6.3	49.1	18.1
Industry	42.1	42.8	19.8	35.4
Services	46.8	50.9	31.1	46.5

Table 10.3
Korea: Forecasts for the 1999–2001 situation

Forecasting institution and date of forecast	GDP growth (%)			CPI inflation (%)		
	1999	2000	2001	1998	1999	2001
International Monetary Fund, October 1999	6.5	5.5	—	0.7	2.8	—
HSBC Asia Economic Weekly, January 2000	9.4	6.3	5.6	0.9	3.6	4.5
Economist Intelligence Unit, 2000:1Q	9.4	7.0	5.2	0.8	3.1	3.3

Having achieved some success in this initial stage of crisis management, Korea has accelerated the pace of structural reform and has initiated measures to stimulate the economy. In particular, expansionary macro policy management since the second half of 1998 has played a key role in enabling the economy to achieve an early recovery. However, with the fiscal deficit increasing and inflationary pressures developing, the expansionary policy stance will have to be moderated in the future. Also, the problem of eliminating a substantial number of bad loans still remains to be resolved. These difficulties suggest that without continuing reform efforts, the current pace of recovery may be short-lived. It also remains to be seen whether the structural adjustments render the economy less vulnerable to future crises.

10.2   Causes and Evolution of the Korean Crisis

Korea had consistently turned in a remarkable economic performance for decades, so the spread of the Asian financial crisis to Korea late in 1997 was a surprising development. Clearly, Korea's economic situation did not fit the mold of the typical balance-of-payments crisis.

Monetary policy had been relatively conservative. The growth rates of M2 were lower in the 1990s than those in the 1980s. The fiscal stance was also prudent: Korea maintained a balanced budget or small surplus since 1994. This is in sharp contrast with the Latin American debt crisis in the early 1980s, which featured the mismanagement of macroeconomic policies: namely, large fiscal deficits and consequent monetary expansion. The Korean crisis was definitely not a result of profligate fiscal and monetary policies.

Widening current account deficits, however, did give cause for concern. Korea incurred current account deficits each year since 1990 except 1993. In 1996, the deficit reached 5 percent of GDP (table 10.1). Nevertheless, Korea's external position was judged to be fairly sustainable. Its current account deficits were used to finance high investment rather than high consumption, and it was thought that the trend of increasing deficits would be reversed quickly as soon as the falling international prices of major export items such as semiconductors, steel, and petrochemical products rebounded.

A sharp export slowdown and a sizable current account deficit in 1996 led many to suspect the possibility of an overvalued exchange rate. Korean currency was effectively pegged to the U.S. dollar. Therefore, the Korean won appreciated sharply against the yen since mid-1995 when the dollar appreciated markedly against the yen. However, during the 1990s as a whole, the real exchange rate of the won did not change much against either the U.S. dollar or the Japanese yen. The overvaluation of won, therefore, was not a major factor of the trade difficulties.

The ratio of total foreign debt to GNP was also fairly low in Korea, compared to such ratios in other Asian and Latin American countries. The ratio had been very high during the early 1980s and then declined steadily. Although the debt–GDP ratio increased over 1994–96 and reached 31.6 percent in 1996, the debt–export ratio remained at a low level by international standards. In sum, the Korean economy did not have any difficulty in servicing its external debt until recently.

Despite sound macroeconomic fundamentals and a fairly sustainable external debt situation, as the currency crisis began to unfold it became clear that the Korean economy possessed a number of structural weaknesses. The impressive macroeconomic performance had served to cover up some serious structural problems, notably weak financial sectors and over-indebted corporate sectors. The financial sector in Korea—as in other developing countries—has been negatively affected by government intervention, connected lending, and lack of prudential regulation and supervision. For many years the Korean government regarded the financial institutions as the ideal instruments for carrying out its industrial policy. State allocation of credit remained little changed after financial liberalization and privatization in the late 1980s (see Borensztein and Lee 1999). The financial institutions did not possess their own credit and risk assessment capabilities and were exposed excessively to key sectors and large corporations.

The key feature of the Korean crisis was a large inflow and a sudden withdrawal of foreign capital. Successful macroeconomic performance and prudent economic management of Korea contributed to the rapid capital inflows into the economy during the 1990s. Though not as dramatic as seen in other Asian countries such as Indonesia and Thailand, capital inflows continued to increase in Korea, reaching 24 billion dollars in 1996 (about 5 percent of GDP). When foreign investors began to lose confidence in the Korean economy, these large inflows turned into sudden outflows. During October–December 1997, capital outflows amounted to about 9.8 billion dollars. It is no wonder that this large-scale shift in financial flows provoked a sudden liquidity crisis.

Huge capital inflows and subsequent capital outflows brought about even more problematic consequences in Korea because financial systems were not well developed. In particular, the rapid financial opening in the 1990s, without adequate prudential regulations, left the financial sector highly exposed to external turbulence. The global integration of the economy accelerated in 1993, partly in an effort to meet the requirements to join the OECD. The number of merchant banks and the volume of their foreign currency business expanded rapidly, but without proper regulation, thereby further affecting the soundness and safety of the financial sector. Merchant banks appear to have invested in high-yield foreign junk bonds with funds borrowed cheaply using Korea's high credit rating in international financial markets. When foreign lenders started to recall loans in late 1997, these assets turned out to be illiquid. Banks were also exposed to large maturity mismatches in their foreign currency operations because they relied on foreign currency denominated short-term borrowing to fund long-term domestic currency denominated loans. The ratio of short-term external debt to total external debt was over 50 percent prior to the crisis, leading to a drastic mismatch between the short-term debts and official foreign reserves. The ratio of short-term external debt to official foreign reserves increased continuously in the 1990s, reaching its historic high of 252 percent in 1997 and far exceeding the ratios of other developing countries (World Bank 1998).

The counterpart to the weak financial sector was excessive investment and high leverage by the corporate sector. The under-regulated financial institutions continued to provide financing to firms, particularly the large conglomerates ("chaebols" in Korean), without appropriate risk assessment. Because chaebols were considered to be "too big to fail," financial institutions believed that the government would protect them from any harm; thus many risky or unprofitable investments were financed. The profit rates (return on assets) in the manufacturing sector had fallen continuously from over 4 percent in 1988 to 0.9 percent in 1996. The decline of rates of return to capital during this period was caused at least partly by excessive and misallocated investment. Fixed investment apparently increased from 30 percent in the late 1980s to over 37 percent of GDP in the 1990s. The major part of investment was concentrated on key sectors such as memory chips, steel and automobiles.

Low profits and soft lending resulted in extremely high leverage among the firms, particularly in the largest chaebols in the economy. Compared to companies in advanced countries, Korean firms rely substantially more on bank finance and less on internal funds (Borensztein and Lee 1999). By 1996 the average debt-equity ratio of firms was over 300 percent and it reached 620 percent for a median firm (World Bank 1998). The ratio exceeded 500 percent for the 30 largest chaebols and reached even 3,000 percent for some chaebols.

Poor corporate governance was also a destabilizing factor for the Korean economy. Because chaebol firms are highly interdependent financially through cross-share holdings and cross-loan guarantees, the financial trouble of one chaebol firm can easily lead to a disaster for the whole group and even for the banking system.

Over-investment, risky projects and high corporate leverage caused serious difficulties for businesses and financial firms when the economy was hit by large unfavorable terms-of-trade shocks in 1995 and 1996. The Korean economy was affected very severely because exports were heavily concentrated in a few sectors such as steel, automobiles and electronics. Semiconductors and steel products accounted for 13 percent and 6 percent of total exports, respectively. The price of major export products fell significantly during the period. For example, the unit export price of memory chips fell by more than 70 percent, and the steel export price dropped by about 30 percent. In 1997 several large Korean firms moved towards bankruptcy. The failure of Hanbo, the fourteenth largest conglomerate, in January was followed by the insolvency of smaller conglomerates including Sammi, Jinro and Dainong. The bigger blow came with the insolvency of Kia Motors, one of the three largest Korean auto companies and the main company of the eighth largest conglomerate. The series of large corporate insolvencies inevitably undermined the health of the financial institutions with large exposure to these conglomerates. According to official estimates, non-performing loans (NPLs) of commercial banks as of the end of 1996 stood at 11.9 trillion won (3.9 percent of total loans made by commercial banks), and they almost doubled to 22.7 trillion won at the end of 1997.

10.3   IMF Adjustment Program

In December 1998, Korea requested financial support from the IMF. The country is still under an IMF adjustment program that is attached to its financial support. The IMF program for Korea can be seen as a mixture of aggregate demand management and structural reform of the financial sector. The choice reflects IMF's view that the crisis originated from structural weakness in the Korean economy, especially from its financial system (IMF 1998). The IMF reform package demanded across-the-board structural changes, including comprehensive dismantling of the old financial system, setting the stage for corporate restructuring and deleveraging, and improving corporate governance and transparency. The reform program also encompassed other measures related to trade liberalization, capital account liberalization and labor market reform.

But the IMF believed that the most urgent task for crisis management should be to restore confidence in the currency by implementing stringent demand management policies. Therefore, the IMF program required a sharp increase in interest rates to stem capital outflows and discourage speculation. In line with this policy, the call rate was raised from 12.5 percent to 21 percent on December 5 and peaked at 35 percent later. Money growth was limited to a rate consistent with containing inflation at 5 percent or less, despite huge inflationary pressures from the sharp depreciation in the exchange rate. The tight fiscal stance for 1998 was called for to alleviate the burden on monetary policy and to provide for the interest costs of restructuring the financial sector (see table 10.4).

However, the IMF policy, which simultaneously pursued structural reform and foreign exchange market stabilization, posed a dilemma. In stabilizing the foreign exchange market in the short run, contractionary fiscal and monetary policies were needed. On the other hand, expansionary policies were required to alleviate the pains from the credit crunch that accompanied structural reform. The recent critiques against the IMF policy argue that the IMF program was too contractionary in the short run, thereby making it very costly to implement the intended structural reform (Radelet and Sachs 1998). It is difficult to determine whether the IMF program exacerbated downturns of the economy that could have been avoided. In our opinion, the fiscal austerity was the "wrong medicine" for an economy that was fiscally sound, while the monetary tightening helped to stabilize the exchange rate and prevent more disastrous consequences.

This is not to deny that the high interest rate aggravated social distress. The tight monetary policy was particularly painful in the Korean economy because most firms were highly indebted. The increase in the cost of credit raised the firms' debt service burden so greatly that a large number of firms, including some that would have been financially viable under normal circumstances, were driven into bankruptcy. In the first quarter of 1998, the average monthly bankruptcy rate of firms reached more than 3,000, more than double the same period in 1997. In the first half of 1998, GDP dropped 5.3 percent year on year. The unemployment rate soared to 7.6 percent in July 1998 from around 2 percent of the previous year, raising the number of job losers to 1.7 million. The sudden job losses caused much social distress because adequate social safety nets were not developed.

Alarmed by the continuous downturn of the economy, the IMF began to soften the stringency of its program. Table 10.4 summarizes the main features of the initial IMF programs and the revised agreements. Starting from the third program (the second review), signed on February 17, 1998, monetary policy was eased. The program allowed for a gradual decrease in the interest rate and a slight increase in the growth of reserve money. In the fourth review, signed on July 28, 1998, the Korean government and the IMF agreed to ease fiscal policy by increasing the target for the budget deficit to 4.0 percent of GDP. In the fifth review as of November 18, 1998, the deficit target was further increased to 5 percent of GDP.

10.4   Corporate and Financial Restructuring Policies

Korea's economic reform program is a coordinated, two-pronged approach that aims to restructure the financial and corporate sectors simultaneously. The government enforced prudential regulations and Bank of International Settlements (BIS) standards in the financial sector, so that financial institutions, in turn, would place corresponding pressure on corporations with regard to their debt reduction and business restructuring.[1]

---

1. See Choi (1999) and World Bank (1999) for the detailed discussion of the process of corporate and financial restructuring.

Table 10.4
IMF programs for Korea

	Standby arrange-ment (5 Dec. 1997)	First review (8 Jan. 1998)	Second review (17 Feb. 1998)	Third review (28 May 1998)	Fourth review (28 July 1998)	Fifth review (18 Nov. 1998)
Growth rate	3%	1–2%	1%	−1%	−4%	—
Inflation	< 5%	~ 9%	9–10%	9–10%	9%	5%
Unemployment rate	3.9%	4.7%	5.0–6.0%	6% range	6% range	—
Current account balance	$4.3 bil.	$3 bil.	$8 bil.	$21–23 bil.	$33–35 bil.	$20 bil.
Usable foreign reserves	—	—	$30 bil. (2/4Q)	$34 bil. (3/4Q)	$41 bil. (4/4Q)	$45 bil. (4/4Q)
Budgetary balance (% of GDP)	Balanced or a little surplus	Deficit permitted	−0.8%	−1.2 to −1.7%	−4.0%	−5.0%
Reserve monetary growth	—	14.9% (1/4Q)	15.7% (2/4Q)	14.2% (3/4Q)	13.9% (4/4Q)	No ceiling
Interest rate	High interest rate	High interest rate	Cautious and gradual decline	Additional lowering	Flexibly adjust	Flexibly adjust

Restructuring and Reform of the Financial Sector

At the end of September 1998, the Korean government had completed the first phase of financial reform: restructuring the financial industry, liberalizing and augmenting its capital market, and strengthening prudential regulation and supervision. In December 1997, 13 financial reform bills were legislated to strengthen the regulation and supervision of the financial sector. In April 1998, an independent Financial Supervisory Commission (FSC) was established. The FSC is playing a pivotal role in the restructuring of the financial sector.

The Korean government has accelerated the liberalization of capital markets to eliminate all controls and restrictions by the year 2000. Most ceilings on foreign equity ownership, foreign takeover of management, and land ownership have been eliminated. To facilitate foreign investment, the existing administrative regulations were simplified into a single legal framework, the Foreign Investment Promotion Act.

The government closed a number of insolvent financial institutions and suspended the operations of other troubled financial institutions. Since the end of 1997, five out of 33 commercial banks and 16 out of 30 merchant banks have had their licenses revoked. As of June 1999, 143 institutions, including 130 credit unions, were either closed or merged, and 19 institutions, including 14 mutual savings and finance companies, had their operations suspended.

The financial restructuring program placed considerable emphasis on the banking sector. The government has written down the debt in two large commercial banks, Korea First Bank and Seoul Bank, and recapitalized them in order to prevent any systematic risk from threatening the settlement system. The FSC requested the submission of rehabilitation plans from the 12 banks which failed to meet the required BIS capital adequacy ratio of 8 percent as of December 1997. The FSC found the plans of five small banks (constituting about 7 percent of total deposits) to be unviable, and ordered them to close and their assets and liabilities transferred to five stronger banks. The remaining seven unsound banks, whose plans were conditionally approved by the FSC, are taking rehabilitation actions, such as disposing of non-performing loans (NPLs), inducing new equity capital, and streamlining business operations.

Viable banks are also implementing measures to further improve their soundness. Some leading commercial banks, e.g., Hanil Bank and Commercial Bank of Korea, merged to strengthen their financial structure and to remain competitive in the domestic market. Over several months in 1998, the FSC established a new system of prudential regulation and supervision with respect to liquidity management, loan classification and loss provisions, and information disclosure of financial institutions. The FSC has been applying basically the same measures and procedures for the restructuring of non-bank financial institutions.

One of the major tasks of financial sector restructuring is to eliminate NPLs. At the end of March 1999, the estimated total of NPLs of all financial institutions, broadly defined to include "precautionary" (non-core) loans of 78.5 trillion won, amounted to 143.9 trillion won (approximately 32 percent of GDP or 25 percent of total outstanding loans). The government aims to dispose all core NPLs of 65.4 trillion won as well as a portion of precautionary loans through two main channels: first, financial institutions' disposal of their own NPLs by either selling off collateral or calling in their loans; second, purchase of the remaining NPLs from the financial institutions at a "market" price (about 50 percent of book value) estimated by the Korea Asset Management Corporation (KAMC). The government is providing fiscal support for the purchase of NPLs by KAMC and for the recapitalization of banks and deposit protection by Korea Deposit Insurance Company (KDIC). As of the end of March 1999, KAMC has purchased NPLs amounting to 44.1 trillion won in book value and plans to spend another 12.8 trillion won to purchase NPLs of 28.3 trillion won in book value. KDIC has provided fiscal support of 22.3 trillion won (as of May 1999) for recapitalization and deposit protection.

The estimated total cost of the government's financial restructuring plan is about 64 trillion won, equivalent to about 14 percent of GDP. Fiscal resources to implement all these restructuring measures are mobilized largely by issuing public bonds, and KAMC and KDIC are the major bond issuers.

To date, the financial restructuring program has progressed well. The reforms have been strengthening the supervisory and regulatory framework, increasing the transparency of financial sector information, improving the mechanisms to deal with troubled institutions and to manage troubled loans, and facilitating the entry of foreign investment and expertise into the system. Most commercial banks have improved their capital adequacy ratio to well above 10 percent. However, the financial institutions' excessive exposure to over-indebted corporations has caused considerable problems in the restructuring process. For instance, in August 1999, when ailing subsidiaries of the Daewoo Group were put on workout programs, the NPLs of the financial institutions increased sharply because of their credit exposure to Daewoo companies, amounting to 45 trillion won. The problem of the NPLs casts a shadow of uncertainty over the progress of the financial sector reform. The stockpile of NPLs will remain high because hidden bad loans will materialize as a consequence of the ongoing restructuring in the corporate sector. Critics say that the NPLs would be greater than the official estimate if NPLs were defined by the international standard, which is based on the borrower's ability to pay back the loans rather than the borrower's history of late interest payments. Estimates of NPLs by private institutions amounted to about 220–300 trillion won, far exceeding the government-tallied amount of 144 trillion won.

Although not directly related to NPLs, recent problems of investment trust companies (ITCs) also illustrate the importance of latent investment loss. One of the main sources of the investment loss of ITCs has been Daewoo securities. As Daewoo's bankruptcy became established, ITCs with an average weighting in Daewoo securities of 10 percent experienced substantial losses in their funds, and interest rates rose in the financial market. In principle, any investment loss of ITCs should be fully borne by their customers. However, any practical action ITCs were to take based on this principle would likely cause full-scale redemption by investors. The government was concerned about the potentially disastrous effect that such redemption might have on the still shaky financial market, so it suspended redemption of the shares of Daewoo-related ITCs. For other ITCs, however, the government has not announced any clear rule of loss bearing.

Despite the progress in financial structural reform, it is unclear whether real practices in banking management and supervision of the financial sector have improved. There are certain human capital constraints in rebuilding the banking system. Bank managers are inexperienced and are unaccustomed to commercial practices. Fundamental behavioral changes to improve the process of credit appraisal and loan allocation requires appropriate guidance and substantial practice over a long period. One way to improve efficiency in the banking institutions is to allow more foreign ownership and placement of foreign expertise at the highest management level. Therefore, the government should move quickly to expedite the sale of two major commercial banks to foreigners. In Korea, financial institutions still remain under the heavy influence of the government. As a result of the recapitalization process, some large banks are effectively nationalized, thus increasing government involvement in the banking system. Strengthening the autonomy of the financial institutions and insulating them from government intervention must be a long-term goal.

Corporate Restructuring Policies

Restructuring of the corporate sector has also progressed, with the Korean government taking the initiative. The corporate restructuring efforts in Korea can be roughly summarized in three points.

First, there have been various regulatory changes aimed at improving management transparency and corporate governance structure. For example, the External Audit Law was revised in early 1998 to require corporations to report combined financial statements in accordance with international standards, starting from 1999. Under the new listing requirements of the Korean Stock Exchange, all listed companies must establish committees of external auditors. By lowering the representation requirement for class action from 1 to 0.01 percent, the government has strengthened legal protection of the rights of minority shareholders. Also, institutional investors will play a more powerful role as monitors of corporate management because the ban on their right to vote in general shareholder meetings has been lifted. To maximize the influence of market forces in corporate governance and exit mechanisms, most of the past regulations on hostile or large-scale mergers and acquisitions have been removed or relaxed.

Second, financial institutions have assumed a leading role in the corporate restructuring. Many analysts agree that one of the main sources of the corporate failures in Korea was the weak financial system. Without proper monitoring by the financial institutions, the corporate sector engaged in highly leveraged and risky investment projects. In recognition of this defect, a group of creditor banks established a formal review committee in May 1998 to assess the viability of 313 client firms showing weak capital structure. The committee classified 55 corporations as nonviable, and took the necessary steps to dissolve these insolvent firms. No new credit has been extended to the nonviable firms by their banks, and bailout from affiliate companies has been prohibited.

However, most financial institutions have been reluctant to act decisively in the corporate exit process, because the legal framework for dealing with illiquid/insolvent firms remains inefficient, i.e., it involves lengthy procedures and high costs, and the balance sheet of the financial institutions themselves may be further weakened by corporate bankruptcies. In addition, fearing that a series of corporate bankruptcies might abort the economic recovery, the government has adopted a gradual approach. Thus, the government and creditor banks have sought to deal with ailing firms by applying workout programs to them under the Corporate Restructuring Accord. As of August 1999, financial institutions have selected 54 subsidiaries of the top 6–64 business conglomerates, and 39 non-chaebol corporations as workout candidates. The scope of the corporate workout program is being extended to include small and medium-sized firms.

The program was originally intended to rehabilitate viable corporations with liquidity problems; however, the desired outcome has been slow in appearing. For example, there have been few debt–equity swaps because banks are hesitant to become more deeply engaged with nonviable firms, and majority stockholders oppose their control over management.

Third, restructuring of the large chaebols has been emphasized. The five biggest chaebols (Hyundai, Samsung, Daewoo, LG and the SK group) accounted for 37 percent of Korea's gross output and 44 percent of total exports in 1997. In fact, because their business activities involve key sectors and they are linked to hundreds of subcontractors, their economic influence is even greater than their size would suggest. Thus, it is not entirely surprising that the chaebols have been a target of more extensive reforms than other corporations. The five largest chaebols and their creditor banks reached an agreement on debt reduction and other restructuring measures based on the agenda for chaebol reform announced in 1998 (Financial Structure Improvement Agreement). There have been considerable improvements in the area of transparency and accountability. For example, cross-debt guarantees among chaebol affiliates in unrelated industries were removed by the end of 1998, and cross-debt guarantees of any kind will be wiped out by March 2000.

There have also been substantial improvements in debt reduction. The debt/equity ratio of the top five chaebols was about 302 percent in mid-1999, compared to about 500 percent at the end of 1998. The progress in debt reduction was made by the chaebols' increased rights-offerings and sales of affiliates not related to core competence. The government has urged the chaebols to reduce their debt/equity ratio to below 200 percent by the end of 1999. One unconventional way to meet this target is through asset revaluation, which would reduce the debt/equity ratio of the top five chaebols to 235 percent in mid-1999. Obviously, the asset revaluation is merely a change in bookkeeping and does not help cure the real problem of over-indebtedness of the corporate sector. The government has not announced yet whether the revised ratios are acceptable.

Recognizing that over-diversification of business activities and duplicate investment in key sectors have caused the low profitability and high leverage of large conglomerates, the government and the top five chaebol leaders announced in September 1998 a framework for mergers and business swaps—referred to as "big deals." [2] However, the deals have not been particularly successful. For example, Hyundai and

---

2. The deals involve seven key industries in which large-scale production is important: semiconductors, petrochemicals, automobiles, aircraft, train car manufacturing, power plant equipment engines and oil refining.

LG Semiconductors have been merged as the government planned, but the merged firm is expanding rather than reducing its capacity, in response to the current boom in the semiconductor industry. The deals seem to be very hastily driven by the government initiative without sufficient consideration of commercial factors. Too much intervention by the government in corporate sector restructuring could bring about bad consequences in the long run. It is not clear that the deals will necessarily reduce overcapacity unless job rationalization is implemented seriously. In an effort to curb rising unemployment, the government keeps asking the chaebols to refrain from conducting massive layoffs. However, it would be impossible to implement comprehensive restructuring and enhance productivity without provoking layoffs, particularly in an industry (such as the automobile industry) with a large labor force. In addition, it is still difficult for the chaebol to close subsidiaries, given the long procedures and high legal and financial costs.

Despite all the comprehensive measures of corporate restructuring, the actual accomplishment in reducing over-indebtedness and improving productivity of the corporate sector is still limited. With the present progress in the restructuring process, it is difficult to expect the debt to equity ratios to decline in the near term to the 200 percent required by the government. It also still remains to be seen whether the structural reform will contribute to enhancing international competitiveness in key sectors.

10.5 Labor Market Reform

Enhancing labor market flexibility is a key goal in Korea's structural reform. An important characteristic of the private employment system in Korea has been a labor force accustomed to lifetime employment. Layoffs were regarded as the last conceivable measure in corporate rationalization. The government and corporations recognize that easing restrictions on layoffs is necessary for financial and corporate restructuring, but they face strong resistance from labor unions. After tripartite negotiations between labor, business and government, the Labor Standard Act was amended in February 1998 to allow layoffs. In addition, the establishment of manpower leasing businesses was legalized in July 1998. This will enhance labor market flexibility by making labor outsourcing an additional option for employment adjustment.

Table 10.5
Korea: Tracking economic developments

	1997:Q1	1997:Q2	1997:Q3	1997:Q4	1998:Q1	1998:Q2	1998:Q3	1998:Q4	1999:Q1	1999:Q2
Growth rate of real GDP (%)	5.7	6.6	6.1	3.9	-3.9	-6.8	-7.9	-4.6	3.7	9.9
Exchange rate (against US$)	897.1	888.1	914.8	1,695.0	1,383.0	1,373.0	1,391.0	1,204.0	1,227.0	1,157.6
Real exchange rate (1990 = 100, WPI based)	88.0	88.1	87.8	153.8	117.6	115.8	116.5	108.4	106.3	100.6
International reserves minus gold (US$ million)	29,893.1	34,069.9	30,389.2	20,367.9	29,683.4	40,835.1	46,912.0	51,974.5	57,385.2	61,920.4
Reserve money growth (%)	-24.7	-12.4	-21.8	-12.5	7.7	0.3	-1.1	-8.1	1.7	3.1
Narrow money growth rate (%)	2.9	4.9	-7.2	-11.4	-20.2	-23.0	-7.6	1.6	16.3	22.9
Broad money growth rate (%)	20.1	17.6	16.4	14.1	12.1	16.3	24.8	27.0	36.3	26.4
CPI growth rate (YOY%)	4.7	4.0	4.0	5.1	8.9	8.2	7.0	6.0	0.7	0.6
Nominal lending rate (%)	11.4	11.4	11.6	13.1	17.3	16.9	14.9	12.1	10.7	9.4
Nominal deposit rate (%)	10.3	10.8	10.6	11.6	16.4	16.3	11.1	9.3	8.7	7.7
Export value (US$ million)	29,724.0	35,532.0	34,182.0	36,727.0	32,284.0	35,342.0	30,931.1	34,722.0	30,254.0	35,764.0
Import value (US$ million)	37,050.0	37,362.0	35,688.0	34,517.0	23,901.0	23,671.0	21,529.3	24,624.0	25,575.0	28,747.0
Export volume (index)	220.8	269.9	273.3	319.7	297.8	334.9	314.3	346.7	315.7	376.7
Import volume (index)	207.4	220.5	209.6	215.4	156.9	169.4	158.6	182.6	195.7	217.5
DS stock market index ($)	116.6	133.1	111.0	39.9	61.7	40.7	41.5	93.4	102.3	159.4
DS stock market index (national currency)	128.8	145.7	125.1	83.3	105.4	69.0	71.1	138.5	154.8	227.4
Korea Composite Index	677.3	745.4	647.1	376.3	481.0	297.9	310.3	562.5	619.0	883.0

To deal with the expected large-scale layoffs from the restructuring process, the government started public work programs and extended unemployment insurance coverage from corporations with at least 10 workers to all businesses, causing the government budget for social safety nets to increase from 5.7 trillion won in 1998 to 8.3 trillion won in 1999.

As the unemployment rate has continued to climb, resistance from the labor unions has intensified, resulting in their withdrawal from the tripartite committee in July 1998 and an organized strike to protest the government's push toward restructuring. In particular, employment adjustments at large conglomerates are not going well because of the resistance from their strong unions. Although the Korean government promised to uphold the laws against illegal strikes and labor practices, it does not enforce them on politically strong labor unions in the large industries. The government tries to prevent massive layoffs in large corporations to stem further increase in unemployment. However, the obstacles to layoffs have not seemed to lower unemployment. Even if the work force is maintained, the hiring of new employees would be slow and the unemployment rate would continue to be high. The improvement of labor market flexibility and business–labor relations will require a long time.

10.6   Prospects for Recovery and Sustainable Growth

Two years after the IMF bailout, the Korean economy shows a strong recovery from the crisis. Various indicators suggest that the economy is now fully out of the crisis. The nation's usable foreign exchange reserves increased to $65 billion in October 1999, up more than seven-fold from November 1997, while its total external liabilities have decreased from $160 billion in 1997 to $143 in August 1999. More importantly, the ratio of short-term debt has dropped to 20 percent of total debt from more than 40 percent in 1997. The won-dollar exchange rate has significantly declined from its historical high of 1,962 won on December 23, 1997 and has been stabilized at around 1,200 for most of 1999. The three-year corporate bond rate, which once topped 25 percent, now stands below 10 percent, and the default ratio of commercial bills has fallen to the pre-crisis level. The real GDP in 1999 is expected to grow by as high as 9 percent (tables 10.3 and 10.6).

Table 10.6
Forecast for the Korean economy, 1999–2000 (year-on-year growth rate, percent)

	1998 P Annual	1999 P 1/4Q	1999 P 2/4Q	1999 P 3/4Q	1999 F 4/4Q	1999 F Annual	2000 F Annual
GDP	−5.8	4.5	9.9	12.3	13.0	10.1	7.8
Consumption	−8.2	5.0	7.3	8.4	8.8	7.4	6.0
Private	−9.6	6.2	9.1	10.3	10.9	9.1	7.0
Government	−0.1	−1.7	−2.3	−1.3	−1.0	−1.5	1.0
Fixed investment	−21.1	−4.3	4.9	6.9	6.9	3.9	9.5
Equipment	−38.5	12.9	37.2	48.0	44.0	35.2	15.7
Construction	−10.2	−13.7	−8.5	−10.0	−7.1	−9.5	5.5
Total exports	13.3	10.3	15.1	22.2	23.5	18.0	11.7
Commodity	15.6	11.9	18.3	25.3	26.0	20.5	10.0
Total imports	−22.0	27.0	26.9	32.0	34.9	30.4	18.1
Commodity	−24.6	26.4	30.8	40.0	41.3	34.9	18.3
Current account	40.6	62	64	66	60	252	126
Trade account	41.6	68	80	72	69	289	170
Exports	132.1	315	357	365	407	1,143	1,593
(%)	(−4.7)	(−3.7)	(3.8)	(16.0)	(21.0)	(9.2)	(10.3)
Imports	90.5	247	277	293	337	1,154	1,423
(%)	(−36.2)	(7.6)	(20.8)	(40.5)	(42.0)	(27.5)	(23.3)
Services, income, transfers (billions of dollars)	−1.1	−6	−16	−6	−10	−37	−44
Price level							
CPI	7.5	0.7	0.6	0.7	1.4	0.8	3.2
PPI	12.2	−3.5	−3.3	−1.9	0.6	−2.0	2.8

Notes: P = preliminary estimate. F = forecast.
Source: Korea Development Institute.

The speedy recovery of the Korean economy is attributed to many factors, such as the early resolution of creditors' panic, the export-oriented industrial structure, and the swift adjustment of macroeconomic policy (Lee and Rhee 1999b). One of the important causes for the V-shaped recovery of the Korean economy is expansionary macroeconomic policies. In September 1998, the government lowered interest rates, extended more credits to small and medium-sized enterprises, and widened the fiscal deficit to revive the economy—despite criticisms that a premature stimulus of the economy might undermine the restructuring process. The call interest rate was lowered to 7 percent in October 1998 and has remained below 5 percent for much of 1999. Korea could pursue the low interest rate policy without destabilizing the exchange rate, because its foreign exchange reserve was growing thanks to a huge current account surplus and successive interest rate cuts in the U.S. Expansionary monetary policy would not have been effective without the financial restructuring, since domestic credit was being constrained by the weak balance sheets of the banking sector.

During the first half of 1999, private consumption and equipment investment increased by 7.5 percent and 20 percent, respectively. Exports continued to grow strongly by about 14 percent during the first half of 1999, but imports expanded more rapidly by about 27 percent during the same period, reflecting strong domestic demand. As a result, the current account surplus is expected to be reduced from $40 billion in 1998 to about $25 billion in 1999. Despite the rapid increase in aggregate demand, consumer prices increased by less than 1 percent in 1999. The exceptionally stable prices can be attributed to the appreciation of Korean won and the fact that aggregate demand is still below aggregate supply capacity.

Recovery of the aggregate economy has not resolved all social problems. The unemployment rate remains high at 5.4 percent (August 1999), with the total number of displaced workers reaching 1.24 million, and it is unlikely to recover its pre-crisis average of 2 to 3 percent in the near future. The typical pattern of employment growth in the previous IMF-program countries indicates that the recovery of employment growth takes more adjustment time, compared with other macroeconomic variables (Lee and Rhee 1999a). The recovery has not been even in every sector of the economy. The recent rapid recovery has concentrated on several manufacturing industries, especially the semiconductor and automobile industries. The service sector, by contrast, remains relatively sluggish. The relative price of services (with respect to total consumer prices) decreased after the crisis, since weak demand for services was accompanied by increased labor supply in the services industry. As many unemployed workers shifted to the services sector, nominal wages in the personal services sector decreased by 3 percent in the first half of 1999, in contrast to the 8 percent increase of the total industry wages. Also, income inequality has widened, thereby reducing social cohesion in a society that was known for its equity as well as its prosperity. It is estimated that the income share of the top 20 percent of households increased from 37 percent prior to the crisis to 40 percent in the second quarter of 1999.

The fast pace of recovery also raises concerns about its sustainability. The recovery is to a large extent an outcome of the initial exchange rate depreciation and the expansionary macroeconomic policies. If, as expected, the government resumes a less expansionary policy stance and the trade account surplus decreases, then the GDP growth rate will decrease in 2000. In fact, most forecasters expect that the economy will grow by about 6 to 7 percent in 2000, three points lower than in 1999 (Asia Pacific Consensus Forecasts, September 1999). Considering recent trends of the economy, these forecasts seem reasonable. The annual growth rate of 6 percent for 2000 implies that the current pace of recovery will slow down to about 1.2 percent quarterly growth starting 2000:1Q. Despite the slowdown of the economy, however, the inflation rate is expected to be 3 to 4 percent in 2000, up from 1 percent in 1999. Lagged effects of the expansionary policy since the second half of 1998, combined with the expected substantial wage increase, will make inflationary pressures more visible in 2000.

However, if structural reform efforts are diluted and the current stance of expansionary macroeconomic policy extends to 2000, the prospects become much more uncertain. The economy may continue its strong growth in the short run, with the inflation rate higher than 4 percent, but in the medium term it may experience another episode of financial instability and recession. To avoid this possibility, the government needs to speed up corporate and financial sector reforms. The stockpile of NPLs in financial institutions is one of the most serious concerns and must be resolved efficiently. To relieve viable firms of their over-indebtedness, debt reduction schemes such as some combination of debt forgiveness and debt–equity swap need to be implemented more actively. Without swift and complete economic reform, the recent pace of recovery cannot be sustained and the economy will be vulnerable to another financial panic and economic crisis.

Another major concern in Korea is fiscal soundness. In restructuring the financial sector and extending the social safety net, the government has rapidly increased its borrowing. The central government debt increased from 13.36 percent of GDP in 1997 to 31.9 percent in 1998. In order to keep the debt at a manageable level, structural reforms need to be pursued more efficiently. Reckless extension of credits to nonviable firms will eventually lead to further increase in the fiscal debt.

The comprehensive restructuring and quick recovery of the economy would not have been possible without political stability. Korea has been very fortunate in having a national consensus for the full-ranged structural reform with the new political leadership of President Daejung Kim. But preserving consensus is certainly more difficult than building it. Now, in part thanks to the quicker-than-expected recovery, the reform is losing full support from many sides of society. The labor unions and large conglomerates are becoming more antagonistic to economic restructuring. Facing a parliamentary election in April 2000, all political parties become less enthusiastic about economic as well as political reform. While we do not foresee that the Korean political situation will worsen and derail the economic recovery, it is inevitable that the reform will slow down.

References

Borensztein, Eduardo, and Jong-Wha Lee. 1999. Financial distortions and crisis in Korea. International Monetary Fund Working Paper, WP/99/20. IMF.

Choi, Bhumsoo. 1999. Lessons of crisis management from the Korean experience. Paper presented at the international forum on "The Korean Financial Crisis," Nov. 18–19, 1999, The Center for International Development at Harvard University and the Harvard Institute for International Development, Cambridge, Massachusetts.

International Monetary Fund. 1998. *World Economic Outlook.* May and October.

Korea Institute of Finance. 1998. *Korea Economic and Financial Outlook,* vol. 3, no. 2 (October).

Lee, Jong-Wha, and Changyong Rhee. 1999a. Social impacts of the Asian crisis: Policy challenges and lessons. Occasional paper, 33, UNDP.

Lee, Jong-Wha, and Changyong Rhee. 1999b. Macroeconomic impacts of the Korean financial crisis: Comparisons with the cross-country patterns. Paper presented at the international forum on "The Korean Financial Crisis," Nov. 18–19, 1999, The Center for International Development at Harvard University and the Harvard Institute for International Development, Cambridge, Massachusetts.

Radelet, Steve, and Jeffrey Sachs. 1998. The onset of the East Asian financial crisis. Discussion paper. Cambridge, Massachusetts: Harvard Institute for International Development.

World Bank. 1998. *East Asia: The Road to Recovery.* Washington, D.C.: World Bank (September).

World Bank. 1999. *Korea: Establishing a New Foundation For Sustained Growth.* Washington, D.C.: World Bank (November).

11

Malaysia: Adjusting to Deep Integration with the World Economy

Dwight Heald Perkins and
Wing Thye Woo

The Asian financial crisis has led to events that have transformed the economic and political landscape in Malaysia. In an unprecedented departure from its long-standing traditions of openness to foreign investment, and of macroeconomic orthodoxy, Malaysia began denouncing foreign hedge funds for economic sabotage in September 1997, and on September 1, 1998, it imposed comprehensive controls on capital outflows. This sharp reversal in policies had as its background an equally sharp economic collapse. Output contracted 7.5 percent in 1998, a drastic change from the average annual growth rate of 8.7 percent in the 1990–97 period, in which the lowest growth was 7.7 percent in 1997.

Other unprecedented events occurred on the political front. On September 2, 1998, Prime Minister Mahathir Mohamad dismissed his designated successor, Deputy Prime Minister Anwar Ibrahim, from the government on the grounds that Anwar was morally unfit to be a political leader. Anwar was subsequently tried and convicted on corruption charges, and he is now on trial for sodomy. Mahathir has also accused his once-designated successor of treason. Anwar's supporters have organized numerous demonstrations since September 1998, some of which turned violent. All of these actions were atypical in the political succession process in Malaysia, where external collegiality had been the norm.

In response to the vocal objections within the Malay (bumiputra) community to his treatment of Anwar, Mahathir called early elections in November 1999 to refresh his political mandate to rule. Although the ruling coalition, Barisan Nasional, again won more than two-thirds of the parliamentary seats, the election results revealed significant opposition within the bumiputra community to Mahathir's continued leadership.

Table 11.1
Malaysia: Pre-crisis situation

	1990–94	1995	1996	1997
Growth rate of real GDP (%)	8.7	9.4	8.6	7.7
CPI growth rate (%)	3.8	5.3	3.5	2.7
Exports (as % of GDP)	72.9	84.6	79.0	80.4
Fixed investment (as % of GDP)	36.7	43.0	42.3	42.8
Gross domestic savings (% of GDP)	35.4	37.2	41.9	41.0
Current account balance (% of GDP)	−5.2	−8.6	−5.3	−5.9
Reserve money growth (%)	21.4	24.7	35.2	27.8
Narrow money growth rate (%)	21.0	13.2	23.7	8.7
Broad money growth rate (%)	19.2	20.0	25.3	17.5
Government expenditure (% of GDP)	26.4	22.5	22.6	21.5
Government budget balance (% of GDP)	−0.7	0.9	0.7	2.4
Foreign debt (as % of GDP)	40.0	42.5	42.1	n.a.
Debt service ratio for all external debt	21.0	17.5	19.2	n.a.
Exchange rate (vis-à-vis US$)	2.7	2.5	2.5	3.9
Real exchange rate (1990=100, WPI based)	93.6	86.1	77.6	106.1
Current account balance (US$ million)	−2,946	−8,469	−4,596	−4,791
Capital account balance (US$ million)	5,587	7,464	9,227	2,503
Foreign direct investment (US$ million)	4,172	4,178	5,078	5,105
Export value (US$ million)	42,071	74,037	78,327	78,903
Composition of export, value of highest four exports (1996 ranking, US$ million)				
Electrical machinery, apparatus and appliances	8,119	16,277	17,953	n.a.
Telecommunications	6,147	12,305	12,157	n.a.
Office machines and automatic data processing	2,592	7,144	9,194	n.a.
Petroleum and petroleum products	4,003	3,671	4,213	n.a.
Import value (US$ million)	42,214	77,751	78,417	79,045
Composition of import, value of highest four imports (1996 ranking, US$ million)				
Electrical machinery, apparatus and appliances	10,942	24,278	25,285	n.a.
Telecommunications	2,919	5,037	4,393	n.a.
Specialized machinery	2,764	4,878	4,353	n.a.
Office machines and automatic data processing	1,464	3,097	4,261	n.a.
Exports' dependence on unaffected markets (%)	35.7	36.5	33.3	n.a

Table 11.1 (continued)

	1990–94	1995	1996	1997
Volume of exports (index)	119.3	165.5	172.4	190.8
Volume of imports (index)	118.0	186.0	195.3	218.9
International reserves minus gold (US$ million)	18,107	23,774	27,009	20,788
Value of total foreign debt (US$ billion)	21.6	34.3	39.8	40.0
Short-term foreign debt (US$ billion)	4.2	7.3	11.1	n.a.
DS Stock Market Index ($)	377.1	510.3	635.5	197.4
DS Stock Market Index (local currency)	415.5	539.1	667.8	319.7
Kuala Lumpur Composite Index	790.5	995.2	1,238.0	594.4
Nominal lending rate (%)	8.3	7.6	8.9	9.5
Nominal deposit rate (%)	6.6	5.9	7.1	7.8
Non-performing loans	14.3	5.5	3.9	6.7

Table 11.2
Malaysia: Changes in labor employment and output composition

	Composition of output		Composition of labor force	
	1986	1996	1970	1990
Agriculture	19.2	12.8	53.7	27.3
Industry	35.5	46.2	14.3	23.2
Services	45.3	41.0	32.0	49.5

Table 11.3
Malaysia: Forecasts for the 1999–2001 situation

Forecasting institution and date of forecast	GDP growth (%)			CPI inflation (%)		
	1999	2000	2001	1998	1999	2001
International Monetary Fund, October 1999	2.4	6.5	—	3.0	2.4	—
HSBC Asia Economic Weekly, January 2000	4.7	5.5	5.0	2.7	3.5	4.0
Economist Intelligence Unit, 2000:1Q	5.1	6.1	5.2	2.8	3.5	4.3

The United Malay National Organisation (UMNO), the bumiputra party headed by Mahathir, has traditionally dominated both the ruling coalition and Parliament. Compared to the 1995 elections, in which UMNO captured 94 of the 162 seats won by Barisan Nasional in the then 192-seat Parliament, in 1997 UMNO won 71 of Barisan Nasional's 148 seats in the now 193-seat Parliament. UMNO's share of Barisan Nasional's seats had declined from 58 percent to 48 percent, and its share of parliamentary seats fell from 49 percent to 37 percent.

For the first time since national elections began in 1955, it is likely that UMNO had received less than half of the Malay votes cast.[1] Also for the first time, UMNO's chief competitor for Malay votes, the Islamic Party (PAS), has broken out of its political isolation in northeast peninsular Malaysia. PAS has won control of one more state government (a total of two states are now under its control), and obtained strong support in Mahathir's home state, Kedah. The implications of UMNO's decline from overwhelming political domination are not clear. Will UMNO be unable to continue to dictate the national socioeconomic agenda to the non-Malay parties in Barisan Nasional, and hence have to settle for a new agenda that would be less discriminatory against the non-Malay communities? Or will UMNO now push for even more radical discrimination against the non-Malay communities in an attempt to attract back the Malay votes that it has lost?

The extraordinary economic and political events are the products of many factors, the foremost being the struggle for political power between Mahathir and Anwar, and their differences in economic policies. Furthermore, these events have causal connections: Mahathir had foreseen that Anwar's expulsion would lead to violent street demonstrations that, in turn, would induce large capital outflow, given the extreme nervousness among investors in the midst of the Asian financial crisis. Hence, the imposition of capital controls preceded the firing of Anwar by a day.

If the capital controls had not been in place when the street demonstrations began, the Malaysian ringgit (MR) and the Kuala Lumpur stock market would most likely have gone into a free fall in the manner that the Indonesian rupiah and the Jakarta stock market did in May 1998, just before Soeharto stepped down from the presidency. Such a free fall, as we shall explain, would have bankrupted many powerful groups within the UMNO, and weakened Mahathir's grip on UMNO.

1. See "Dr. M's grim results," December 2, 1999 in http://www.freemalaysia.com.

Another important reason for the imposition of capital controls was that the government could undertake expansionary fiscal and monetary policies to boost employment and the stock market without significantly worsening the balance of payments. The short-term interest rate has dropped from 11.06 percent on June 10, 1998 (when Anwar was in charge of economic policy) to 6.58 percent on December 16, 1998, and then to 3.16 percent on February 2, 2000. The stock market has rebounded in line with the fall in interest rate; for the same dates, the stock market index has risen from 489.9 to 543.0 and then to 942.9.[2]

The imposition of capital controls and the political unrest following the ousting of Anwar raise the need for a fresh look at two questions that have usually been answered optimistically:

1. What is the short- and medium-term outlook for Malaysia's economic growth?

2. What is the underlying international competitiveness of Malaysia's economy at present, and how is it likely to evolve in the future?

To answer these questions adequately, it is necessary to keep in mind that nearly three decades ago, Malaysia's political leaders took a large gamble. The gamble was that the nation could simultaneously restructure its economy to increase the ownership share of Malays in the industrial and modern service sectors, and continue to enjoy rapid increases in per capita income for all. By any reasonable standard, this gamble paid off. The economy achieved a large degree of restructuring, and growth continued at an annual average per capita rate of between 4 and 5 percent per year over two and a half decades. If per capita GNP (measured in purchasing power parity) in Malaysia continues to grow at 4 percent per year, by the year 2020 Malaysia will have a per capita GNP nearly equal to that of the United States in 1993.

Success in the past, however, does not guarantee success in the future. The achievements of 1970–96 were partly due to effective national leadership, but there was also luck involved. Malaysia had an unusually rich natural resource base on which it could rely as it began its restructuring. Just as the restructuring got underway, that resource base got

---

2. There is, of course, no simple negative relationship between the interest rate and the stock market index: factors such as political instability and expectations of the future also matter. For example, the stock market index fell to 294.6 on September 2, 1998, the day that Anwar was sacked, even though the short-term interest rate on that day was 9.5 percent, lower than on June 10.

even richer with the development of the offshore extraction of petroleum and natural gas. With petroleum and timber channeling large funds into government and private coffers, Malaysia could make mistakes and still do well. As it turned out, Malaysia did not make that many mistakes so it did very well. Natural resources, however, will not carry the Malaysian economy into the future, because its share of total output and exports has shown a clear downward trend in the last 15 years.

To identify Malaysia's prospects for economic growth and worldwide competitiveness, we turn to examine the economic policies, business organizations, and business leaders that contributed to Malaysia's successes.[3]

11.1   State Ownership from the Race-Based Economic Policies of the 1970s and 1980s

In many ways, the breakthrough from import-substituting industries to the export of manufactures occurred with the establishment of free trade zones, first in Penang in 1970 and then around Kuala Lumpur in 1971.[4] The subsequent arrival of many Japanese and American firms was not so much the result of actions taken by the Malaysian government as it was of external factors. Japanese and American firms could no longer stay competitive in much of their electronic assembly work if they continued to rely on high-cost labor at home. The issue was not whether to go abroad but where to go. Malaysia was an attractive choice: it was stable politically, foreigners could live there comfortably, and the Malaysian government welcomed foreign investment (unlike Taiwan or South Korea).

The other major development of the first half of the 1970s in the industrial sphere was the discovery and development of petroleum. Petroleum, like electronics, was another new industry developed for the most part with foreign investment and technology.

In the context of this booming economy Malaysia began to implement policies to achieve 30-percent bumiputra ownership of modern sector assets. Up to the mid-1970s, the path chosen to raise the bumiputra ownership share was the creation of state-owned enterprises. These efforts, however, had only a limited impact.

---

3. A more detailed historical analysis of Malaysia's policies that were aimed at changing the racial distribution of corporate ownership is presented in Perkins (1998).
4. In a free trade zone, exporters can bring in inputs without paying duty, provided that such imports are re-exported as finished products.

To accelerate the rise in bumiputra ownership, in 1995 the government introduced the Industrial Coordination Act (ICA). The ICA required that all enterprises with equity over a certain limit had to sell 30 percent of their shares to bumiputras. There were loopholes. The most important one was that firms that exported over 80 percent of their output were not subject to the bumiputra ownership requirement. None of the Kuala Lumpur and Penang electronics firms, therefore, felt any impact from the ICA. The Chinese-Malaysian and foreign businesses complained vociferously about the ICA from the outset. These complaints gradually led to modifications in the legislation, mainly the raising of the asset limit and the lowering of the export requirement.[5]

Table 11.4 presents data on ownership of modern sector firms in Malaysia in 1974 and 1993, and it shows that the ethnic makeup of the Malaysian-owned companies has changed dramatically in two decades.

While half of the share capital of the top 80 firms in 1974 was in the hands of foreigners (excluding Singaporeans from the "foreigner" category), foreigners owned only 10.7 percent of the shares of the top 100 firms on the Kuala Lumpur Stock Exchange (KLSE) in 1993. In the mid-1970s, the private local ownership was mostly Chinese. By the early 1990s, Chinese-Malaysians controlled only 13.9 percent of the top 100 company shares, and Indian-Malaysians owned a minuscule 0.1 percent. Bumiputra direct ownership in 1993 was 6.3 percent, but the unit trusts, which were primarily designed to provide bumiputras with share ownership, accounted for another 17.6 percent, bringing the bumiputra total to 23.9 percent in 1993. The Malaysian government directly controlled 40.5 percent of the market capitalization of these firms in the 1990s, in contrast to only 6.3 percent in 1974. The race-based economic policies had caused the Malaysian government to dominate "the commanding heights of the economy"—an economic ownership pattern that is similar to that of state socialism![6]

---

5. In 1975 the asset limit was initially set at MR250 thousand, a level that included all but the smallest non-bumiputra enterprises. It has been creeping upward since; e.g., the limit was MR2.5 million in 1986, but this was still low enough to include most enterprises above the level of a single proprietor with one or two dozen employees. The export requirement was changed so that firms exporting 50 to 80 percent of their output could have foreign ownership of over 50 percent, but the bumiputra share still had to be 30 percent. In effect, if exports constituted over 50 percent of output, a foreign firm could reduce the non-bumiputra local ownership share.

6. The state-owned capital should be included in the bumiputra ownership totals, since the government was staffed mainly by bumiputras and these companies had hiring policies that gave strong preferences to bumiputras. In addition, government companies relied heavily on bumiputra suppliers and vendors.

Table 11.4
Market capitalization of the top KLSE companies by ownership category

Nationality or ethnicity	Percent share (1974)	Percent share (1993)
Foreign-controlled companies [a]	49.11	10.7
Malaysian-controlled companies		
Government A [b]	6.3	40.5
Government C	17.7	
Chinese (private local) [c]	27.0	13.9
Bumiputra (private local)		6.3
Indian (private local)		0.1
Institutions		10.4
Unit trusts	—	17.6
Nominees	—	0.7
Total	100.0	100.0

a. Foreign-controlled companies in 1974 do not include Singapore-controlled companies. If Singapore companies were included, the foreign share would be 61.1 percent of a larger total. Singapore companies were excluded because of complications connected with the way Singapore (and Malaysian) companies were cross-listed in the early years in both Singapore and Kuala Lumpur.
b. Government A companies were those under government control in 1974. Government C companies were those under foreign control in 1974 but were taken over by the government by 1977.
c. Private local ownership in 1974 was mostly Chinese.
Sources: The 1974 data were derived from Tan (1982). Ms. Veena Loh constructed the 1993 data under the supervision of Tan Tat Wai.

A major question from the outset was how to distribute the bumi-putra shares. Few bumiputras had experience with corporate shares, and most lacked the money to buy them. The initial approach was for the Ministry of Trade and Industry to draw up a list of names to whom the shares should be distributed. The chosen individuals typically bought the bumiputra shares at a significant discount from the other shares in the same company. Share allocation, therefore, became a vehi-cle for political patronage.

However, if the favored bumiputras were to realize their profits quickly by turning around and selling off the discounted shares that they had just received (an action engaged in by many), then the 30-percent target of bumiputra ownership would be very difficult to achieve. So, over time, a large part of the discounted bumiputra corporate shares were given to the unit trusts set up by Permodalan Nasional Berhad (National Equity Corporation or PNB). PNB formed its first unit trust, Sekim Amanah Saham Nasional (ASN), in 1981. The ASN unit trust was a quick success because it had a number of special features. PNB, using funds allocated to it by the government, guaranteed each share of MR10 a bonus of MR90, but the MR90 could not be withdrawn until regular earnings had accumulated to an equivalent amount. A rate of return of 10 percent was guaranteed, plus there were bonuses if investments did better than that. As things turned out, ASN paid an average annual rate of return of 18 percent.

By the early 1980s Malaysia was well into the process of restructuring the race ownership of the modern sector of the economy. The commodity price boom of the late 1970s not only ameliorated the disincentive effects of ownership restructuring, it also helped lay the groundwork for a government-led effort in the 1980s to change Malaysia's industrial structure by establishing a number of heavy industries. The core of the plan was the construction of a new cement plant (Kedah Cement), a new steel mill (Perwaja Steel), and an automobile plant (Proton Saga). These heavy industry projects were financed to a large degree by a new state-owned corporation, HICOM, which undertook massive external borrowing to do so.

11.2 Privatization in the 1990s

By the 1990s large numbers of Malaysians, including many government leaders, had become increasingly disillusioned with state-owned enterprises as vehicles for achieving growth and social goals. Many of the state-owned enterprises made sustained losses, even though private enterprises in the same lines of business were doing well. Government oversight of the state-owned firms was so weak that the government itself did not even know how many firms there were!

The first step toward changing the ownership structure of many of the large state-owned enterprises was corporatization, which started in the mid-1980s with the listing of Malaysian International Shipping (MISC) and Malaysian Airlines (MAS), but did not get underway on a broader basis until the 1990s.

The second step was the privatization of new infrastructure projects (e.g., the North-South highway and cellular phone projects) through a process that awarded the contract on what was called an invited bid or involuntary bid, which usually meant that the contract went to the first proposal. The awarding of these contracts has been controversial from the outset. The ethnic makeup of those who won the contracts was reasonably balanced; however, the process was not transparent, only a limited number of firms was involved, and the terms of the contracts were widely perceived as being overly generous. For example, Renong Berhad, which used to be the main investment vehicle for UMNO and now is controlled by Halim Saad, won eight of the thirteen large national projects that Malaysia has awarded since 1992.

The third step was the outright privatization of existing large state firms. The scope of the effort was broad, and by 1993 even HICOM was sold. Privatization in Malaysia, however, has involved objectives not found in similar efforts elsewhere, such as in Great Britain under Margaret Thatcher. Privatization in Malaysia was only partly driven by considerations of efficiency. In an important respect, privatization was the continuation of UMNO's social redistribution policies in another form, and was a means of strengthening bumiputra loyalty to UMNO. Since most of these companies were already corporatized, share prices were already determined by market forces, and so the price at which shares were sold was not a major issue. On the other hand, the government did issue a controlling block of shares to favored individuals, generally allocating 32 percent or less of the total number of shares, because under the law any higher percentage required a general offer.

The entrepreneurs who received these shares, such as Tan Sri Yahya Ahmad, who took control of HICOM, and Tan Sri Tajuddin, who took control of MAS, were mainly bumiputras and members of UMNO. Realistically speaking, given the political background of many of these firms, it is doubtful whether anyone other than a bumiputra entrepreneur could have done the vigorous cost cutting that was required, and which did occur after privatization in the cases just cited. Who else could have cut the bloated staffs (mostly bumiputras) of these companies or removed inefficient bumiputra vendors from their lists?

While the acquisition of assets by UMNO members strengthened their allegiance to the top ministers, it also rendered their support of the existing UMNO leadership to be disproportionately influenced by the state of the economy in general, and by the state of the stock market in particular. This second implication of the massive asset redistribution program, we shall see, lies at the root of the two extraordinary economic and political events mentioned at the beginning of this paper.

11.3   Enhanced Vulnerability to Financial Panics and High Interest Rates

It turns out that the headlong plunge to accelerate bumiputra ownership of the corporate sector made the bumiputra business community particularly vulnerable to financial downturns. The financial vulnerability was created by the government's lax regulations on collateral-based loans and by the government's directions to the state banks to extend investment loans to bumiputras. The generous flow of bank loans enabled the bumiputra community to buy the discounted shares and to invest in the more profitable unit trusts, and made it possible for the politically connected bumiputra entrepreneurs to buy controlling shares in state companies. The newly purchased assets, in turn, constituted a large proportion of the value of the collateral that the bumiputra borrowers pledged for their bank loans.

The high economic growth of the 1990s, supplemented by large foreign capital inflows, caused the stock market to boom. The Kuala Lumpur Stock Exchange Composite Index went from 506 in 1990 to 1238 in 1996. The rise in share prices allowed Malaysians to borrow more from the banks to acquire more assets. The outcome was that the domestic debt/GDP ratio in Malaysia in mid-1997 stood at 170 percent, which is among the highest in the world.

The reversal of foreign capital flows in mid-1997, and its acceleration at the end of 1997, exacerbated the decline of the Malaysian stock market that had started at the end of 1996.[7] Besides crashing the stock market, the capital outflow also depreciated the ringgit significantly against the U.S. dollar, from MR2.5/US$ in 1997:2Q to MR3.9/US$ in 1997:4Q, and then to MR4.2/US$ in 1998:2Q.

Anwar, who was in charge of economic affairs up to almost the end of June 1998, reacted to the acceleration in capital flight in the final months of 1997 by implementing an IMF-style high interest rate policy to stabilize the exchange rate. The annualized growth rate of reserve money went from over 25 percent in all four quarters of 1997 to –6 percent in 1998:1Q and then to –15 percent in 1998:2Q. As a result of the significant tightening of credit in early 1998, the lending rate, which had been inching up since the start of the Asian financial crisis in July 1997 from 8.9 percent in 1996:4Q to 10.0 percent in 1997:4Q, jumped to 12.2 percent in 1998:2Q. The high interest rate policy could not halt the

---

7. The Kuala Lumpur Composite Index had fallen from 1238 in 1996:4Q to 1077 in 1997:2Q.

decline of the ringgit, however. Worse yet, it reduced investment spending further and contributed to the downslide of the stock market index to 455 in 1998:2Q from 1238 in 1996:4Q.

In Anwar's defense, it could be argued that the efficacy of his high interest rate policy was undermined by Mahathir's occasional excoriation of conspiratorial speculation by foreigners. The ringgit fell sharply after each outburst by Mahathir, possibly because jittery investors interpreted his strong condemnation as the prelude to the imposition of capital controls. One should note, however, that similar high interest rate policies in Indonesia, Thailand, Korea and Russia had also failed to stop their currencies from falling further after an initial sharp devaluation, despite the absence in these countries of denunciations of foreign speculators by high government officials.

The collapses in the domestic stock market and the foreign exchange market were also accompanied by a large decline in aggregate demand. Private consumption and private investment, especially housing investment, plunged because of the abrupt withdrawal of foreign funds, the high interest rates, and the pessimism about quick economic recovery in East Asia. Furthermore, the positive effects from the depreciation of the ringgit were more than offset by the depressed demand conditions in the region, making exports in the first half of 1998 (US$35 billion) lower than in the first half of 1997 (US$39 billion).

The fall in profits and in share prices rendered many large bumiputra conglomerates financially illiquid or insolvent. The decline in their share prices reduced the value of the collateral pledged against their bank loans, and the drop in profits caused by the economic slowdown made them unable to service their bank loans.

Possibly, the most well-known rescue attempt of a politically connected conglomerate in 1997 was the November 17 announcement by United Engineers Berhad that it had just used borrowed funds to acquire 32.6 percent of the shares of its parent company, Renong Berhad. United Engineers had done this without consulting its minority shareholders. Furthermore, the government had to issue a waiver to exempt United Engineers from having to make a general offer for Renong shares that it did not own. Because United Engineers' move was widely seen as bailing out the indebted majority shareholders of Renong to the detriment of minority shareholders in both companies, the share prices of both companies plummeted after the announcement of the acquisition.[8]

The continued general downslide in profits and share prices led to a second bailout of Renong. In October 1998 Renong defaulted on its debts, and the government paid off MR10.5 billion of Renong's short- and medium-term bank debt by issuing an equivalent amount of long-term bonds. Renong promised to repay the government from its future earnings.

Most large bumiputra conglomerates shared Renong's financial difficulties over the last year. Quite a few of them, especially the politically connected ones, also received state assistance to weather the financial storm. The difficulties that Malaysia's conglomerates (both bumiputra-owned and non-bumiputra-owned) had in servicing their large bank debts severely damaged the balance sheets of Malaysia's banks. Bank Bumiputra, a state bank, was pushed into bankruptcy for the third time since its establishment in 1966. The government had to put in at least MR2 billion as capital in order for Bank Bumiputra to meet the minimum risk-weighted capital adequacy ratio. Sime Bank and RHB Bank, two banks with strong ties to UMNO members, merged in mid-1998 and received an infusion of MR1.5 billion from Danamodal, a state company recently established to recapitalize troubled banks.

An estimate by Lehman Brothers in October 1998 put Malaysia's problem loans at the median of key Asian market economies experiencing banking crises. The proportion of problem loans in total bank loans was 13 percent for Japan, 33 percent for Malaysia and South Korea, 48 percent for Thailand and 61 percent for Indonesia.[9] Standard & Poor estimated that the amount of funds required to recapitalize Malaysian banks would exceed 40 percent of GDP.

11.4   Reflating the Economy

It was clear by the end of June 1998 that the forecast of 2.5 percent growth in 1998 released in May by the IMF was too high. Salomon Smith Barney predicted in June that 1998 growth would be –3 percent,

---

8. Later, in February 1998, the Kuala Lumpur Stock Exchange reprimanded United Engineers for not reporting accurately that the shares had actually been purchased over a period of time up to November 17, 1997, rather than on November 17 itself. This is probably the major reason why the Renong shares were bought at MR3.24 per share, about 12 percent higher than the closing price of MR2.90 on 17 November. A fine of MR100,000 was levied on United Engineers for inaccurate reporting.

9. "Little Help in Sight," *Far Eastern Economic Review*, October 15, 1998.

while the Economist Intelligence Unit (EIU) predicted 0.8 percent growth in its 1998:2Q issue. It was in this atmosphere of deepened pessimism, and after Mahathir's political leadership was indirectly challenged by Anwar at the annual UMNO meeting in June, that Mahathir appointed Daim Zainuddin to formulate an alternative to Anwar's high interest rate policy.

Reflation through lower interest rates in July 1998 was a risky policy however, because the unsettled global financial markets made the outcome uncertain. There was a chance that a significant lowering of interest rates would stimulate aggregate demand to rise substantially to raise output, restore corporate profits, and renew confidence in the underlying strength of Malaysia's economy. The culmination of this positive scenario would be the repatriation by domestic investors of their overseas holdings to undertake capacity expansion, the return of foreign capital to the stock market, and the stabilization of the ringgit.

On the other hand, there was also a chance that lowering interest rates considerably would worsen the July 1998 situation. Instead of stimulating private spending, the lower interest rates would end up stimulating capital flight. Speculators would borrow ringgit at the lower rates, and buy foreign currencies to bet against a further depreciation of the ringgit. A massive substantial injection of money would thence set the ringgit on a downward spiral, which would bankrupt even more Malaysian banks and businesses that had foreign debt.

Given the uncertainty of the outcome from lowering interest rates, and the ongoing capital flight from the region, a "wait-and-see" policy emerged by default, along with a small reduction in interest rates. The short-term interest rate on August 26, 1998 (one week before implementation of capital controls) was 10.0 percent, down from 11.1 percent on July 1, 1998. Output, the stock market, and the ringgit continued to fall in July and August. It soon became clear that GDP had fallen an annualized 6.8 percent in the second quarter of 1998, and that the decline in the third quarter would be even greater. Incremental adjustments on the policy front were no longer acceptable, either politically or economically.

Malaysia put on capital controls on September 1, fixed the exchange rate at MR3.8/US$, started reducing interest rates substantially, and announced an expansionary government budget on October 23, 1998. Infrastructure spending was increased to raise the general government budget deficit to 4.2 percent of GDP in 1999, a major reversal of the budget surplus tradition, which had produced surpluses of 4 percent in

1997 and 0.7 percent in 1998.[10] The non-financial public enterprises became an important vehicle of the reflation effort. The state oil company, Petronas, kept financially precarious firms operating by acquiring them, e.g., the country's largest shipper (Malaysian International Shipping Corporation) and the national car company (Petronas). The deficit spending of the non-financial public enterprises caused the budget surplus of the consolidated public sector to go from 4 percent in 1996 and 6.3 percent in 1997 to –1 percent in 1998, –5.4 percent in 1999, and (expected) –4.5 percent in 2000.

Mahathir and Daim also announced that bailouts of troubled firms would increase, and they urged banks to boost their lending. Two new state agencies, Danaharta and Danamodal, were established to restore the banking sector to financial solvency so that bank lending would resume. Danaharta would take over the bad bank loans, and Danamodal would recapitalize the banks. The central bank even imposed a mandatory target of 8 percent growth for bank loans in 1998.[11] In February 2000, the central bank introduced a MR300 million subsidized loan program targeted at small and medium-sized firms owned by bumiputras.

The injection of liquidity, with leakage minimized by capital controls, lowered the short-term interest rate steadily from 11.1 percent on July 1, 1998—after Daim just took over the economic portfolio—to 6.6 percent on December 9, 1998, and then to 3.17 percent on December 21, 1999. The stock market index rose steadily from 471 on July 1, 1998 to 522 on December 9, 1998, and then to 791.2 on December 21, 1999.[12]

The pegging of the ringgit at MR3.8 per US$ since September 1998 has rendered it undervalued vis-à-vis the other major currencies in the region. The results were a surge in Malaysian exports from US$72 million in 1998 to US$82 million in 1999, and a surge in foreign investment in the semiconductor industry. Foreign direct investment was also

---

10. General government comprises federal, state and local governments. The budget balance as a percent of GDP was calculated from estimates in pages 6, 7 and 23 in the 1999:4Q issue of the Economist Intelligence Unit report on Malaysia. Nominal GDP in 1999 and 2000 was calculated by assuming a nominal growth rate that equaled the real growth rate plus the CPI inflation rate minus 1.

11. The 1998 target was rescinded in early December, when it became clear that it would not be reached because the deep slump had reduced the demand for credit too much. This 8 percent target is mandatory for 1999.

12. The short-term interest rate in early February 2000 is very much below the interest rate on July 2, 1997 when the Thai crisis began: 3.2 percent and 7.5 percent, respectively. However, the stock market index in early February 2000 (about 943) is still way below the pre-crisis level of 1085.

helped by the exemption of new foreign-owned firms from bumiputra ownership requirements, regardless of the export orientation of the new foreign-owned firms.

The reflation measures, together with the natural bounce-back from the regional financial panic, gave Malaysia a 4.7 percent growth rate in 1999; this was higher than the 3.9 percent growth in Thailand but lower than the 9.4 percent growth in Korea.[13] The success of the reflation program would have been predicted by any standard macroeconomic model, because the output decline in 1998 was caused by a reduction in aggregate demand and not by a loss in production capacity.

There is, however, a very important issue concerning the use of bailouts in the reflation. If the bailouts were mostly for bumiputra firms that were rendered illiquid by the financial panic (e.g., companies that were unable to roll over their short-term debt), then the underlying growth of the economy will be unaffected. But if the bailouts covered mostly bumiputra firms that had their insolvency hastened by the high interest rates and lower aggregate demand, then the survival of these low-growth potential firms will lower the trend growth rate. Furthermore, these inefficient firms are likely to weaken the future fiscal situation by requiring more subsidies, and to raise the costs for downstream firms by obtaining increased import protection in the future.

In conclusion, the government's reflation policies did reduce the output loss inflicted by the Asian financial crisis. However, the sustainability of the present recovery will hinge crucially on the Mahathir-Anwar political conflict not escalating to either dampen private spending or reduce foreign investment. Furthermore, the long-term benefits from the reflation program will depend crucially on whether it was accompanied by a restructuring of the industrial and financial sectors to weed out the less efficient firms. If no such weeding occurred, then the short-run reflation program might have lowered the long-run growth rate.

11.5   Capital Controls and Future Growth

Since the primary reason for the imposition of the capital controls was to prevent funds from rushing out in response to the anticipated demonstrations by Anwar supporters, it was only natural that the capital controls were reduced as the political protests became less frequent.[14]

---

13. Estimates are from HSBC, *Asia Economic Weekly*, January 24, 2000.
14. See Mahani (forthcoming) for a fuller discussion.

On February 15, 1999, the government divided foreign capital into two categories: (a) funds that had entered before that date and (b) funds that would come in after that date. For the first category, the repatriated principal would be taxed if it had been in residence less than a year; and for the second category, only the profits would be taxed. In effect, the government was exempting new capital flows from exchange controls.

Finally, on September 21, 1999, the above two-tier system was replaced by a flat tax rate of 10 percent on repatriated profits. Repatriated principal is now neither taxed nor subject to legal impediments; thus, Malaysia has abandoned the practice, if not the rhetoric, of capital controls.

Relatively little outflow of foreign capital has occurred since the easing of capital controls in February 1999: less than US$350 million flowed out between mid-February and the end of September. This is not surprising because the Malaysian stock market had rebounded substantially; the output recovery was fairly robust; and Morgan Stanley Capital International had announced on August 12, 1999, that Malaysia would be re-included in its Emerging Markets Free Index and the All Country Free Index. The last development is especially noteworthy, because it confirms international recognition that capital controls are no longer binding in Malaysia.

The important question for Malaysia is whether its temporary use of capital controls has permanently turned a large proportion of foreign investors away from Malaysia toward the many developing countries that are now welcoming foreign capital as never before. Given how dependent Malaysian growth and competitiveness have been on foreign direct investment in the past, the continued high inflow of foreign capital (and hence technology) will be necessary to maintain the high trend growth rate of the last two decades. We think that the extensive Latin American experiences with capital controls provide grounds to be optimistic that foreign capital will return over time to Malaysia, albeit possibly with a higher risk premium being paid by Malaysia for several years. Of course, the return of foreign capital is fundamentally conditional on the underlying social stability in Malaysia not being affected by the current Mahathir-Anwar political fight.

Table 11.5
Malaysia: Tracking economic developments

	1997:Q1	1997:Q2	1997:Q3	1997:Q4	1998:Q1	1998:Q2	1998:Q3	1998:Q4	1999:Q1	1999:Q2
Growth rate of real GDP (%)	9.2	8.4	7.5	6.0	−2.8	−6.8	−10.9	−10.3	−1.3	4.1
Exchange rate (against US$)	2.5	2.5	3.2	3.9	3.6	4.2	3.8	3.8	3.8	3.8
Real exchange rate (1990 = 100, WPI based)	71.4	73.9	90.9	106.1	93.9	104.7	96.8	102.3	97.6	96.8
International reserves minus gold (US$ million)	27,709.9	26,586.3	22,159.3	20,788.2	19,803.9	19,701.6	20,702.4	25,559.4	27,139.8	30,571.3
Reserve money growth (%)	28.7	25.7	25.6	27.8	−6.3	−15.0	−39.6	−38.6	6.2	24.6
Narrow money growth rate (%)	23.4	20.3	15.1	8.7	−14.2	−18.9	−30.6	−29.4	−17.3	−3.7
Broad money growth rate (%)	22.6	23.0	21.6	17.5	8.9	3.1	2.8	−1.4	3.6	13.2
CPI growth rate (YOY%)	3.2	2.5	2.3	2.7	4.3	5.7	5.7	5.4	4.0	2.6
Nominal lending rate (%)	9.2	9.3	9.6	10.0	11.2	12.2	10.9	8.2	8.0	7.4
Nominal deposit rate (%)	7.2	7.3	7.7	8.9	9.4	10.0	8.7	5.9	5.6	3.8
Export value (US$ million)	19,696.9	19,698.8	20,443.2	19,064.9	17,579.3	17,914.8	19,292.1	20,000.8	18,225.5	20,490.5
Import value (US$ million)	18,882.6	21,606.6	19,955.7	18,601.0	15,345.2	14,472.2	585.0	549.4	550.3	616.8
DS stock market index ($)	629.8	543.0	321.8	197.4	241.6	136.5	121.6	168.8	167.5	303.1
DS stock market index (national currency)	649.7	570.2	434.0	319.7	365.9	235.6	192.3	381.5	331.1	532.3
Kuala Lumpur Composite Index	1,203.1	1,077.3	814.6	594.4	719.5	455.6	373.5	586.1	502.8	811.1

11.6   International Competitiveness

We now turn to the microeconomic level to examine the international competitiveness of each sector of Malaysia's economy. We group Malaysian industries into four categories: manufactured export industries, manufactured import-substituting light industries, heavy industries and modern service industries.

Manufactured Export Industries

Malaysia's manufactured export industries have shared two characteristics that are important to achieving international competitiveness. First, ethnicity-oriented ownership policies have played only a minor role in these industries because most have been exempted from the ownership requirements of the ICA. Second, the great majority of firms in this sector are foreign-owned, either wholly or in controlling part. The ICA ownership policies played little role because the government recognized early on that there are few rents to redistribute in the export of manufactures. International competition largely eliminates rents in this sector, and profits thus reflect returns on business skill and entrepreneurship. Any effort to divert a substantial share of these profits to those not contributing to their creation kills the incentive to develop the business in the first place. Where foreign ownership is involved, it is a simple matter for the owner to decide to set up business in some other country.

Malaysia's electronics sector, by far the most important manufactured export sector in the country, illustrates how Malaysia's manufactured exports have developed to date. The electronics sector is two distinct groups of industries, both of which sell most of what they produce outside of Malaysia. Large American firms such as Intel and Hewlett-Packard dominate the semiconductor, computer and peripherals industries. These firms are not listed on the Kuala Lumpur Stock Exchange, so the precise size of their Malaysian operations is not public information; however, several firms, notably Intel, have investments in Malaysia that exceed US$1 billion. What started as highly mobile firms employing cheap labor have become enterprises participating in a wider range of activities in Malaysia. Furthermore, management and the technical staff of these plants are now largely drawn from the local population. Ownership, on the other hand, is entirely foreign.

The other part of the electronics sector produces consumer electronics, such as television sets, VCRs, air conditioners and refrigerators. Brand names matter with these products, and most of the firms in this sector are wholly owned by large Japanese conglomerates such as Matsushita, Sony, Hitachi and Sanyo. Japanese firms differ from those of the Americans and Europeans in that top management in Malaysia is usually staffed by Japanese who rotate in and out from their home offices in Japan. These plants cannot be easily relocated to other countries because they involve substantial investments and have been in Malaysia a long time, but they are less firmly rooted than the semiconductor manufacturers. However, one should not overstate how firmly rooted are the semiconductor firms, given the rapid pace of technological change in the industry.

If Malaysia's future is like its past, future manufactured export growth will depend on the following actions:

• retaining foreign exporting firms already in the country,

• continuing to attract new foreign direct investment (FDI), and

• avoiding actions that would discourage existing foreign firms from branching out into new and more advanced areas of business as their existing lines become obsolete or uncompetitive.

But can foreign direct investment alone carry an economy that is no longer generating much growth from its rich natural resource sector? Singapore and Hong Kong have experienced FDI-led growth for long periods, but they are much smaller countries or territories than Malaysia and have an unusually strong financial and commercial infrastructure. Malaysia is more comparable in size and infrastructure to Taiwan, but Taiwan's manufactured export industries were led by Taiwanese, with FDI playing only a small role. Thus, there is a plausible basis for concern that foreign direct investment alone will not be able to carry Malaysian manufacturing to ever higher levels of production and exports sufficient to sustain rapid GDP growth.

Manufactured Import-Substituting Light Industries

Most of the firms in this category are small or medium-sized. Three companies in this category are listed in the top fifty on the Kuala Lumpur Stock Exchange. Two are foreign-owned (Nestle and Rothman) and one is local, Perlis Plantations (of the Robert Kuok group), which includes sugar manufacturing among its diversified activities. In the next fifty firms listed by size, there are only six more in this category and most of them are foreign (R.J. Reynolds, Guinness and Carlsberg) or local franchises of foreign operations (Kentucky Fried Chicken). The exception is Federal Flour, also part of the Robert Kuok group.

Chinese-Malaysians own the great majority of the firms in this category. Some of these firms will no doubt grow enough to become suppliers to more than the Malaysian domestic market, but few firms outside of the textile industry played such a role in the mid-1990s. As they grow larger, however, they become subject to the rules of the Industrial Coordination Act, and if they do not become larger, they are not likely to be able to export. But if many of these local light industry firms do not grow up to international status, which firms will?

The incentive structure rooted in the ownership legislation thus inhibits the development of an export capacity among import-substituting light manufacturers. This situation is common to many developing countries, particularly in the Philippines. Very small firms often prosper and grow out of sight of government regulatory and tax authorities until they reach a certain size, when they are suddenly faced with a raft of government interventions. Those firms with foresight often avoid this problem by staying small.

In short, light manufactures currently in the import-substituting sector do not appear to be promising sources for the export-oriented entrepreneurs of Malaysia's future, and this is in part because the ICA discourages non-bumiputra-owned firms from expanding the scale of their operations.

Heavy Industries

Oil and gas
Malaysia currently has oil and gas reserves plus the realistic prospect of future discoveries of new fields that will allow the country to extract substantial rents from this source for several more decades. The sector, however, is not a dynamic source of future growth either in domestic value-added terms or in terms of exports. If domestic demand for petroleum and gas continues growing at current rates, Malaysia will eventually become a net importer of these products.

Petrochemicals

The petrochemical sector is dominated by Petronas, the state company that controls all the oil and gas fields and receives most of the rents from them. In the mid-1990s, worldwide profit margins in petrochemicals were extremely low. Petronas's downstream efforts may also have had low or no profits, but there is no way for an outsider to know because profits from downstream activities are not separated out publicly from the profits (and rents) to the company as a whole. The Malaysian situation is further complicated by being next to Singapore, which entered the industry early and made itself the petroleum and petrochemical center for all of Southeast Asia. In addition, Singapore has defended that position with vigorous price cutting and similar measures to prevent or cripple the rise of potential competitors.

Cement

Cement is an industry in which transport costs provide significant natural protection for what, in most countries, is an industry oriented toward the domestic market. Scale economies can be achieved at one or two million tons of output per year, and the Malaysian market in 1996 was already around 12 million tons, more than big enough for Malaysia's six major producers. The largest producer is APMC, a joint venture between the MUI group of Khoo Kay Peng and the Blue Circle Group of the U.K. Most of the other cement firms have close ties to the government.

Because infrastructure and concrete products (as inputs) affect the cost of export products only in a small and indirect way, the question of whether local Malaysian-produced cement is fully competitive with imported cement only becomes an issue if the domestic plants are extremely inefficient, and Malaysia's are not. Malaysia, in fact, might well become an exporter of cement, particularly to Singapore, which regularly imports several million tons a year. However, the export market for cement is neither large nor growing rapidly, in part because it is a favorite target for the import-substituting industrial policies of many developing countries.

Steel

The steel manufacturing industry is very different from the cement industry. The technology is more complex; scale economies are important in the case of some products; and steel is both a potential export product and a major input into other actual and potential exports, notably automobiles. The Malaysian government has tried to help develop a modern steel sector, but it has experienced decidedly mixed results. Malayawata was the government's first attempt. The government's second try (Perwaja Steel) resulted in large financial losses. The 30-percent tariff rate on steel products has produced two prosperous private steel mills, ASM and Southern Steel.

Automobile manufacturing
The case of the car manufacturer Proton Saga is complex. Proton has a large advantage in the Malaysian market in that, unlike its domestic competitors, Proton does not have to pay either the excise tax or the 40-percent duty on the import of completely-knocked-down kits. Informed guesses put the Proton price at about 20 percent above that of comparable automobiles on the unprotected world market, which is not a particularly high percentage as developing country auto production costs go, but is not an internationally competitive price either.

If one takes a longer view, to the year 2020, the case for Proton may prove to be stronger. All late-developing automobile sectors, including that of the Japanese, take a long time to become competitive. If Proton's costs do not come down, the consoling thought is that expensive cars do not generally raise the costs to other manufacturers the way expensive intermediate inputs do. Nonetheless, an uncompetitive car industry would be a drag on overall economic performance.

The engineering firms connected with the automobile sector are not yet capable of standing on their own as exporters of auto components, as is the case, for example, of many auto parts manufacturers in Taiwan.

On the whole, even an optimist would agree that it will be several years before Malaysia's heavy industries can realize their potential to be internationally competitive.

The Modern Service Sector

Malaysia's service sector has a long way to go before it will be capable of playing a leadership role in the economy and becoming a major source of foreign exchange earnings. Malaysia's banking sector is a clear case in point. The large-scale banking sector, if one excludes the foreign-owned banks, is owned by either the government or large bumiputra interests with close ties to government. The private Chinese-Malaysian banks are small and getting smaller. Their decline did not come about because of government coercion. For the most part, mismanagement by the banks' founders got the banks into trouble, and the central bank was forced to step in. Once the government intervened, however, the eventual result was often the sale of the banks' assets to bumiputra interests. Restrictions on the opening of new branches by existing smaller banks have had a similar effect.

Among the bumiputra banks, there are strong institutions such as the Arab Malaysian Bank of Tan Sri Azman Hashim. Others are considerably less successful, notably Bank Bumiputra. The problem with banks with close ties to government, such as Bank Bumiputra, is that the competitiveness of these banks is undermined from two directions. On the one hand, they are expected to lend to government-supported enterprises even when those enterprises are in deep trouble, as was the case with Perwaja Steel. On the other hand, these banks have good reason to believe that, because of their close ties to government, they will be rescued if they make mistakes. Banks with this set of constraints and incentives are never likely to be internationally competitive.

The service sector in Malaysia also includes tourism, hotels, gambling and related services. Malaysia is already a major international presence in the hotel business, with such notable international chains as Shangri La and Equatorial (even if the headquarters of the former has now moved to Hong Kong). Malaysia does not have the historical sights of Bali or Thailand, but it has other major tourist assets and it is well along in developing them.

Some portions of Malaysia's service sector have the potential to become internationally competitive, but a service sector capable of supporting broad and sustained growth of the economy and of foreign exchange earnings has yet to be developed.

11.7 Conclusion

We have reviewed the evolution of Malaysia's industrial policy and industrial structure as part of an effort to identify sources of future competitiveness and growth in the manufacturing and service sectors. We found that the internationally competitive parts of the manufacturing sector are mostly dominated by foreign-owned and foreign-controlled firms. A few domestically owned and controlled firms also have become successful exporters of manufactures and even a few services, and their numbers increased modestly in the mid-1990s. Most manufactures and services are oriented toward the domestic market, and many still require some protection from international competition.

The size of the Malaysian domestic market is not particularly large, however, so firms whose growth is based solely on that market will not be able to take advantage of many economies of scale. Furthermore, industries that depend indefinitely on protection from foreign competition tend to work more at maintaining that protection than at raising their own productivity. Import-substituting growth, therefore, is likely to be slow growth over the long haul. If Malaysia is to enjoy continued rapid GDP growth, many of these import-substituting firms will have to become exporters of goods and services.

There is nothing really unusual about this future challenge, except for two special features of the Malaysian economy. The first special feature is the important role of Malaysia's rich natural resource base. This natural resource base has made a major contribution to Malaysia's growth in the past and has played a central role in helping fund some of the country's industrial and social experiments. But Malaysia's natural resources are a steadily declining share of GDP, of exports, and of government revenue, and will soon play a minor part in the Malaysian growth story, much as tin and rubber have become relatively minor sectors of the overall economy.

The second special feature of Malaysian industrial and service sector development is the emphasis on ownership restructuring and income redistribution. In the view of Malaysia's leaders, and even from the perspective of many who had to help pay for this restructuring and redistribution, the change was necessary to ensure a stable society in which benefits are widely shared and occupations are not identified with ethnicity. By any reasonable standard, ownership restructuring has been highly successful. By the mid-1990s it was not possible to identify many large sectors of the economy as belonging to any one ethnic group.

However, ownership restructuring was not without its costs. Malaysia's internationally competitive manufacturing sectors are precisely those sectors that have been exempted from the ownership requirements and are dominated by direct foreign investors. Local Malaysian firms, as is usually the case in most countries, have started by concentrating on the domestic market; hence they have been subject to ownership restructuring throughout their history. Some have grown and prospered under the requirements of laws such as the ICA, but the number of these firms that have grown to be truly international is not large.

Probably the least successful strategy of the ownership restructuring was the reliance on state ownership to implement social objectives. The government itself realized some years ago that state firms tended to be inefficient, and undertook privatization of most of them. Privatization, however, generally meant sale to bumiputras, not sale to the highest bidders, in order to create a group of bumiputra billionaires. The goal of creating bumiputra billionaires is being achieved in part by giving selected individuals exclusive licenses to build key elements of Malaysia's infrastructure. In some cases, the license has mainly generated rents for the license holder. The more this type of situation occurs, the greater the danger that Malaysian costs of doing business will rise to uncompetitive levels. A worrying example is the 1997 increase in electric power rates, which are now at a level that makes Malaysia the second most costly producer of electric power in the region.

The crucial question in the Malaysian context is whether the newly created bumiputra billionaires have acquired the right kind of experience to be able to match the earlier performances of the more successful Korean chaebols. Few of these individuals, for example, came to their tasks with much experience of either manufacturing or exporting. If these new holders of great wealth can make the necessary transition to industrial and international entrepreneurship, Malaysia's future looks bright. If they cannot make this transition, then Malaysia has two (not mutually exclusive) choices. The economy can continue to depend on foreign direct investors to play this role or it can attempt to look elsewhere locally for entrepreneurial talent. For the most part, the incentive structure needed to stimulate foreign direct investors can arguably be said to be in place despite the recent temporary capital controls. The same, however, cannot be said with respect to a mechanism to encourage new sources of local entrepreneurial talent.

There exist fast-acting solutions to the present economic malaise and to the long-run problems of maintaining high growth and increasing international competitiveness, but considerable statesmanship and political skill will be required to overcome resistance to these quick-relief solutions.

The first politically sensitive reform is to relax the ownership restrictions of the ICA to enable the needed recapitalization of the banks and large firms. UMNO must make a credible commitment to the permanence of the ICA reforms if the troubled firms are to succeed in issuing new shares. The ICA reforms will also have the salubrious effect of encouraging the small and moderate (import-substituting) firms owned by non-bumiputras to expand their capacities and eventually become big exporters.

The second politically sensitive reform is to revise the state industrial policies to include expiration dates for state subsidies and import protection. The government must institute a weeding-out process within its infant industry program to prevent high-cost inputs from undermining international competitiveness. This "tough love" approach will help the protected firms to focus on improving productivity.

Our suggestion for the reform of the ICA is actually neither radical nor politically infeasible. The National Economic Recovery Plan unveiled by Daim Zainuddin in July 1998 included just such a proposal. In its essence, the suggested ICA reforms in Daim's plan are similar to the "graduation requirement" we recommended for incorporation into the national industrial policy. The government clearly has succeeded in creating a professional and entrepreneurial bumiputra community that equals the non-bumiputra community in competence and competitiveness. By most indications, Malaysia now has a large, well-educated bumiputra middle class that is actively engaged in nearly all industrial and modern service activities. Furthermore, there is no reason to think that explicit industrial policies, backed by state subsidies and import protection, are needed to guide the investments of well-informed bumiputra entrepreneurs.

Of course, assessments differ as to whether the Malay professional and entrepreneurial classes are now able to compete with non-Malay Malaysians. On the eve of the 1997 elections, in a speech to government officials, Mahathir rejected the arguments for meritocracy advanced by some successful bumiputras:

[With the implementation of meritocracy] the Malays and the bumiputras will become manual workers and will not be able to hold high positions they are holding today. ... Let us not think that we have reached this level because of our own ability.[15]

Although there is disagreement over the readiness of the Malays to compete, there is agreement that the government subsidies retard the progress of Malays toward parity in competitiveness with the non-Malays and, equally important, toward parity in competitiveness with the rest of the developed world. In his advice to the Malay community after the 1999 elections, Deputy Prime Minister Abdullah Ahmad Badawi warned:

---

15. The Straits Times Interactive, "Malaysia not ready for merit system: Mahathir," July 30, 1999; http://straitstimes.asia1.com.sg/reg/region.html/.

[Because of the excessive dependence by Malays on government subsidies], for every step taken by Malays, the non-Malays take 10 steps... [Even then] this economic structure is changing and bumiputras must be aware of globalization and its effects on our economy...We must prepare ourselves to compete in a bigger arena... It is time for more bumiputra entrepreneurs and businessmen to attain excellence through their own efforts.[16]

Herein is the Malay dilemma: the government subsidies that promote the socioeconomic mobility of the Malays in the short run may end up harming the long-run competitiveness of this race unless the government can ensure that the Malays do not become addicted to these subsidies. The Malay leadership is caught between short-run political expedience and long-run economic competitiveness. The economic future of the Malays (and of the country) and their relative position in the world economy hinge on how UMNO will react to the significant Malay desertion from UMNO in the 1999 elections. Would UMNO be too weak to take a farsighted view of the interests of the Malay race in a global economy, or would UMNO convert this crisis into an opportunity to implement policy changes that would enable Malay entrepreneurs and professionals to stand on their own feet on the world stage?

These are extraordinary times in Malaysia, and extraordinary political leadership is important. Part of extraordinary leadership is the political courage to assess objectively whether the continuation of the race-based programs and the industrial policies has more to do with ensuring political patronage than with providing "infant industry protection" to "disadvantaged" bumiputra professionals and businesses. If holding onto political power is the real motivation behind these policies, then the economic costs from a rigid ICA are not serving the cause of social justice, which is the defensible motivation behind the race-based policies. It is then time to throw away the crutches that are getting in the way of the economy advancing faster. A fast-growing and fiercely competitive economy will do more to enrich the bumiputra community than state-generated rents can ever hope to do.

16. The Straits Times Interactive, "Abdullah warns of new Malay dilemma," January 31, 2000; http://straitstimes.asia1.com.sg/reg/regional.html/.

References

Mahani, Zainal-Abidain. (forthcoming). Implications of the Malaysian experience on the future international financial arrangements. *ASEAN Economic Journal.*

Perkins, Dwight. 1998. Ownership and control of Malaysian industry and business services: Rents versus profits. Development discussion paper no. 617, Harvard Institute for International Development, Harvard University, January.

Tan, Tat Wai. 1982. *Income Distribution and Determination in West Malaysia.* Kuala Lumpur: Oxford University Press.

12

Thailand and the Crisis: Roots, Recovery and Long-Run Competitiveness

Frank Flatters

12.1 Introduction and Overview

The unpegging of the Thai baht from the U.S. dollar in July 1997 and the baht's subsequent collapse are commonly regarded as the triggers of the Asian crisis. The floating of the baht was made necessary by the exhaustion of Thai foreign exchange reserves, after months of futile efforts to stave off necessary policy adjustments and financial sector reforms. The crisis was preceded by an investment bubble, especially in real estate and stock markets, by widespread structural and prudential problems in the financial sector, and by a very rapid buildup of short-term foreign debt liabilities. Foreign borrowing and lending behavior was encouraged by a false sense of security about the fixed exchange rate, and possibly as well by confidence that downside risks would be covered by sovereign assumption of private debt obligations.

Denial and unwillingness to adjust preceded the floating of the baht by at least six months and arguably up to two years, and persisted for at least several months afterwards.[1] The two major policy blunders were the stubborn determination to protect the fixed exchange rate and the bleeding of the treasury to prop up failing financial institutions without requiring or facilitating necessary structural adjustments in the financial and banking sector. These failures made the crisis much worse and the recovery much longer than necessary.

The author thanks Wing Thye Woo for comments on an earlier draft, Popon Kangpenkae for assistance with data, and Duangkamol Chotana for many helpful discussions and observations, and for insisting on clarity.
1. See the report of the Commission Tasked with Making Recommendations to Improve the Efficiency and Management of Thailand's Financial System (1998) (Nukul Commission Report), especially chapter 2, for an excellent account of the government's mishandling of financial and exchange rate policies in 1996–97. The report is also interesting for its account, based on evidence from Thai officials, of the IMF's extensive efforts to alert the government to emerging problems, and of the government's refusal to take advantage of this advice.

Table 12.1
Thailand: Pre-crisis situation

	1990–94	1995	1996	1997
Growth rate of real GDP (%)	9.2	8.7	6.4	–1.3
CPI growth rate (%)	4.8	5.8	5.8	5.6
Exports (as % of GDP)	29.2	33.5	30.0	37.5
Fixed investment (as % of GDP)	40.1	41.8	40.8	35.6
Gross domestic savings (% of GDP)	35.4	36.2	35.3	34.0
Current account balance (% of GDP)	–6.5	–8.0	–7.9	–4.6
Reserve money growth (%)	16.1	22.6	13.5	15.8
Narrow money growth rate (%)	14.7	12.1	9.1	1.5
Broad money growth rate (%)	18.7	17.0	12.6	16.5
Government expenditure (% of GDP)	15.2	15.8	16.1	18.1
Government budget balance (% of GDP)	3.2	2.9	2.3	–0.6
Foreign debt (as % of GDP)	40.1	50.4	50.3	59.6
Debt service ratio for all external debt	14.2	10.4	12.1	15.8
Exchange rate (vis-à-vis US$)	25.3	25.2	25.6	47.2
Real exchange rate (1995=100, WPI based)	94.7	89.6	80.1	123.8
Nominal wage index	130.5	189.7	189.3	217.1
Real wage index	118.1	150.1	141.4	148.0
Current account balance (US$ million)	–7,121	–13,554	–14,691	–2,916
Capital account balance (US$ million)	10,599	21,908	19,486	–15,440
Foreign direct investment (US$ million)	1,948	2,068	2,335	3,028
Export value (US$ million)	33,174	56,458	55,720	57,533
Composition of exports, value of highest four exports (1996 ranking, US$ million)				
Office machines and automatic data processing	2,551	5,557	9,310	n.a.
Electrical machinery, apparatus and appliances	3,050	6,404	6,106	n.a.
Fish, crustaceans, and mollusks	3,227	4,472	3,852	n.a.
Telecommunications	1,884	3,049	3,020	n.a.
Import value (US$ million)	42,407	70,775	72,331	62,853
Composition of imports, value of highest four imports (1996 ranking, US$ million)				
Electrical machinery, apparatus and appliances	4,786	9,691	8,367	n.a.
Road vehicles	3,060	5,392	4,877	n.a.
Specialized machinery	2,860	4,502	4,434	n.a.
General industrial machinery and equipment	2,648	4,761	4,294	n.a.

Table 12.1 (continued)

	1990–94	1995	1996	1997
Exports' dependence on unaffected markets (%)	45.8	36.7	37.8	n.a.
Volume of exports (index)	135.9	202.0	193.0	n.a.
Volume of imports (index)	121.3	175.0	170.3	n.a.
International reserves minus gold (US$ million)	20,997	35,982	37,731	26,179
Value of total foreign debt (US$ billion)	45.2	83.2	90.8	91.7
Short-term foreign debt (US$ billion)	17.5	41.1	37.6	n.a.
DS Stock Market Index ($)	662.4	963.4	609.6	141.7
DS Stock Market Index (local currency)	660.9	958.4	617.4	269.4
Bangkok SET index	1,052.1	1,280.8	831.6	372.7
Nominal lending rate (%)	12.8	13.3	13.4	13.6
Nominal deposit rate (%)	10.4	11.6	10.3	10.5
Non-performing loans (% of total loans)	8.6	7.7	9.0	20.0

Table 12.2
Thailand: Changes in labor employment and output composition

	Composition of output		Composition of labor force	
	1986	1996	1970	1990
Agriculture	15.7	10.7	79.8	64.1
Industry	33.1	39.8	6.0	14.0
Services	51.3	49.5	14.2	22.0

Table 12.3
Thailand: Forecasts for the 1999–2001 situation

Forecasting institution and date of forecast	GDP growth (%)			CPI inflation (%)		
	1999	2000	2001	1998	1999	2001
International Monetary Fund, October 1999	4.0	4.0	—	0.5	2.0	—
HSBC Asia Economic Weekly, January 2000	3.9	4.3	4.0	0.3	2.5	2.5
Economist Intelligence Unit, 2000:1Q	4.0	4.7	5.3	0.2	2.0	4.0

Following a change of government in November 1997, however, Thailand worked closely with international financial agencies to design and implement a crisis management and economic recovery program. The initial program focused on tight monetary and fiscal policies, aimed at stemming the collapse of the baht and restoring confidence. As time progressed, the government showed flexibility and pragmatism in adjusting the program to changing circumstances and to new knowledge about the crisis and the impacts of its policies. Thailand became the IMF's "star" partner in dealing with the crisis.

The baht collapsed from 25 to the dollar on June 30, 1997 to 55 in mid-January 1998. It then began to recover and stabilized at about 39 to 40 in March 1998. In a major policy turnaround, the government began a substantial easing of monetary policies in August 1998. Since then, bank lending rates have fallen almost continuously. Although all real economic indicators were abysmal throughout 1998, the baht and the stock exchange index showed surprising strength in the latter part of the year and in early 1999. In early 1999, the government introduced a major short-run tax-expenditure stimulus package, confirming and reinforcing the gradual easing of its fiscal stance that had begun the previous year. By mid-1999, some of the real economic indicators had begun to stabilize, and the first quarter of 1999 showed the first positive growth in quarterly GDP since the first quarter of 1997.

Nevertheless, full recovery is still some way off. Significant gaps remain in the government's economic program, especially in dealing with corporate debt restructuring, and with bank recapitalization and the large and growing non-performing loans (NPLs) in the banking system. Political factors and social pressures have impeded progress in these important areas. But failure to act has also aggravated social tensions and continues to threaten future stability. The immediate needs of the crisis, "reform fatigue," and now the prospects of recovery have all distracted attention from fundamental long-run problems of Thai competitiveness.

12.2   The Evolving State of the Economy: An Overview

Lead-Up to the Crisis

The first indicators of the impending crisis were evident in the trade data. Import and export growth stopped in 1996; exports resumed very sluggish growth in 1997, and collapsed again in 1998. Imports showed the most dramatic drop, from 31.8 percent growth in 1995 to a 37.2 percent decline in 1998.

The simultaneous fall in exports and imports in 1996 left the current account almost unchanged. The following year, however, saw a huge reversal in capital flows, from a surplus of $19.5 billion in 1996 to an $8.7 billion deficit in 1997. Almost all of this was accounted for by net private capital flows, which changed from an inflow of $18.2 billion in 1996 to an outflow of $8.8 billion the next year.

The collapse of capital flows reflected a sudden crisis of confidence.[2] The investment bubble that had been created in the first half of the 1990s was self-sustaining as long as growth continued to justify expectations. However, growth could not be maintained on the basis of expectations alone. Among the factors contributing to the vulnerability of the system were the following:

• large and growing short-term foreign liabilities relative to foreign exchange reserves, which themselves were rapidly diminishing as the Bank of Thailand (BOT) tried to maintain the baht's peg;

• the increasing oversupply of real estate, especially in Bangkok, which hurt the property and construction sectors directly, and also threatened the value of the principal form of collateral used in much bank lending;

• falling stock market values as prices outran growth in the earnings capacities of listed companies;

• underlying problems of corporate governance and serious weaknesses in the regulation of financial markets;

• macroeconomic mismanagement, especially unwillingness to float the baht; and

• the realization that overvaluation of the baht, together with more fundamental problems of human resource development, and protection of special interests, were eroding Thailand's competitiveness in labor-intensive exports and undermining its ability to move "up the ladder of comparative advantage."

---

2. The Thai crisis of confidence is broadly consistent with the characterization provided by Radelet and Sachs (1998).

Table 12.4
Thailand: Tracking economic developments

	1997: Q1	1997: Q2	1997: Q3	1997: Q4	1998: Q1	1998: Q2	1998: Q3	1998:Q4	1999:Q1	1999:Q2
Growth rate of real GDP (%)	7.0	7.5	-4.2	-4.4	-8.0	-12.3	-12.5	-5.8	0.8	3.5
Exchange rate (against US$)	26.0	25.8	36.5	47.2	38.8	42.3	39.3	36.7	37.6	36.9
Real exchange rate (1990 = 100, WPI based)	75.1	75.5	100.7	123.8	95.9	101.1	95.3	95.1	95.0	93.4
International reserves minus gold (US$ million)	37,073.8	31,361.0	28,621.8	26,179.5	26,892.5	25,784.8	26,578.0	28,825.1	29,230.0	30,722.8
Reserve money growth (%)	18.3	31.0	19.8	15.8	1.0	-10.8	-3.3	-4.5	1.3	-2.2
Narrow money growth rate (%)	2.3	0.8	-1.9	1.5	-5.7	-3.3	-1.1	4.9	13.0	17.1
Broad money growth rate (%)	10.0	11.9	16.6	16.5	15.6	13.8	12.7	9.7	8.6	6.2
CPI growth rate (YOY%)	4.4	4.3	6.2	7.5	9.0	10.3	8.1	5.0	2.7	-0.4
Nominal lending rate (%)	13.0	12.8	13.9	14.9	15.3	15.3	14.8	12.3	10.2	8.9
Nominal deposit rate (%)	9.8	9.3	11.5	11.5	12.0	12.2	11.6	6.8	5.4	4.9
Export value (US$ million)	14,128.8	14,028.1	14,548.8	14,827.8	13,872.4	12,939.5	13,237.3	13,395.4	12,674.1	13,662.1
Import value (US$ million)	17,487.2	17,206.3	15,203.4	12,956.7	11,082.1	9,308.3	9,090.3	9,038.6	9,005.6	10,390.9
DS stock market index ($)	517.9	391.2	292.3	141.7	205.4	117.2	124.9	246.5	232.7	336.2
DS stock market index (national currency)	531.4	400.3	419.2	269.4	318.5	195.8	195.0	353.8	345.3	489.8
Bangkok SET index	705.4	527.3	544.5	372.7	459.1	267.3	253.8	355.8	352.0	521.8

The bleeding of the country's foreign exchange reserves and of its Financial Institutions Development Fund (FIDF)[3] proceeded in tandem, with the most damaging withdrawals on both accounts taking place in the first half of 1997. The difficulties of the financial sector were well recognized by major market participants. And yet the government played a purely passive role—financing the liquidity shortfalls without insisting on any structural adjustments.

Effects of the Crisis[4]

The huge reversal of capital flows between 1996 and 1997 required major economic adjustments. The government delayed floating the baht until net foreign exchange reserves had been exhausted. Since many domestic debts were denominated in foreign currency, the baht's depreciation aggravated the already serious non-performing loan (NPL) problems in the banking and financial system. In June 1997, prior to the float, 16 finance companies were shut down. To reassure creditors and depositors and to avoid financial panic, the government stated that remaining banks and finance companies were financially sound and all their credits and deposits would be guaranteed by the government. By the end of 1997 the FIDF had provided more than Bt1.2 trillion (about $30 billion) in liquidity support to banks and finance companies, of which maybe a quarter will be recoverable.

The main goal of macroeconomic policy after July 2 was to stem the free fall of the baht, mainly through tight monetary policies and correspondingly high interest rates. This further aggravated NPL problems of banks and finance companies, and 42 more financial institutions were shut down "temporarily" in August.

Restoration of financial market stability finally became the other top policy priority. Measures implemented or being planned included tightening of NPL reporting and provisioning rules; deadlines for and measures to encourage recapitalization of banks and finance companies according to international capital requirements standards; introduction

---

3. The FIDF had been established in 1985, as a juristic institution under the Bank of Thailand, with a mandate and very broad powers "to rehabilitate and develop financial institutions and to improve their stability." Prior to 1996, short-term liquidity support had been rarely used by FIDF. See chapter 5 of the Nukul Commission Report for a brief history of the role of FIDF and for a critique of its emergency measures, including massive liquidity injections, in 1997.
4. For further discussion of the origins and the effects of the crisis in Thailand, see Siamwalla (1997) and Flatters (1999).

of workable bankruptcy and foreclosure laws, and of complementary debt workout systems; disposal of assets of closed companies; and reorganization of good and bad assets of remaining firms. The negative wealth effects of the depreciation and the collapse of asset markets, together with the failure of credit markets due to the financial turmoil, depressed domestic demand. The export slump continued, as did the even more severe contraction of imports, in order for the current account to adjust to the net capital outflows. GDP started to decline in the second half of 1997 and continued through 1998. The effects are mirrored in the decline of manufacturing output.

The social implications were serious. Labor market adjustment took several forms. The number of unemployed tripled from 1996 until the end of 1998. There also were major reductions both in hours worked and in nominal wages.[5] While the initial labor force impacts were largely in urban areas, the effects were also felt in the countryside through both return migration of urban workers and reduced remittances. On the other hand, agriculture benefited from depreciation-induced increases in domestic currency prices of tradeable goods. Fortunately, CPI inflation was remarkably low, despite the large depreciation in the baht.

Thailand does not have a well-developed formal social safety net. There is no unemployment insurance. Many basic social benefits, such as health care, are tied to employment and, until very recently, ceased when employment with the firm ended. The main "social insurance" systems have been the extended family and the informal labor market. These have been severely tested in the crisis. Arguably, the most important government contribution to social insurance has been the severance penalties specified in Thai labor law, which make it costly for firms to lay off workers. This is the main explanation for the high proportion of labor market adjustment that has occurred through reduced wages and hours, rather than unemployment. This has ensured a certain amount of "income spreading" that could not have been accomplished under the formal social security system.

---

5. Significant decreases in wages and hours worked are widely acknowledged. Wage reductions of 20 to 30 percent have been common in many sectors. However, poor labor market data make it difficult to make reliable quantitative estimates of the overall incidence or magnitude of these decreases. See Kakwani (1998) for some preliminary evidence on the importance of wage decreases and underemployment in the adjustment of labor markets to the crisis.

12.3   Evolution of Policy Responses

Phase I: Fiscal and Monetary Orthodoxy

In the midst of the crisis, when the ruling coalition lost the confidence of Parliament in November, Thailand had a peaceful and orderly change of government. Unlike its predecessors, the leading party in the new government had a reputation for being relatively corruption-free, and it appointed several widely respected economics and business experts to the cabinet.

The government's initial program followed the IMF orthodoxy quite closely—tight monetary and fiscal policies and strict enforcement of high standards of financial sector governance. The initial Letters of Intent (LOIs) with the IMF trumpeted the government's pride in its strict fiscal and monetary discipline, with increases in the VAT rate and cuts in planned government expenditures. By this standard, monetary and fiscal policies were quite successful. An immediate symptom was the sharp and continuing rise in interest rates. Unfortunately, as a result of the spread of the financial crisis to other countries in the region and of continued (and justified) concerns about the health of the financial sector, the baht tumbled further in early 1998. It finally began to stabilize in March.

Financial sector reform and recapitalization, debt restructuring, and the implementation of effective bankruptcy and foreclosure laws proceeded much more slowly. A bankruptcy law was passed in February, but in response to pressures from influential debtors it had been watered down to the point of almost complete ineffectiveness.

Phase II: Monetary Easing and Financial Restructuring

While initial forecasts were of a speedy V-shaped recovery, it became increasingly apparent that the recession would be deeper and much longer lasting than had been predicted.

One result had been the gradual relaxation, in consultation and agreement with the IMF, of official fiscal targets, especially on the revenue side. The relaxed fiscal targets, however, were more in the nature of a passive recognition of the devastating effects of the crisis on revenues than an active attempt to provide a fiscal stimulus.[6]

---

6. The fiscal deficit targets had been gradually easing over the successive LOIs. The target in the first LOI had been for a surplus of 1 percent of GDP. In the fourth, fifth and sixth LOIs the target was reduced successively to –2.5 percent, –3.5 percent, and –5 percent of

By August 1998, there was widespread and increasingly vocal public pressure on the government to reverse its strict monetary policies, which were seen as a major cause of the alarming contraction of the real sector and the continuing growth of NPLs. In response to and in general sympathy with this view, the government and the IMF agreed, as part of the fifth LOI, on a major relaxation of monetary policies. The goal was to switch from exchange rate to monetary growth targets and thus to stimulate the real sector through lower interest rates. Lower interest rates were also seen as a means of easing loan payment burdens on debtors.

The monetary and fiscal easing had the predicted effect on interest rates, as both lending and deposit rates began to fall substantially and rapidly.[7] This led to a resurgence of stock market investment and a significant increase in the Stock Exchange of Thailand (SET) index in the fourth quarter. Slightly more surprising was a further strengthening of the baht, which the BOT attempted to restrain. Falling interest rates and improvements in the baht and the SET index led some observers to suggest that the Thai economy had bottomed out and that recovery was on the horizon. However, while there were some small promising signs (foreign direct investment was beginning to return and was significantly higher than in 1997), most of the real economic indicators, such as exports, imports, bank lending, manufacturing output, investment and employment, still showed little sign of turning around.

At the same time as the reversal of monetary policies, the government announced additional initiatives intended to speed up the recapitalization of the banks, restructure corporate debts, and increase bank lending. By that time, NPLs accounted for about 40 percent of loans in the banking system, and were still rising. By early 1999 the NPL rate for the entire banking system had reached 47 percent, and remained at that level throughout most of the year. Increasing numbers of the bad loans were reported to be "strategic NPLs," i.e., debts on which borrowers were refusing to make payments as a matter of choice rather than financial necessity. The absence of adequate foreclosure laws was a major factor in this regard.

GDP, excluding the costs of financial sector assistance. Until the fifth LOI, monetary targets had been expressed primarily in terms of the interest rates needed to try to maintain exchange rate stability. The fifth LOI changed the emphasis towards a substantial easing of interest rates and liquidity in order to stimulate domestic demand.

7. Because of the profit squeeze on banks from NPLs, however, lending rates have not fallen nearly as quickly as those on deposits.

The tightening of NPL reporting rules and the phasing in of new loan provisioning requirements were putting increased pressure on bank profits, and this would continue until the rules came fully into effect in 2000. As losses ate into the banks' equity, recapitalization became even more urgent. However, as NPLs expanded, it became increasingly obvious that full provisioning would effectively wipe out most, if not all, existing shareholders' equity, even for the most healthy of the remaining banks. It is understandable, therefore, why banks were reluctant to adjust.

The August 1998 measures were aimed at providing government recapitalization support to the banks, subject to conditions related to increased bank lending and more immediate provisioning for bad loans. They did not include any attempts to separate the massive NPLs from the banks' books. The recapitalization measures were voluntary—banks were not required to join the government scheme, and could continue to follow a gradual provisioning schedule laid out much earlier in the reform program. They could continue to postpone necessary adjustments, including further write-downs of shareholders' capital. Given this option, banks were extremely reluctant to join the recapitalization program. The influence of some of the largest banks, through their close links with the military and other highly influential and respected parties, has made it difficult for the government to force them to absorb large losses and make other adjustments necessary for recapitalization and restructuring.

Paralleling the bank recapitalization program were two sets of measures to encourage debt restructuring: the reform of some basic economic laws and the introduction of incentives to enter a government-assisted voluntary debt restructuring program. Effective bankruptcy and foreclosure laws are essential to an orderly resolution of debt restructuring problems. Thailand's laws were completely ineffective—with no teeth to force delinquent debtors to the bargaining table. Foreclosure procedures could routinely take five to ten years to complete, and a debtor could restart the clock at any time by making a single interest payment. In light of the obvious need for changes in these and related business laws, the government had committed with the IMF to pass a set of "basic economic laws" by the end of October 1998. Once again, the influence of vested interests interfered with the process. Most important in this regard was a group of some of the largest corporate debtors, well represented in the Thai Senate, who mounted a strong and very public nationalistic campaign to delay and dilute the new measures. The government was very slow to respond to this challenge, and as a result, passage of the laws was delayed until well into 1999. The absence of an effective legal framework for bankruptcy and foreclosure was one of the causes of the crisis. Delays in implementing these laws have been a major obstacle to progress on debt restructuring.

In mid-1998 the government also introduced a voluntary debt restructuring program, labeling it the "Bangkok approach." This Thai version of the "London approach" is an informal and voluntary system, supervised by the Bank of Thailand and a new Corporate Debt Restructuring Advisory Committee (CDRAC) under which creditors and debtors agree to a schedule and a set of steps for reaching agreement on debt restructuring. The scheme is supported by tax incentives and is meant to be both a substitute for (in the sense of being invoked earlier) and complementary to (in the sense that it does not replace them if they become necessary) formal bankruptcy and foreclosure procedures.

As with the August bank recapitalization program, the debt restructuring exercise has had very limited success. Even by late 1999, only a small portion of the debts identified for treatment under the program had been resolved, and a growing number were going to have to go to the new bankruptcy courts for resolution. Even more worrisome is that most debts that have been settled in this manner have involved mainly a rescheduling of the debts and very little true restructuring. An indicator of the failure of the process to date is that a number of debts that had been "restructured" in this manner had already become non-performing again in the second half of 1999.

Phase III: Further Fiscal Stimulus

The government launched several new spending initiatives in 1999. At the end of March, it announced a number of major social spending programs funded with external loans from the ADB, IMF, World Bank and Japan. By the time of the seventh LOI in March 1999, the 1998–99 fiscal deficit was targeted at 6 percent of GDP, not including another 1 percent in non-budgetary expenditures under the Miyazawa Plan[8] to be disbursed in the final six months of the fiscal year (ending in September).

The fiscal stimulus programs have suffered from the usual "long and variable lags" in implementation. Three-quarters of the way through the fiscal year, only 50 percent of the planned budget had been disbursed, and only 6 percent of the Social Investment Program (SIP) budget had

---

8. The Miyazawa Plan was a bilateral aid plan announced by Japan's Finance Minister Miyazawa to help the crisis countries in Asia.

been allocated. More than a third of the Miyazawa Plan money was allocated to the Ministry of Interior, ensuring relatively more rapid disbursement, but offering little assurance as to the productivity of the resources employed. There has been some controversy over the foreign financing of budget deficits, especially in the face of very high levels of domestic liquidity and when most of the foreign borrowing was on commercial terms.

12.4   The Current Situation and Longer Term Prospects

Current Situation

By late 1999, most indicators show that the Thai economy has finally bottomed out and has started on the road to recovery. Positive GDP growth at a rate of 0.8 percent was reported in the first quarter, and this increased to 3.5 percent in the second quarter. However, it should be noted that these rates were made higher by a further downward revision in 1998 growth estimates (from –8 to –9.4 percent). The growth of manufacturing production turned positive in January and has been slowly accelerating; the rate of decline of consumption has been falling steadily through the year; and imports started growing again in May, and exports in June. As of August 1999, private investment was still falling, but at a decreasing rate. Capacity utilization was gradually increasing, but was still less than 60 percent in August.

High levels of excess capacity in manufacturing and real estate mean that short-term recovery will not be investment-led. On the other hand, this means that rapid production growth could be achieved at relatively low cost. The rate of short-term growth will depend on consumption and exports, and signs are hopeful on both these fronts.

While the worst is almost certainly over, there remain some significant threats to recovery in both the short and longer terms.

12.5   Remaining Obstacles to Recovery

Financial Restructuring

The principal obstacle to Thailand's full and speedy economic recovery is its shattered financial system.[9] Thailand's crisis has been largely a

9. See also Flatters (1998) and Flatters (1999).

financial crisis. A full recovery will require resolution of problems paralyzing the financial sector. The two necessary elements here are bank recapitalization and resolution of outstanding NPLs. Despite major reductions in interest rates, NPLs remain stubbornly high, and even more importantly, bank lending continues to shrink.

It can be argued that once the die was cast in the first half of 1997, a slow and very arduous recovery of the financial sector was inevitable. However, the absence of essential bankruptcy and foreclosure laws and associated weaknesses of the legal framework, and delays in dealing with these obvious problems, have deepened the damage and impeded necessary restructuring. A major casualty, at least in the short run, has been Thailand's debt culture. Acrimonious senate debates and public discussions, and the actions of vested interests in the financial community, have politicized essential legal and economic functions. Problems of corporate governance and outright looting of corporate and banking assets have become increasingly widely reported.

The government has taken many of the right steps. However, the costs of its failure to effect a speedy removal of bad debts from bank balance sheets will be hotly debated for some time. The government faced a large political risk in being seen to be bailing out rich bankers by taking over bad debts. In the uncertainties of the early days of the crisis, it certainly would have been very difficult to place "fair" values on these assets, and that was the major problem. In addition, it was the government's view that leaving the bad loans with the banks would ensure more effective management of these portfolios. Thailand has adopted a much more market-oriented approach to bank recapitalization and financial sector restructuring than most other countries.

A major failure of the debt restructuring process has been the absence of incentives for the banks or other creditors to take significant "haircuts" (i.e., to write down the value of the loans). Faced with large operating losses and increasing capital adequacy requirements, such radical "haircuts" would threaten the financial survival of current bank shareholders. And under existing financial laws, debtors had little incentive to agree to disadvantageous settlements. The August 1998 banking package had the potential to force more speedy adjustment on the banks, but participation was made voluntary. Instead, most banks took advantage of beneficial new capital definitions to convert deposits into "capital," and avoided debt write-offs by agreeing to debt rescheduling rather than restructuring. These actions helped solve short-run balance sheet problems, but have only put off necessary adjustments to the future.

Political Stability

Thailand had the good fortune to have undertaken a major constitutional reform just prior to the crisis. As a result, and unlike Indonesia for instance, Thailand accomplished a peaceful, legitimate, constitutional change of government in the midst of the crisis. The competence and legitimacy of the new government have been very beneficial to Thailand. A principal goal of the new constitution and of the current government is to root out longstanding traditions of "money politics" and of bureaucratic corruption. Whether these goals will be met is still unclear.

As a democratic government, however, the ruling coalition has been pressured by competing and sometimes very powerful special interests. The government's very slim parliamentary majority made it difficult to overcome vested interests or implement unpopular measures. This was seen in the weakness of the initial new bankruptcy law, in continuing difficulties passing new economic laws, and in lack of aggressiveness with financial sector restructuring and recapitalization. In October 1998 the government found it necessary to admit another large and influential party to the coalition. This provided a safer parliamentary majority, but also expanded the range of interests and competing forces that must be satisfied within the coalition. The government has suffered a gradual diminution of its respectability as it has been tainted by new scandals and the slow economic recovery. Many of the old pros from Thailand's money politics regime are still in the game—some are in the current cabinet—and there is no guarantee that they will not win the next election.

In the face of political pressures from many directions, the government has often forsaken the economic high road in order to satisfy particular interests. This might be viewed as a sign of a healthy democracy, but it will also impose longer term economic costs. One immediate outcome has been the accumulation of quite significant public sector indebtedness—a relatively new feature of Thai economic life.

The External Environment

The external environment will play an important role in determining the speed and sustainability of recovery. Simultaneous recovery of the crisis-stricken economies will help to provide a virtuous circle of mutually reinforcing external demand. However, such a circle will be of much smaller magnitude, even under the best of circumstances, than the contagion that worked in the opposite direction in 1997–98. Capital flows will certainly pick up as recovery becomes more certain. However, notwithstanding the unfortunate herd instincts that are sometimes seen in international capital flows, domestic and international investors have learned some new lessons as a result of the crisis, and this will cause higher risk aversion and higher standards of economic management and corporate governance than in the past.

Japan and China remain large question marks on the immediate horizon, and the sustainability of U.S. growth will be equally important to Thailand's recovery.

Problems of Long-Run Competitiveness

Even before the crisis, Thailand faced some serious problems with long-run competitiveness. While overall productivity growth was moderate, most of it was in agriculture or arose from inter-industry shifts. There was little indication of growth of technological capabilities, or movements "up the ladder of comparative advantage." [10] Among the widely recognized barriers to growth in competitiveness were very low levels and quality of education, serious deficiencies in infrastructural development, and a policy regime at the microeconomic level that was too much geared to creating and preserving rents rather than fostering market competition.[11] Monopolies in basic services (e.g., telecommunications) and protection of upstream industries (steel and petrochemicals) were among the most obvious and egregious examples of misguided protectionism. While prudent macroeconomic policies had always been regarded as an area of strength in Thailand, the financial and macroeconomic mismanagement that led up to the crisis have called that into question as well. Political and bureaucratic corruption has been another continuing source of concern.

While the crisis has drawn attention to some of these issues and has provoked some policy improvements, many of the problems have been left "on hold," and some have become worse. One immediate effect of

---

10. See Tinakorn and Sussankarn (1996).
11. For an early review of these challenges to Thailand's competitiveness see Akrasanee, Dapice and Flatters (1991).

the crisis has been a reduction in school enrollments, which will lower rather then raise future education levels. Education budgets have suffered under the crisis, and bureaucratic and political energies have been diverted from educational reform to more immediate problems. While the government has attempted to exempt major export industries from the costs of upstream protection, it has done little to attack the protection problem directly. The Board of Investment, while reluctantly reducing reliance on selective income tax incentives, still devises plans to provide "temporary" protection in the form of tariffs, exemption from competition laws and other incentives for "strategic" sectors. There has been considerable talk and some action in dealing with corruption in various ministries, and yet there has been little progress in systematic public service reform and introduction of realistic wage systems.

This is a very tough policy agenda, and it is not surprising that progress has been difficult in the crisis environment. But resolution of these problems is essential to the restoration and sustainability of Thailand's long-term growth and competitiveness. And the hope of recovery, coupled with looming elections, is very likely to dampen both the demand for and the supply of needed policy reforms.

12.6   Conclusion

Thailand is better equipped in many respects than most other countries in the region to face the challenges of the new, post-crisis global environment. This is especially true of its relatively stable constitutional and political framework. Reform fatigue and immediate electoral concerns will reduce the drive for necessary reforms. Vested interests have delayed and sidetracked appropriate crisis responses. However, openness of debate about economic and political issues, while sometimes slowing down reform in favor of special interests, does at least keep the discussion in the public arena.

References

Akrasanee, Narongchai, David Dapice and Frank Flatters. 1991. *Thailand's Export-Led Growth: Retrospect and Prospects.* TDRI Policy Study. Bangkok: Thailand Development Research Institute.

Commission Tasked with Making Recommendations to Improve the Efficiency and Management of Thailand's Financial System. 1998. *Analysis and Evaluation of Facts Behind Thailand's Economic Crisis (Nukul Commisssion Report).* Bangkok: Nation Multimedia Group. March.

Flatters, Frank. 1998. *ASEAN and the Economic Crisis: Lessons for Vietnam.* UNDP-Funded Research Report No. 7, VIE/95/015. Hanoi, Vietnam. October.

Flatters, Frank. 1999. *Thailand, the IMF and the Economic Crisis: First In, Fast Out?* Presented at the Brookings Institution/Chung Hua Institute for Economic Research Conference on the Asian Financial Crisis and Taiwan's Role in the Region, Washington, D.C., 5 April (forthcoming in conference volume to be published by Brookings Institution).

Kakwani, Nanak. 1998. *Impact of the Economic Crisis on Employment, Unemployment and Real Income.* Bangkok: National Economic and Social Development Board. September.

Radelet, Steven and Jeffrey Sachs. 1998. *The East Asian Financial Crisis: Diagnosis, Remedies, Prospects.* Harvard Institute for International Development. April.

Siamwalla, Ammar. 1997. Can a Developing Democracy Manage its Macroeconomy? The Case of Thailand. J. Douglas Gibson Lecture, Queen's University, Canada. October.

Tinakorn, Pranee and Chalongphob Sussangkarn. 1996. *Productivity Growth in Thailand.* TDRI Research Monograph no. 15. Bangkok: Thailand Development Research Institute.

Index